LAWYERS AND MEDIATORS

Do lawyers make matters worse, or do they provide information, advice and support which can help to prevent disputes arising or manage them when they do? Do mediators enable parties to communicate and reach agreements tailor-made to their needs? Or working outside the legal framework, do they find it difficult to protect weaker parties and access expert advice? What happens when lawyers become mediators? This book will describe the structure of service provision and the day-to-day work of lawyers, mediators, and lawyer mediators, drawing on empirical work carried out between 2013 and 2015 immediately after the recent changes to the management of divorce and separation within the family justice system. The reduction in legal aided help in 2013 and the failure of mediation to fill the gap in 2014–15 have given rise to a difficult debate. This book aims to provide an account of some of the practical effects of these policies through a description of the daily work of practitioners in the sector. It raises the question of whether we need to choose between traditional legal services and the new processes of private ordering or whether intermediate positions might be possible.

Lawyers and Mediators

The Brave New World of Services for Separating Families

Mavis Maclean
and
John Eekelaar

·HART·
PUBLISHING
OXFORD AND PORTLAND, OREGON
2016

Published in the United Kingdom by Hart Publishing Ltd
16C Worcester Place, Oxford, OX1 2JW
Telephone: +44 (0)1865 517530
Fax: +44 (0)1865 510710
E-mail: mail@hartpub.co.uk
Website: http://www.hartpub.co.uk

Published in North America (US and Canada) by
Hart Publishing
c/o International Specialized Book Services
920 NE 58th Avenue, Suite 300
Portland, OR 97213-3786
USA
Tel: +1 503 287 3093 or toll-free: (1) 800 944 6190
Fax: +1 503 280 8832
E-mail: orders@isbs.com
Website: http://www.isbs.com

British Library Cataloguing in Publication Data
Data Available

Library of Congress Cataloging-in-Publication Data

Names: Maclean, Mavis, author. | Eekelaar, John.

Title: Lawyers and mediators : services for separating families / Mavis
Maclean and John Eekelaar.

Description: Oxford ; Portland, Oregon : Hart Publishing Ltd, 2015. |
Includes bibliographical references and index. | Description based on print
version record and CIP data provided by publisher; resource not viewed.

Identifiers: LCCN 2015042676 (print) | LCCN 2015041542 (ebook) |
ISBN 9781509904846 (Epub) | ISBN 9781509904822 (hardback : alk. paper)

Subjects: LCSH: Divorce mediation—England. | Practice of law author.—England,

Classification: LCC KD764 (print) | LCC KD764.M325 2015 (ebook) |
DDC 346.4201/66—dc23

LC record available at http://lccn.loc.gov/2015042676

ISBN: 978-1-50990-482-2

Typeset by Compuscript Ltd, Shannon
Printed and bound in Great Britain by
TJ International Ltd, Padstow, Cornwall

Preface

In the Preface to our first study of the main legal personnel involved in the provision of family justice, *Family Lawyers: the Divorce Work of Solicitors* (Hart Publishing, 2000), we wrote that from about the mid-1990s, the nature of the debate about legal processes in relation to family matters seemed to have changed. 'What did seem different … was the intensity of feeling that the legal process had not simply gone wrong, or was in need of improvement, but that it was somehow in its nature completely inappropriate as the mechanism for dealing with family disruption and conflict'. We therefore thought it important to assemble empirical evidence so that 'if significant change was to be brought about … we should at least understand rather better what it was we would be departing from'. It was with this objective that we examined the work of solicitors in that book, followed later with a description of the relevant work of barristers (*Family Law Advocacy: How Barristers Help the Victims of Family Failure* (Hart Publishing, 2009)) and the judiciary (*Family Justice: The Work of Family Judges in Uncertain Times* (Hart Publishing, 2013)).

Our sense that a sea-change was occurring in at least official perceptions of the nature and place of law in family matters where the state was not directly involved has been amply confirmed in the years that followed. Official action could not prevent individuals consulting lawyers or using legal processes (though compulsory attendance at Mediation Information and Assessment Meetings was intended to signal the availablity of an enticing alternative), but they could withdraw financial support from those who needed it for those purposes. So when pressures for financial constraint following the financial crisis of 2008 bore down on legal aid funding, private law family legal services were an obvious target. This did not seem to be a purely financial policy. It seemed to be driven also by the attitude we had noted in the 1990s that the law was out of place in this area. This seems to be confirmed by official attempts to encourage the use of mediation in its place, even by making some public funding available for this purpose. Yet, despite the enthusiasm and energy of its advocates, family mediation was an unproven procedure and lacked a coherent institutional framework. There were even sharp divisions about important aspects of its practice.

The landscape of family legal services in the two years immediately following the drastic reduction in family legal aid from April 2013 could be likened to a wartime panorama of destroyed edifices. Yet there is still a population needing some provision, and a range of new legal structures is slowly emerging together with the new player, mediation, though this is still struggling to establish itself. It seemed to us to be of the greatest importance to try to examine this new scenario as closely as we could so that we could understand better what was happening, how these different elements relate to each other and what they were providing for the public.

The method employed was essentially the same as in our previous studies: meeting with the protagonists and as far as possible observing their work, although it differed in some ways, as explained in our text, because of the diversified and developing nature of the services provided. We have to admit that we found trying to bring all the pieces together into some kind of coherent whole very difficult. While we felt much regret at the passing of what we consider to have been a humane vision demonstrating community responsibility towards the needs of people experiencing serious difficulties, we do not think the current position is without hope. There are many actors determined to help families experiencing separation, and a willingness to explore new processes. We have put forward a suggestion of our own which we think brings together the strengths of both those trained in the law and in mediation, though for that very reason may cause some disquiet in both those camps. But it is made in a spirit of respect for them all.

We express our thanks to all those, who for reasons of protecting the anonymity of the cases studied cannot be named. Our gratitude is equalled by our respect and admiration for those working in this difficult field at this difficult time with courage, energy, skill and great integrity.

Contents

1

Family Legal Services and the State

I. FAMILY LAW, THE ROLE OF SOLICITORS AND LEGAL AID

T HIS BOOK IS about the way the legal system responds when individuals face problems in their family relationships which are serious enough to involve separation. It does not cover the issues which arise when the state, usually through social services departments, becomes involved in family matters. In that event the engagement of people's legal rights is not disputed, and policy makers in the United Kingdom have, so far, accepted that when those affected do not have sufficient means to obtain the assistance of legal professionals, the state should make a contribution through the legal aid system. That does not mean that state funding in that context has escaped the demands of austerity following the financial crisis of 2008, and the strict eligibility criteria can leave some people affected without legal representation in these situations.[1] But they have mostly taken the form of structural and procedural reform of the court process and restrictions on the use of expert evidence (Ryder 2012).

But when the state is not directly involved (in 'private' law cases, as opposed to 'public' law cases) the UK government in 2010 took a very different view about contributing to legal assistance for those with insufficient means to access it. This view is encapsulated in the statement from the Ministry of Justice that 'there is a range of other cases which can very often result from a litigant's own decisions in their personal life. Where the issue is one which arises from the litigant's own personal choices, we are not likely to consider that these cases concern issues of the highest importance' (Ministry of Justice 2010: para 4.19). This book is about those issues. There are very many of them. In a survey, conducted on behalf of the Legal Services Board in 2012, of 4017 individuals, 10 per cent claimed to have experienced a legal need within the previous three years regarding divorce, 9 per cent regarding problems relating to relationship breakdown and 6 per cent regarding domestic violence. Ten per cent equates to about 4 million people in England and Wales (Legal Services Board 2012: 9–11).

---

[1] See, eg, *Re D* [2014] EWFC 39.

The nature of the substantive law dealing with family problems (in short, family law) changed markedly over the last quarter of the twentieth century. In the United Kingdom this has been expressed as follows:

> [O]ne might say that the earlier law was based on a constructed vision of the world, one in which people lived, or were expected to live, according to neat moral and behavioural categories imagined by law. Essentially the law tried to maintain, or even create, a type of social structure, and was designed to reward conformity with that structure, and penalise aberrations from it. Put another way, upholding that actual, or imagined structure, took precedence over the well being of individuals (Eekelaar 2013: 420).

However, the modern law had moved away from seeking to uphold actual or imagined social structures or practices towards seeking to protect and enhance individual well-being when problems arose in personal relationships. Observations of the way the lower-level family courts work (Eekelaar and Maclean 2013) support the view that a predominant role of the courts is to find solutions to real-life problems within the general principles of the law. The result has been that, while there remain 'deficiencies and contentious areas' and the law 'may well have become less clear cut',

> it seems that on the whole the current substantive family law engages well with people's problems and offers a framework for resolving them (Eekelaar 2013: 422).

However, while the substantive law provides a 'framework' for resolving those problems, its effectiveness depends on the legal and other services available whereby people can have access to that framework. It must also be remembered that

> [t]he very fluidity and complexity of 'real life' family problems meant that neat solutions cannot always be found, and that it may take time to move to work towards the most satisfactory (or sometimes the least worse) solutions (Ibid: 422).

John Dewar has made a similar observation about the role of family law in the Australian context:

> Family law presents primarily a regulatory rather than an adjudicative task, in the sense that it provides guidance mostly to lay people in the practical resolution of issues or disputes (Dewar 2010: 385).

But Dewar goes on to observe that 'this fact is not recognised in the way we write family laws. Indeed, as we have seen, current law in Australia is so complex that many lawyers struggle to make sense of it.' This problem is aggravated by the variety of contexts in which issues potentially involving family law may arise: in courts, when seeking legal advice, in mediation, in Family Relationship Centres (for Australia), or simply in private discussion and negotiation between parties. Thus, Dewar says, family justice systems are 'fragmented, horizontalised, dispersed, and are "high reach, low intensity" systems of mass dispute settlement (ie many people see their problems as legal ones, but use very low intensity legal mechanisms, in multiple fora, to solve them)' (Ibid: 378).

A similar proliferation of points at which some form of access to assistance relating to matters that engage family law might be found has occurred in England and Wales. The main reason for this is that one of the major sources from which people experiencing family difficulties could obtain advice or guidance—namely, solicitors—has become much more difficult as a result of the legal aid limitations. In our earlier examination of the work of family solicitors (Eekelaar, Maclean and Beinart 2000), we noted that their practice reflected well the modern character of substantive law described above in its engagement with real issues faced by people with family problems in all their complexity. It had the following features:

1. A high degree of interactivity: that is, 'interaction with the client and others involved in the case'. This interactivity took various forms, the most important of which were providing support for the client (in terms of reassurance, information, facilitating or making contact with third parties such as banks, utilities and creditors, and practical advice) and negotiating a position with the client (that is exploring and settling with the client a preferred outcome which best represents the clients' wishes and interests with the 'normative standards' indicted by the law) (Ibid: chs 4 and 5).
2. Ongoing support, which might be described as managing the client through difficult times, giving them 'empowerment' through the legal system (Ibid: cases discussed at 104–08).

Work with legally aided clients could at that time be likened to 'a mixture of a general medical practitioner and a social worker with clout' (Ibid: 63).

The cases observed for that study showed how these solicitors accepted a broadly defined responsibility for helping their client to make plans for a new stage in their life, to negotiate these with the other party and move on with their lives. This kind of support appeared to potentially avoid escalation from lack of agreement to dispute, and was concerned as much with solving problems about finding affordable housing, settling debts, and giving financial advice, as with engaging in disputes about property sharing or arrangements for children. The provision of legal information, advice and support extended beyond dispute resolution and focused on moving towards settlement, not disagreement. The solicitors negotiated with their clients to try to reach a position which a court would find acceptable. If both parties had solicitors performing this function, agreement would probably be reached. If difficulties remained, an application to court might be invoked strategically in attempts to move the negotiations along, but litigation in the sense of taking a matter to a contested final hearing was and remains rare. This was acknowledged in the Consultation Paper making the proposals for the legal aid changes, where it is stated that, in 2008, 73 per cent of ancillary relief orders were uncontested (Ministry of Justice 2010: para 4.157). Since that refers only to outcomes following an application to court and resulting in an order, the settlement rate for *all* issues dealt with by lawyers would have been much higher. Statistics for orders made from April to June 2014, using two sets of data, showed a similar pattern. Financial orders were contested in 25 per cent of cases in one set, and 30 per cent in another set, and adjudication occurred in only 5 per cent in one set and 7 per cent in the other (Hitchings, Miles and Woodward 2014). Similar findings had been made in the 1990s (see Davis, Pearce, Bird, Woodward and Wallace 1999).

We summarised the solicitors' role in this way:

(1) Help to achieve change of legal status; (2) help with the redistribution of resources in an equitable manner; (3) help in the transformation of one household into two bearing in mind both the welfare of any children involved, and the impact on the public purse. These tasks were accomplished by: (1) providing knowledge about potential adjudication and the practical experiences of others so that clients can plan ahead, perhaps needing to transform their objectives in line with what is possible both legally and practically; (2) facilitating contact with third parties such as banks, utilities, and creditors; (3) constructing narratives from the chaos of events and acts; (4) speaking for the client, marshalling arguments and being unemotional in negotiation; (5) offering support and guidance, both emotional and practical; (6) carrying out formal acts (Eekelaar, Maclean and Beinart 2000: 79–80).

It is evident that only a small part of this activity (and then only for few clients) involved assistance in actual litigation. The court may have been used as a place where further negotiation could take place, or to register an agreement in the form of an order of the court by consent in order to ensure enforceability if the arrangement broke down. But contested final hearings, ie trials, were, and remain, rare. A significant amount of the solicitor's work took place outside the meeting with the client. We particularly drew a distinction between 'legal aid' and 'private client' practitioners, noting that the work of the former 'in many ways resembled that of a social worker or general practitioner', whereas the latter practitioner 'looks more like the adversarial commercially minded stereotypes of the divorce lawyer, largely because he accepts his client's instructions rather than negotiating a strategy with him' (Ibid: 79). Our later observations of family law cases also revealed an important supporting and helping element in the work of barristers and even judges (Maclean and Eekelaar 2009; Eekelaar and Maclean 2013).

However, as we will see, despite this reality, in the bid to reduce legal aid expenditure, government sources have consistently ignored this supportive role of lawyers, especially when seeking to direct people to use mediation rather than resort to lawyers, equating the use of lawyers either with litigation or, at best, 'arm's-length' negotiation, both of which were said to 'heighten conflict'. The curious and continuing contrast between government views of the work of solicitors in family cases and the findings of a number of research studies, including our study mentioned above, was set out by PSC Lewis (2000), who compared policy statements with empirical research results. Lawyers were criticised by policy makers for conducting arm's-length negotiation which often reduced communication and increased tension and conflict, providing only legal advice, seeking their client's interests at the expense of the other party, and unpicking or interfering with agreements reached in mediation. In contrast, empirical research cited by Lewis reported that 'not all clients, and perhaps not even a majority, will see increased hostility and attempts to over-reach', and sometimes solicitors were used to solve problems with third parties on the client's behalf. Others[2] found that although solicitors were reluctant to let a client accept less than what is 'fair' in mediation, they were not in any way hostile to the process and were extremely reluctant to litigate; that parties may need arm's-length negotiation where there is a power imbalance between the parties or high conflict, and that people even in mediation wanted to know what a court would award and what options were available.

II. LEGAL AID AND FAMILY MATTERS

A. The 1990s

Under the previous system, any lawyer could take a case and, provided the eligibility criteria were met, submit a bill to the Legal Aid Board for payment. This increasing expenditure of public money on private quarrels came under strong pressure during the period of the Thatcher government, and alleviation was sought in the introduction in 1990 of conditional fees, whereby the lawyer receives no fee if the case is lost but is paid an enhanced fee if it is won.[3] But these were not brought in for family cases, and the legal aid scheme was becoming, at a time of rapidly increasing divorce rates,[4] in Stephen Cretney's words, 'the victim of its own success' (Cretney 2003: 318). By 1996/97 the net cost of civil legal aid was £807.3 million of which 48.5 per cent was spent on matrimonial and family cases.[5] So pressure for reform continued, with the added support of the Social Market Foundation think tank which in 1994[6] had raised the question of supplier-induced demand for professional services (see Bevan 1996; Moorhead 1998;

---

[2] Davis, Cretney and Collins (1994); Ingleby (1992); Walker, McCarthy and Timms (1994). The same reluctance by lawyers to litigate, and preference to reach agreement, has been observed in Scotland: Myers and Wasoff (2011: 7, 100).

[3] Courts and Legal Services Act 1990, s 58.

[4] The divorce rate (number of divorces in relation to every 1,000 of the ongoing married population) increased from 2.4 (1951–60) to 13.0 (1997): see Gibson (2000: 44).

[5] See Legal Aid Board Annual Reports 1996/97, 2.

[6] *Law Society Gazette*, 20 July 1994, 3.

Webley 2015). The Labour government, elected in 1997, while recognising the importance of legal services, was determined to control expenditure and secure value for money. In 1997, Lord Irvine, the Labour Lord Chancellor from 1997 to 2003, commissioned a review of civil justice and legal aid by Sir Peter Middleton (Middleton 1997). Middleton took up the idea of supplier-induced demand, and to ensure value for money recommended control over legal aid expenditure through block contracts between the Legal Aid Board and providers of legal services. He also favoured extending the scope of conditional fees (see Abel 2003, especially ch 8, 'Labour ends legal aid as we know it').

Under the Access to Justice Act 1999, a 'cap' was placed on legal aid expenditure for the first time, which primarily affected civil work, as criminal work where the liberty of the accused is at risk was prioritised.[7] The Act set up the Legal Services Commission (LSC) to establish, maintain and develop a Community Legal Service which replaced the legal aid fund in civil and family cases.

> The Commission will use the resources of the fund in a way that reflects priorities set by the Lord Chancellor and its duty to secure the best possible value for money, to procure or provide a range of legal services. The Commission will also have a duty to plan what can be done towards meeting need for legal services, and to liaise with other funders of legal services to facilitate the development of co-ordinated plans for making the best use of all available resources. The intention is to develop comprehensive referral networks of legal service providers of assured quality, offering the widest possible access to information and advice about the law and help with legal problems.[8]

From January 2000 legal aid work could be provided only under contract with the LSC, the objective being to reduce drastically the number of legal aid providers in the interests of efficiency by concentrating them into far fewer firms. In the 2010 tendering round, the number of contracts for family law work was reduced by nearly a half, 'with good firms losing out altogether and new, untried firms getting the cases for which they bid' (Paterson 2012: 95–96). The Commission operated a Funding Code which strictly specified the types of work for which public funding might be provided. It was predicted that the number of firms taking on legal aid work in family matters would diminish, and aspects of practice were likely to change. For example, a fresh application to the LSC would need to be made if the service to a client was to extend beyond advice (Legal Help) to assistance (Approved Family Help) or Legal Representation (see Eekelaar, Maclean and Beinart 2000, ch 1).

---

[7] Personal injury claims were removed entirely from legal aid in the expectation that legal provision would be available through conditional fee arrangements: see Paterson (2012: 90–93).

[8] Access to Justice Act 1990, Explanatory Memorandum, para 9.

In the case of family law, the government had long been promoting mediation as a way of reducing public funding in family matters. The use of mediation, in the sense of 'reconciliation', had been urged by the Denning Committee (1947), and was given fresh impetus under the name 'concilia-tion' (assistance in reaching agreement) by the Finer Committee (1974) after changes to divorce law in 1971 made this easier (see Eekelaar and Maclean 2013: 32–35). This became central to the Conservative government's policy towards divorce in the 1990s, in particular in the Consultation Paper *Looking to the Future: Mediation and the Ground for Divorce* (1993). In the ensuing White Paper (1995: para 5.8) with the same title, the Conservative government described mediation as an alternative to 'negotiating matters at arm's length ... and to litigating through the courts'. A new process for obtaining a divorce was enacted in the Family Law Act 1996, but its imple-mentation was suspended until the results of pilot 'information meetings', designed in part to entice people away from lawyers towards mediation, were known. The meetings failed to achieve that objective, and eventually the proposed divorce reform was abandoned (see Eekelaar, Maclean and Beinart 2000: 1–9). However the policy in section 29 of the 1996 Act, which required a party seeking legal aid in family proceedings (with some excep-tions) to first attend a meeting with a mediator to assess suitability for medi-ation, survived in the Funding Code issued by the LSC.[9] Legal aid might be refused if the mediator considered the matter suitable for mediation. But the take-up of mediation remained low (only one in three or four cases) partly because it was not possible to compel the other party to attend, so the gov-ernment was funding largely non-productive assessments (Dingwall 2010).

Nevertheless, the association of lawyers with 'litigation' by the previous administration continued and was reinforced by a speech in June 1999 by the Labour Lord Chancellor, Lord Irvine, when he said of mediation: 'Par-ties are more likely to adhere to agreements they have made themselves rather than orders that have been imposed from outside.'[10] The role of legal advisers in supporting and guiding parties who may not even be in dispute was once again ignored. As we will see, the Coalition government returned to this theme in the context of further legal aid reforms in 2010.

B. 2010 and Beyond

A new assault on publicly funded family law work was launched in 2010 with the Coalition government's proposals for legal aid reform, which not

---

[9] Access to Justice Act 1999, s 8. Funding Code 3C-454, specifying that 'the client must attend a meeting with a mediator or otherwise satisfy the requirement under Criterion 11.12.2 before funding by way of Family Help (Higher), Legal Representation will be granted'.

[10] Speech to UK Family Law Conference, Inner Temple, London, 25 June 1999.

only sought spending cuts which reduced the scope of the scheme, but embraced such changes as being not only necessary but right in returning responsibility to the individual (Ministry of Justice 2010: para 4.19). In these proposals the government set out what were described as 'principles' according to which certain areas of law could be removed from the scope of the legal aid scheme. The relevant one here is the statement that 'there is a range of other cases which can very often result from a litigant's own decisions in their personal life. Where the issue is one which arises from the litigant's own personal choices, we are not likely to consider that these cases concern issues of the highest importance' (see Eekelaar 2011). The logic supporting this alleged 'principle' cannot withstand scrutiny: there are many instances in a market-driven world where people make personal choices (such as purchasing consumer goods or choosing jobs) and where it turns out they suffer some wrong for which they are owed legal redress. It can only be seen as an indirect way of announcing the neo-liberal policy stance that considers the role of law to be at best largely irrelevant in the family context and at worst undesirable in building a society where self-reliance and self-sufficiency are prioritised (see Cabinet Office 2010). This approach is not restricted to the United Kingdom. It is currently found in other jurisdictions, such as Canada, New Zealand and Spain.[11]

The only exception made from this exclusion is where it is necessary to protect the 'vulnerable'. But 'vulnerability' is understood primarily in terms of violence and abuse bringing about or risking injury to health (see Hunter 2011). Being involved in family breakdown is not in itself considered to create vulnerability, despite the emotional stress commonly suffered by those who experience it. Justice, on this view, is replaced by a kind of 'welfare' provision, and rationed accordingly. The proposals were enacted in the Legal Aid, Sentencing and Punishment of Offenders Act 2012 (LASPO), which took effect from 1 April 2013.

The argument is different where state authorities become involved in family life. Legal aid remains available in child care and protection cases ('public' law family cases where the state is a party). But where family members themselves are in conflict, the general provision is that legal aid should be available only when 'in relation to a matter arising out of family relationship between A and another individual B there has been or is a risk of domestic violence between A and B, and where A was, or is, at risk of being the victim of that domestic violence'.[12] 'Domestic violence' is defined in paragraph 12(9) as 'any incident, or pattern of incidents, of controlling, coercive or threatening behaviour, violence or abuse (whether psychological, physical,

---

[11] See Maclean, Eekelaar and Bastard (eds) (2015: chs 1 (Treloar), 2 (Atkin), 3 (Rogerson) and 11 (Picontó-Novales)).
[12] Legal Aid, Sentencing and Punishment of Offenders Act 2012 (LASPO), Schedule 1, para 12(1).

sexual, financial or emotional) between individuals who are associated with each other'.[13] There is an equivalent[14] provision for procedures regarding children when a child is 'at risk of abuse'. There is a marginal extension to 'home rights, occupation orders and non-molestation orders under Part 4 of the Family Law Act 1996' (which usually arise in the context of domestic violence cases).[15]

The only circumstances outside those contexts where legal aid is available in family matters are in relation to forced marriage protection orders,[16] proceedings connected with certain international instruments,[17] to assist a child in the (rare) cases where a child is a party to the proceedings[18] or proceedings where an individual is seeking to prevent the unlawful removal of a child from the UK or the return of a child so removed.[19] Finally, the Legal Aid Agency (LAA) (which replaced the LSC, bringing the administration of legal aid under closer government control), may make an 'exceptional case determination' that it is

> necessary to make the services available ... because failure to do so would be a breach of (i) the individual's Convention rights (within the meaning of the Human Rights Act 1998), or (ii) any rights of the individual to the provision of legal services that are enforceable EU rights, or that it is appropriate to do so, in the particular circumstances of the case, having regard to any risk that failure to do so would be such a breach.[20]

The key Convention right is in Article 6, which states: 'In the determination of his civil rights and obligations or of any criminal charge against him, everyone is entitled to a fair and public hearing within a reasonable time by an independent and impartial tribunal established by law.' Further guidance from the Lord Chancellor imposed a qualifying 'threshold' in cases alleging breaches of human rights requiring that 'withholding of legal aid make(s) assertion of the claim practically impossible or lead(s) to an obvious unfairness in the proceedings'.[21] This attempt to impose an additional threshold of 'exceptionality' when Convention rights are at stake was struck down by the Court of Appeal in December 2014 as being too restrictive, the court stating that it was not necessary to establish that there was 'substantial' risk

---

[13] LASPO, Schedule 1, para 12(9) as amended by Legal Aid, Sentencing and Punishment of Offenders Act 2012 (Amendment of Schedule 1) Order 2013/748, art 4(1).

[14] Ibid, Schedule 1 para 13.

[15] Ibid, para 11.

[16] Ibid, para 16.

[17] Ibid, paras 17, 18.

[18] Ibid, para 15.

[19] Ibid, para 10.

[20] Ibid, ss 8–10 and Schedule 1, Part One.

[21] *Lord Chancellor's Exceptional Funding Guidance (Non-Inquests)*, para 10 (February 2013). http://legalaidhandbook.com/2013/02/26/lord-chancellors-guidance-published/.

or 'high degree of probability' that Convention rights would be breached in order to make an exceptional case determination.[22]

Not surprisingly, the exemption from exclusion from the scope of legal aid through definition as an exceptional case was initially little used. The Legal Aid Agency planned for 5,000–7,000 applications for such exemption in the first year but received only 1,520, of which 69 (5 per cent) were granted (Ministry of Justice and Legal Aid Agency 2014b: 7, Key Finding 15). Only 125 applications for Exceptional Case Funding (ECF) for family matters are reported in the quarterly *Legal Aid Statistics, England and Wales, April to June 2014*, and only seven were granted. The House of Commons Justice Committee (2015: para 45) concluded that 'the exceptional cases funding scheme has not done the job Parliament intended, protecting access to justice for the most vulnerable people in our society'.

In June 2015 the Lord Chancellor amended the previous guidance. This in turn was strongly criticised by Collins J,[23] who said that he was 'satisfied that the scheme as operated is not providing the safety net promised by Ministers and is not in accordance with s 10 [of LASPO] in that it does not ensure that applicants' human rights are not breached or are not likely to be breached'.[24] As regards family cases, he was even more forthright, saying:

> It is difficult to imagine a family case, particularly when there are contested issues about children, in which there would not be an interference with the Article 8 rights of either parent or the children themselves. Thus unless the party seeking legal aid could albeit unrepresented present his or her case effectively and without obvious unfairness, a grant of legal aid would be required. That does not mean that every case will require it: some may be sufficiently simple for the unrepresented party to deal with. Obviously if there is a lack of capacity even such cases may require legal aid. That issue I will have to consider in further detail later. But I am bound to say that I believe that only in rare cases, subject to means and merits if properly applied, should legal aid be denied in such cases. As it is now applied, the scheme is clearly wholly deficient in that it does not enable the family courts to be satisfied that they can do justice and give a fair hearing to an unrepresented party. While the problem may perhaps be less acute in other civil cases, I have no doubt that the difficulties I have referred to in family cases apply.[25]

The government subsequently stated that it would carefully consider the judgment.[26]

---

[22] *Gudanaviciene and Others, R (on the application of) v The Director of Legal Aid Casework and Another* [2014] EWCA Civ 1622 paras 32, 45, 181–82.

[23] *IS v the Director of Legal Aid Casework and the Lord Chancellor* [2015] EWHC 1965.

[24] Ibid, para 107.

[25] Ibid, para 40.

[26] *Government Response to Justice Committee's Eighth Report of Session 2014–15: Impact of changes to civil legal aid under Part 1 of the Legal Aid, Sentencing and Punishment of Offenders Act 2012*, July 2015, 7. There was a slight increase in grants of exceptional funding in January to March 2015 over the previous quarter. Of 102 determinations in family matters, 21 were successful: Ministry of Justice and Legal Aid Agency, *Legal Aid Statistics in England and Wales January to March 2015*, Figures 31 and 32.

Where the claim for publicly funded legal assistance is made on the basis of actual or risk of domestic violence, one of the following categories of evidence is required:[27]

(a) a relevant unspent conviction for a domestic violence offence;

(b) a relevant police caution for a domestic violence offence given within the twenty-four month period immediately preceding the date of the application for civil legal services;

(c) evidence of relevant criminal proceedings for a domestic violence offence which have not concluded;

(d) a relevant protective injunction which is in force or which was granted within the twenty- four month period immediately preceding the date of the application for civil legal services;

(e) an undertaking given in England and Wales under section 46 or 63E of the Family Law Act 1996 (or given in Scotland or Northern Ireland in place of a protective injunction)—

    (i) by the individual ('B') with whom the applicant for civil legal services ('A') was in a family relationship giving rise to the need for the civil legal services which are the subject of the application; and

    (ii) within the twenty-four month period immediately preceding the date of the application for civil legal services, provided that a cross-undertaking was not given by A;

(ea) evidence that B is on relevant police bail for a domestic violence offence;

(f) a letter from any person who is a member of a multi-agency risk assessment conference [MARAC] confirming that—

    (i) A was referred to the conference as a victim of domestic violence; and

    (ii) the conference has, within the twenty-four month period immediately preceding the date of the application for civil legal services, put in place a plan to protect A from a risk of harm by B;

(g) a copy of a finding of fact, made in proceedings in the United Kingdom within the twenty-four month period immediately preceding the date of the application for civil legal services, that there has been domestic violence by B giving rise to a risk of harm to A;

(h) a letter or report from a health professional who has access to the medical records of A confirming that that that professional or another health professional—

    (i) has examined A in person within the twenty-four month period immediately preceding the date of the application for civil legal services; and

    (ii) was satisfied following that examination that A had injuries or a condition consistent with those of a victim of domestic violence;

(i) a letter from a social services department in England or Wales (or its equivalent in Scotland or Northern Ireland) confirming that, within the twenty-four month period immediately preceding the date of the application, A was assessed as being, or at risk of being, a victim of domestic violence by B (or a copy of that assessment);

---

[27] Civil Legal Aid Procedure Regulations 2012, s 33, as amended by the Civil Legal Aid (Procedure) (Amendment) Regulations 2014.

(j)   a letter or report from a domestic violence support organisation in the United Kingdom confirming—

    (i)   that A was, within the twenty-four month period immediately preceding the date of the application for civil legal services (and, where relevant, that period commences with the date on which A left the refuge), admitted to a refuge established for the purpose of providing accommodation for victims of, or those at risk of, domestic violence;

    (ii)   the dates on which A was admitted to and, where relevant, left the refuge; and

    (iii) that A was admitted to the refuge because of allegations by A of domestic violence;

(k)   a letter or report from a domestic violence support organisation in the United Kingdom confirming—

    (i)   that A was, within the twenty-four month period immediately preceding the date of the application for civil legal services, refused admission to a refuge established for the purpose of providing accommodation for victims of, or those at risk of, domestic violence, on account of there being insufficient accommodation available in the refuge; and

    (ii)   the date on which A was refused admission to the refuge;

(l)   a letter or report from—

    (i)   the person to whom the referral described below was made;

    (ii)   the health professional who made the referral described below; or

    (iii) a health professional who has access to the medical records of A, confirming that there was, within the twenty-four month period immediately preceding the date of the application for civil legal services, a referral by a health professional of A to a person who provides specialist support or assistance for victims of, or those at risk of, domestic violence;

(m)   a relevant domestic violence protection notice issued under section 24 of the Crime and Security Act 2010, or a relevant domestic violence protection order made under section 28 of that Act, against B within the twenty-four month period immediately preceding the date of the application for civil legal services;

(n)   evidence of a relevant court order binding over B in connection with a domestic violence offence, which is in force or which was granted within the twenty-four month period immediately preceding the date of application for civil legal services.

Similar provisions apply in cases where the application for legal aid is based on child abuse.

These are formidable conditions which could operate as a deterrent for fearful victims. Yet, although accepting that there was 'a good arguable case that some victims of serious domestic violence, who are genuinely in need of legal aid, cannot fulfil the requirements', the Divisional Court held that they had been lawfully made within the purpose of LASPO.[28] Most of

---

[28] *R (on the application of Rights of Women) v The Lord Chancellor and Secretary of State for Justice* [2015] EWHC 35 (Admin), para 38.

the circumstances refer to previous proceedings or agency involvement, and would not cover a situation arising after two years from the original incident. So if a perpetrator has been released after serving a custodial sentence of over twenty-four months for a domestic violence related offence, the victim could be in fear but not be eligible. Of the types of evidence required, perhaps the most accessible is the letter from a 'health professional' who may be a 'nurse'.[29] The letter must confirm that the claimant has been examined in person[30] by a nurse and to have suffered from injuries or a condition 'consistent with those of a victim of domestic violence'. There must be doubt as to how far these requirements allow all the kinds of behaviour that could fall within the definition of domestic violence in the amended paragraph 12(9) of LASPO ('any incident, or pattern of incidents, of controlling, coercive or threatening behaviour, violence or abuse (whether psychological, physical, sexual, financial or emotional) between individuals who are associated with each other') to be established for the purposes of obtaining legal aid. A survey by the group 'Rights of Women' suggested that 39 per cent of women who were victims of domestic violence had none of the forms of evidence required to qualify for legal aid.[31]

The provisions underline the conception of law as being important in relationship disputes only when one party's physical health needs to be protected against some form of behaviour by the other party. It could be seen as supplementary to the health service. It has nothing to do with ideas of 'fair dealing' or 'sustaining social norms': in short, nothing to do with justice between individuals. But, as Alison Diduck (2014: 619) has pointed out, 'for reasons of gender and generational fairness, justice should begin in the family, not be banished from it'. Like Lucinda Ferguson (2013: 132–33) and Bill Atkin (2015), she observes that this gives the way 'private' family disputes are settled a 'public' dimension.

These legal aid changes do not mean that law has disappeared from family relationships. It is only that government does not currently consider it sufficiently important that it should be accessible to all. We have moved a long way from the concept of state funding for legal services as a necessary condition for the full and equal exercise of the civil rights described by TH Marshall (1963) in his lecture 'Citizenship and Social Class' given in Cambridge in 1948[32] at a time when the pressing need for help with divorce

---

[29] Civil Legal Aid Procedure Regulations 2012, s 33(3).

[30] In our research we were told that the Co-operative Legal Services had tried to provide a service to help women in this position to access legal aid by offering a phone interview with a trained nurse who would then, if appropriate, provide a letter in accordance with the requirements for a reasonable fee. But this was not accepted by the Legal Aid Agency, which required that any such assessment must be made in person.

[31] See House of Commons Justice Committee (2015: para 67). See also Coy, Scott, Tweedale and Perks (2015).

[32] See Maclean (2000).

following the social stress of World War II was providing a key stimulus for the development of the legal aid system. Fifty years later assisting people through private troubles is no longer held by government to be a proper use of public monies. After LASPO, those with the means to do so can of course use the services of the legal profession. Those without such means (even if the other party does have the means) must use other means. This could involve gathering such information as they can from the internet, or from advice centres, seeking alternative means of dispute resolution or finding themselves in court from choice as applicants or involuntarily as respondents without advice or representation, or simply giving up.

III. MEDIATION AND THE ABANDONMENT OF LEGAL SUPPORT

These legal aid changes were accompanied by a renewed drive to promote mediation. A Practice Direction of 2011 from the President of the Family Division[33] stated an 'expectation' that applicants in most family proceedings will have contacted a mediator before making an application to the court for an 'information meeting about family mediation and other forms of alternative dispute resolution' (known as a mediation information and assessment meeting (MIAM)). But it is not compulsory for the respondent in such a case to attend, or for the parties to undertake mediation itself. It is hoped that attending a MIAM will divert disputes away from courts into mediation. The measure does not attempt to discourage access to legal services at an earlier stage. But the government's ambition for the use of mediation goes well beyond merely diverting cases from the courts. The perception that the only options available to people with family difficulties are mediation or litigation (or at best expensive arm's-length negotiation) expressed in the 1990s has re-surfaced. The government's terms of reference for the panel appointed in 2010 to review the family justice system included the following among its 'guiding principles':

> Mediation and similar support should be used as far as possible to support individuals themselves to reach agreement about arrangements, rather than having an arrangement imposed by the courts.

This repeated a long-standing, and incorrect, assumption that if the parties failed to settle a disagreement among themselves and had resort to lawyers, the matter would inevitably reach the courts. The panel was to examine

> how to increase the use of mediation when couples separate as a preferred alternative to court processes (Family Justice Review 2011: Annex A).

This is notable by its omission of any reference to the role of lawyers, especially solicitors, in achieving settlement without going to court, and of their

---

[33] Practice Direction 3A, *Pre-Action Protocol for Mediation Information and Assessment.*

role in providing the kind of assistance and support mentioned earlier. In fact, in its final report the panel was supportive of lawyers and recognised the importance of legal advice,[34] and simply recommended that 'attendance at a MIAM and (Separated Parents Information Programme (SPIP)) should be required of anyone wishing to make a court application', though mediation itself would not be compulsory (Family Justice Review 2011: Executive Summary paras 115–19). Thus the 'expectation' referred to in the Practice Direction of 2011 became a legal requirement in the subsequent legislation.[35] This time, however, the government wielded a financial weapon in an attempt to ensure that mediation was used at an even earlier stage. As mentioned above, apart from some special cases, no legal aid would be available for any 'private law' family matter, whether in the form of advice or other forms of legal help, or representation in court. However, as the panel put it, 'the Government recognised the value of legal advice *alongside mediation*' (Family Justice Review (2011: para 4.96) (our emphasis)). Legal advice was not seen by government as sufficiently valuable in itself. Therefore funding would be available for eligible individuals for undergoing mediation, with limited amounts also available for legal advice both during and immediately after the mediation,[36] but not before or in place of it.

Consistently with the subordination of the role of lawyers demonstrated by the government's terms of reference to the panel, the website 'Maintenance Options', developed by the government, gives this advice to parents who may be 'struggling' to agree on child maintenance:

> If you're struggling to reach agreement with your child's other parent, mediation might help. As a last resort, you can use the courts or the statutory child maintenance service to arrange child maintenance.

It then proclaims:

> Mediation can: help you make decisions before or after you've separated or divorced; help you both work together to decide what's best for your child; reduce conflict between you and your child's other parent; make a flexible, lasting agreement on issues such as child maintenance; be cheaper than going to court.[37]

Once again, the only option mentioned other than mediation for those finding it difficult to reach agreement is 'going to court'. Nor is there any reference to the guidance lawyers might provide when parties may not be in conflict, but may need support and guidance. It is not surprising, then, that from 1 April 2013, under the provisions of LASPO, when public funding was withdrawn from most 'private' family issues, some funding was retained for mediation, and a small amount for legal advice if given in support of

---

[34] Family Justice Review (2011: paras 2.223, 4.95; Executive Summary para 51).
[35] Children and Families Act 2014, s 10 (1).
[36] LASPO, s 9(1) and Schedule 1, Part 1, clause 12.
[37] Accessed 23 January 2015.

mediation.[38] But that could only be accessed once mediation had started, and only applies if there is a 'family dispute'. The possibility that help may be needed to clarify the parties' entitlements and possibly *prevent* a dispute from arising does not seem to have been considered by policy makers.

Since then the perception that the only significant alternatives are 'going to court', implying a contested hearing, or mediation seems to have hardened. In 2014 a Ministry of Justice Task Force on Mediation, despite saying that dispute resolution services 'could include psychologists, counsellors, child consultants, financial advisers and in particular, legal advisers' (Family Mediation Task Force 2014: para 16), thought that mediation was likely to be the 'primary option', adding that 'in looking towards this pattern of choices and provision we do not want to downplay the continuing role of the judiciary and the courts' and that 'the role of the judiciary in promoting mediation and other forms of out of court dispute resolution at every stage of the litigation process is also crucial not only so that appropriate cases move out of litigation into mediation but also so that the general public and legal profession is constantly reminded by the judiciary itself that the court may not be the best option' (Family Mediation Task Force 2014: paras 24, 25). Also in 2014 a government-supported document advising mediators how to promote themselves states at one point: 'The Government is committed to encouraging more people to resolve their disputes outside of the courtroom, which is why it is introducing legislation to require people to consider mediation before going to court', and at another: 'You do not necessarily have to see a lawyer as a first step when you decide to separate or divorce—you can go straight to a mediator' (Ministry of Justice and Family Mediation Council 2014: 19).

IV. IMPACT OF THE LEGAL AID CHANGES OF APRIL 2013 ON SERVICES FOR INDIVIDUALS CONTEMPLATING SEPARATION

On the face of it, the policy was devised in order to reduce the number of legally aided family cases going to court for adjudication, although, as we have seen, it has also cut away the public funding given for the advisory and supportive function of lawyers. Yet those who consulted solicitors have only rarely required judicial resolution. The overwhelming majority of issues raised with solicitors were resolved without it. As stated earlier, legal aid has been retained in public law cases and in private cases in specific circumstances where a party is deemed to be 'vulnerable' (largely as a result of violence, for which there must be objective evidence), certain international cases and 'exceptional circumstances' where failure to provide

[38] LASPO, Schedule 1, para 14.

legal aid would breach someone's rights under the European Convention on Human Rights.[39]

The National Audit Office (NAO), which is charged with scrutinising public spending for Parliament, and is independent of government, has reported that the legal aid changes did result in a significant overall reduction in the provision of legal aid. Indeed, the NAO calculated that the Ministry of Justice was likely to exceed the savings of £268 million it would be expected to make as a result of the changes by another £32 million because it was funding even fewer matters than anticipated (Ministry of Justice and Legal Aid Agency 2014b: Summary, Key Finding 5). As regards family law, the total number of private law family court cases started in April–June 2014 was about 41 per cent lower than for April–June 2013 (public law cases remaining stable) (Ministry of Justice, September 2014: 13). However, the NAO report noted that the number of family court cases starting (including those eligible for legal aid) where neither party had legal representation was 30 per cent higher in the financial year 2013–14 compared to 2012–13, and that in the January–March quarter of 2014 both parties were represented in only 20 per cent of cases starting in the family courts compared to 27 per cent for the same quarter in 2013 (immediately prior to the implementation of LASPO) (Ministry of Justice and Legal Aid Agency 2014b: para 1.25 and Figure 3). The report went on to observe that the increased number of cases in the family courts where neither party was legally represented could generate £3 million additional costs for HM Courts and Tribunals Service, which finances the courts (Ibid: Key Finding 6).[40]

Even more notable is the information that in the financial year 2013–14 the Legal Aid Agency agreed funding for legal help (that is, legal advice) in 161,623 fewer family cases than in the previous financial year before the reforms, a drop of 79 per cent, and for legal representation in 38,018 fewer family cases, a drop of 30 per cent (Ibid: para 2.7 and Figure 6). This indicates the extent of the devastation wrought on the supportive work of legal aid solicitors described earlier in this chapter. The expectation that this would be replaced by mediation was not realised. In fact between 2012–13 and 2013–14 publicly funded mediation assessments and mediation starts fell by 17,246 (56 per cent) and 5,177 (38 per cent) respectively (Ibid: para 2.8). Expenditure on family mediation fell by just over a half. Legal aid figures show that in the financial year 2013/14 there were 13,423 publicly funded mediation 'assessments' (a drop of 56.2 per cent from the previous year) leading to 8,432 mediation starts (a conversion rate of 62.8 per cent). However, the number of assessment *meetings* was much larger (30,447 in 2013–14 where parties were seen together, separately or alone, a drop of

---

[39] LASPO, ss 8–10 and Schedule 1, Part One.
[40] For more data, see (2014) *Family Law*, November, 'Update' and Ministry of Justice and Legal Aid Agency (2014a).

60 per cent from the previous year). So the number of meetings where mediators discussed the possibility of mediation exceeded actual mediations by nearly 3:1. Of the 9,672 mediation outcomes over that period, 65 per cent reached full agreement while 31 per cent failed to reach agreement (Ministry of Justice and Legal Aid Agency 2014a, calculated from Tables 7.1 and 7.2; Family Mediation Task Force 2014: 8). Figures from National Family Mediation (NFM) give 27,000 formal referrals (that is, any referral by a third party, such as a court, lawyer, counselling agency, GP, or Citizens Advice Bureau, as opposed to self-referral) to NFM members for 2013–14, a drop of 31 per cent from the previous year, and that 6,200 (18.2 per cent) of all referrals (34,000, formal and self-referred) proceeded to full mediation, a 14 per cent decrease from the previous year. Of these mediations, just over one half were fully successful, while one-third failed to reach agreement (National Family Mediation 2014).

There could be a number of reasons for the fall in mediation assessments and assessment meetings, including that the need to make a referral as a condition for obtaining legal aid for representation fell away as such legal aid was virtually abolished, that lawyers may have thought they could resolve matters without recourse to the added time and cost of attempted mediation and that people were using lawyers less often as legal aid for advice was seldom available so there were fewer clients whom lawyers could refer to mediation. The modest extent to which referrals proceed to mediation perhaps supports this view. The generally low level of mediation starts shows that mediation has not taken the place of the drastically reduced availability of legally aided advice by lawyers, despite the government's willingness to fund such mediation. This is an inevitable consequence of the government's misunderstanding of the role lawyers were playing, and failure to appreciate that this could not simply be replaced by mediation.

Concerns that these events would have harmful consequences for mediation providers led the government to appoint the Task Force referred to above as part of an attempt to 'gather ideas for how to improve the mediation picture' (Family Mediation Task Force 2014: para 5). Perhaps its most practical suggestion, accepted by the government,[41] was that for a period of three years both parties who attend a MIAM should receive public funding for the first session of the mediation even if only one qualified for it (Ibid: para 49), but mainly it concentrated on ways of promoting public understanding of mediation in the hope that this would bring about a 'cultural shift' (Ibid: paras 27, 28). Its more radical suggestion that government should make all MIAMs free irrespective of the parties' means for a

---

[41] See *Government Response to Justice Committee's Eighth Report of Session 2014–15: Impact of changes to civil legal aid under Part 1 of the Legal Aid, Sentencing and Punishment of Offenders Act 2012* presented to Parliament by the Lord Chancellor and Secretary of State for Justice by Command of Her Majesty July 2015, 18.

period of 12 months (Ibid: para 43) was not accepted although the House of Commons Justice Committee (2015: para 158) repeated this suggestion. Subsequently the government and Family Mediation Council launched a desperate-looking attempt to advise mediators how to sell their product and 'get a "bigger bang for your buck"' in a document that treats it solely as a business (Ministry of Justice and Family Mediation Council 2014: 15).

The NAO report's observation that 'the Ministry implemented the reforms without a good understanding of why people go to court to resolve their disputes' (Ministry of Justice and Legal Aid Agency 2014b: 7, Key Finding 11) and its reference to an even more significant failure to understand why people 'access legal aid' (Ibid: 8, Key Finding 17) seem well founded. The report suggests possible damaging consequences:

> There may ... be costs to the wider public sector if people whose problems could have been resolved by legal aid funded advice suffer adverse consequences to their health and well being as a result of no longer having access to legal aid (Ibid: 6, Key Finding 6).

> The Ministry reduced fees for providers without a robust understanding of how this would affect the market and monitoring has been limited (Ibid: 7, Key Finding 14).

This echoes the findings in the report commissioned by the Law Society from Cookson (2011), drawing on data from the English and Welsh Social Justice Survey and the Legal Services Commission (see also Cookson 2013).

As regards the impact on the legal services market, there is a real danger that, despite the innovative measures taken by some solicitors described in the next chapter, the willingness of solicitors to continue with, or enter, family law practice will be severely damaged. Even before LASPO family legal aid provision was being restricted. The Legal Services Commission had offered only 1,300 contracts for family work in 2010 instead of the previous total of 2,400, favouring bigger firms, which were considered more efficient, but devastating the smaller local firms where specialists in family work were often found.[42] A joint study by the Law Society, the Ministry of Justice and the Legal Services Board in 2012 found that 31 per cent of legal aid firms indicated that they were likely to cease doing legal aid work during the next three years (Pleasence, Balmer and Moorhead 2012: ii). It must be remembered that, in addition to the removal of much private family law work from the scope of legal aid provision, years of freezing rates of pay for legal aid work had been followed by a reduction of these fees by 10 per cent, so that the National Audit Office report discloses that many providers said that the fees paid for legal aid work did not meet the costs

---

[42] See Resolution Survey 2010 of all solicitors offering legal aid work, reported by Natalie Hanman in *The Guardian*, 17 August 2010; also *Family Law Week*, www.familylawweek. co.uk/site.aspx?i=ed64464 (accessed 15 April 2015).

of providing it. A survey reporting the responses of 275 practitioners found that 68 per cent reported that their ability to balance the books had decreased over the previous year, compared with 3 per cent reporting an increased ability, and 11 per cent reporting no change (Ministry of Justice and Legal Aid Agency 2014b: paras 3.20–21 and Figure 12).

The NAO recommended that

> the Ministry should develop measures to evaluate the impact of the reforms more fully; continuing to monitor the use of mediation and considering what further action it should take if take up does not increase in line with expectations; should establish the extent to which those who are eligible for civil legal aid are able to access it; should develop its understanding of the challenges facing civil legal aid providers and the provision of support across the country [and] use this improved understanding to ensure sustainability in the market and coverage across the country (Ibid: 8, Recommendations).

Unless this is done, the report concluded, 'implementation of the reforms to civil legal aid cannot be said to have delivered better overall value for money for the taxpayer' (Ibid: 8, para 17). The House of Commons Justice Committee (2015: paras 87–89) agreed:

> 87. We were not impressed by the Minister's response to our concerns about the impact of the legal aid reforms on providers of publicly funded legal services. We share the concerns of the National Audit Office, concerns we raised in our report in 2011, that the legal aid reforms were carried out without adequate evidence of the likely impact on the sufficiency and sustainability of the legal aid market.
>
> 88. The National Audit Office found that fourteen local authority areas saw no face to face civil legal aid work at all in 2013–14, and very small numbers of cases were started in a further 39 local authority areas. We are deeply concerned that this may indicate the existence of a substantial number of 'advice deserts'.
>
> 89. We urged the Government in 2011 to carry out research into the geographical distribution of legal aid providers to ensure sufficient provision to protect access to justice. Not only did the Ministry of Justice fail to heed our warning, it has also failed to monitor the impact of the legal aid reforms on the geographical provision of providers. We do not know for certain if there are advice deserts in England and Wales, and nor does the Ministry of Justice. This work needs to be carried out immediately because once capacity and expertise are lost the Ministry of Justice will find it difficult, and potentially expensive, to restore them. In some areas it may already be too late.

V. CONSEQUENCES OF LACK OF REPRESENTATION

Prior to the establishment of the single family court,[43] a Report by Mr Justice Ryder, on behalf of the Judiciary in England and Wales, recognised the

---

[43] Crime and Courts Act 2013, s 17.

importance of providing support for litigants in person (LIPs) (also known as self-represented litigants (SRPs)) in private law family cases, saying:

> The Family Justice Council is collaborating with professionals with expertise in assisting self representing litigants and Government to provide advice and materials to assist courts and self representing litigants in the conduct of private law and financial remedy proceedings. These materials will be available in a variety of formats (Ryder 2012: para 58).

However, research carried out for the Ministry of Justice, completed in September 2013 and published a year later (Trinder et al 2014), identified considerable needs for support for LIPs across several dimensions. The authors found that the main reason for appearing in person was lack of funds, and that only a small minority of LIPs were able to represent themselves competently in all aspects of their family law proceedings. A range of vulnerabilities was identified. These caused problems for the court by reason of non-appearance, refusal to engage with the proceedings, and sometimes violent and aggressive behaviour.[44]

Unmeritorious and serial applications did not appear to be brought more often by LIPs than by represented parties. But pre-hearing preparations were not adequate. Such preparations included determining the legal merits of a case, translating a dispute into a legal form, considering mediation, making an application correctly, and possibly negotiating with the other side in the waiting room and subsequent handling of the case in matters such as disclosure and filing statements. All of these issues raise problems for court staff, as the court system is predicated on an adversarial model with full representation. Preparing court bundles and conducting cross-examination were beyond the capacity of most LIPs without help. In some cases the hearings were managed satisfactorily when the lawyer for one side in effect worked for both parties, or a third party such as a lawyer for the children acted as broker, or the judge took on a fully inquisitorial role, or if the LIPs were competent. But in other cases, hearings had to be adjourned when they became disrupted by LIPs, or took longer and extra hearings were needed, or LIPs were unprotected and unable to explore concerns or present their case.

The authors (Trinder et al 2014) made a number of suggestions for ameliorating the situation. They recommended that all relevant forms, practice directions, templates and pro forma documents should be re-evaluated from the perspective of the LIP, that judges should be encouraged to give LIPs

---

[44] In September 2014 unrepresented litigants in Canada published a frank open letter to the judiciary, saying they were tired of being treated as 'annoying obstacles unworthy of compassion and understanding' when they stand before the courts and are advised to get a lawyer when they simply cannot afford one. They said 'the most important and simple reason that we are representing ourselves is that we cannot afford, or can no longer afford, the cost of legal services': www.lawtimesnews.com/201409224205/headline-news/unrepresented-litigants-make-plea-for-compassion (accessed 27 January 2015).

clear verbal instructions and guidance on process and procedure, that court staff should be available for face-to-face inquiries, that a single family member or friend should be able to accompany the LIP, and that a mechanism should be introduced to enable judicial recommendation for the provision of publicly funded representation in the interests of justice when needed.

During 2014, the President of the Family Division sought to resolve the unfairness that could arise in private law cases which did not qualify for funding, and in public law cases which did, but where a party only marginally failed the means test for eligibility by assuming that the Family Procedure Regulations, which proclaimed their overriding objective as being to ensure fairness, and a statutory provision allowing the court to 'cause' questions to be put to a witness, empowered judges to order that representation be provided for a litigant at the expense of a public body, perhaps a local authority or the court service.[45] This solution was, however, eventually rejected by the Court of Appeal.[46] That court suggested that in some cases unfairness could be avoided by judges acting in a more inquisitorial manner and posing questions on behalf of LIPs, or through funding lawyers through exceptional case determinations.[47] However, Adrian Zuckerman has powerfully argued that it is a misconception to think that 'inquisitorial' processes make the use of lawyers unnecessary (Zuckerman 2014).

Some support for LIPs can be found in helpful counter staff on court premises. One of us, when trying to help a friend with her petition, after trying for some weeks to seek clarification on how to complete the form by letter, and having called many times by telephone, finally got through to a member of the counter staff who gave excellent advice, confirming the information required but advising not to post anything as so much gets lost. Instead he suggested faxing the information to a number for his attention, and promised that he would sit by the machine until it appeared and call back to confirm, and did so, at 4.30 on a Friday afternoon. Sadly this part of the court service is also under pressure and subject to austerity measures.

In October 2014 the Ministry of Justice announced plans to allocate £2 million over the next two years (between £1.4 million and £1.6 million in 2014–15) and between £1.4 and £1.6 million in 2015–16 to support LIPs in family and civil courts through the use of voluntary sector personal support units in courts, funding community law centres to give initial legal advice and improving online information (Ministry of Justice and Legal Aid Agency 2014: para 1.30). Evaluation of the contribution of the voluntary sector is limited so far. A report (Sefton, Moorhead, Sidaway and Fox 2011) on the service provided by the Citizens Advice Bureau at the Central Family Court in London describes 35 family law clients being helped with up

---

[45] *Q v Q* [2014] EWFC 31; *Re D* [2014] EWFC 39.

[46] *K & H (Children)* [2015] EWCA Civ 543.

[47] See also *Gudanaviciene and Others, R (on the application of) v The Director of Legal Aid Casework and Another* [2014] EWCA Civ 1622, para 185.

to three 45-minute appointments with a solicitor from private practice (an Honorary Legal Adviser) working mainly on procedural aspects of the case rather than giving advice on the merits, and able to refer to the Bar Pro Bono Unit for representation if required. Over half the clients using this service had wanted help with the divorce process, and many were vulnerable as a result of health problems, difficulties with language, or reported being victims of domestic abuse. They were advised to be concise, to avoid contentious language, to check facts, prepare schedules for the contact arrangements they sought, and to focus on immediate issues, putting the interests of the children first. Advisers were confident that their work was of benefit, and clients confirmed this, comparing it favourably with online and published guides to legal problems.

In 2014 the then Minister concerned with family justice, Simon Hughes announced that in November 2014 CAFCASS (the Children and Family Court Advisory and Support Service) would pilot a free telephone helpline, the 'Supporting separating parents in dispute helpline', for six months. It aimed to put separating parents 'who have been unable to resolve disputes and want to avoid court battles over their children or who need help in doing so' in touch with an experienced professional

> who will act as their single point of contact throughout the dispute. They will talk through the difficulties being faced, assess what support the parent needs and will offer impartial information and guidance. This will include putting callers in touch with the relevant local professionals and support services, including mediation.

CAFCASS will follow up with the parent to see how efforts to resolve the dispute are progressing and, if necessary, will provide further assistance.[48]

A local initiative in Bristol co-ordinates the work of six voluntary agencies (a Law Centre with a voluntary solicitor scheme, a Citizens Advice Bureau, a Personal Support Unit which uses volunteers to support people on court premises, a Multi-Faith Support Group, a group of postgraduate law students who provide 'assistance', and the Samaritans) (see Wildblood, Goldingham and Evans 2014). How far these schemes address the real needs of LIPs remains to be seen.

VI. WHAT FOLLOWS

In the light of these concerns, Chapter 2 will first look in more detail at the changing structure of the legal profession after the deregulation which followed the Legal Services Act 2007. We then set out the findings of our small study of the front-line response from the profession, drawing on data from a sample of Resolution members' websites, and the development of working arrangements with web-based services.

---

[48] See www.cafcass.gov.uk/news/2014/october/minister-announces-new-cafcass-out-of-court-pilots.aspx (accessed 29 July 2015).

2

The Marketisation of the Legal Profession

T HE NEW LANDSCAPE for delivering legal services in family matters has been described in the preceding chapter in terms of resources and ideology, the combined impact of the recession and the implementation of neo-liberal policies. This chapter will look at how the legal profession is responding to these challenges, drawing first on published data on deregulation and its effect on the market for legal services, and then on data from our small survey of what solicitors are promising on their websites, and how they are working with the internet as it develops into a new provider of legal information and advice.

I. DEREGULATION AND FREEING THE MARKET

Following the report of the Family Justice Review (2011: 49–63) in November 2011 there has been less talk of courts and lawyers and more of a Family Justice Service which covers a wider range of interventions and services, including various forms of alternative dispute resolution, advice and support. The judicial response in a report by Mr Justice Ryder (2012) focused on the court system. It made recommendations about how the work of the proposed single family court that was envisaged under the then Crime and Courts Bill (subsequently the Crime and Courts Act 2013) would be carried out. The key proposals were for strong judicial management, which would control the deployment of specialist judges in the network of courts that would comprise the single family court and the allocation of cases to them, and the development of case management procedures which would accelerate progress, especially of public law cases. There were also recommendations for developing support for self-represented litigants.

But while these steps have been taken to unify and rationalise the family court system, the landscape for the delivery of family justice outside the courts has become increasingly fragmented. The previous chapter described the gradual restriction of public funding of legal services culminating in the Legal Aid, Sentencing and Punishment of Offenders Act 2012 (LASPO). But alongside this was the parallel attempt to deregulate the work of the legal professions and work towards establishing a free market in legal services, which was seen to have the potential to bring down legal costs. Signs of this appeared in Margaret Thatcher's period in office with the removal of the solicitors' monopoly in conveyancing by allowing the practice to be carried out by licensed conveyancers[1] and by building societies for non-borrowers.[2] But it was taken up in earnest by Lord Mackay, Lord Chancellor from 1987 to 1997, especially in three Green Papers published in 1989. These discussed bringing to an end the limitation of advocacy to members of the Bar, further extending conveyancing by non-lawyers, allowing multidisciplinary partnerships and advertising by lawyers, and reducing legal aid costs by shifting the cost of litigation from legal aid to the parties under conditional fees (though these did not operate in family cases) (see Abel 2003: especially ch 2; Abel 2005: ch 1; Boon 2010).

Despite strong resistance by the legal profession, the Courts and Legal Services Act 1990 enacted provisions regarding advocacy rights,[3] the extension of conveyancing services,[4] and conditional fees.[5] Turning to court procedure, an inquiry into access to civil justice led by Sir Harry Woolf, which reported in 1996 (Woolf 1996), sought to simplify, speed up and reduce the cost of civil litigation with the introduction of pre-action protocols designed to enhance the prospect of achieving settlement prior to initiating proceedings, and increased judicial case management if that failed. As mentioned in the previous chapter, the Labour government went on to fundamentally change the way legal aid was funded in the Access to Justice Act 1999. This also widened the scope of conditional fees (but they were still not permitted in family cases), extended the Woolf reforms to the appeal system, and further broadened the scope for granting rights of audience to non-barristers.

Subsequently, a report from Sir David Clementi (2004), commissioned by the then Department of Constitutional Affairs (now the Ministry of Justice), recommended far-reaching changes in the regulation of the legal profession. In the Introduction to his report, Clementi noted that 'certain' lawyers 'see a conflict between lawyers as professionals and lawyers as business people'. He responded that 'the idea that there is a major conflict is in my view misplaced. Access to justice requires not only that the legal advice given is sound, but also the presence of the business skills necessary to provide a cost-effective service in a consumer-friendly way' (Ibid: Introduction, para 10). The Clementi report made two recommendations that were fundamental to the structure of legal services. One was to remove the regulatory function from the professions' representative bodies (the Bar Council and the Law Society) to an independent Legal Services Board, and the other was to

---

[1] Administration of Justice Act 1985.
[2] Building Societies Act 1986.
[3] See Courts and Legal Services Act 1990, ss 27–33.
[4] Ibid, ss 34–53.
[5] Ibid, s 58.

permit non-lawyers to manage, and have ownership interests in, firms that deliver legal services (later known as alternative business structures (ABSs)) and also that those ABSs might provide a mixture of legal and non-legal services (multi-disciplinary practices (MDPs)). Both of these were implemented in the Legal Services Act 2007 (LSA). The Legal Services Board has general oversight over approved, independent regulators of providers of legal services such as the Solicitors Regulation Authority (SRA) for solicitors, the Bar Standards Board (BSB) for barristers, CILEx Regulation (for legal executives), the Council for Licensed Conveyancers (for conveyancers) and some others. The regulation extends only to the carrying out of 'reserved legal activities'. These are the exercise of rights of audience (that is appearing as an advocate before a court); the conduct of litigation (that is issuing proceedings before a court and commencing, prosecuting or defending those proceedings); reserved instrument activities (that is dealing with the transfer of land or property under specific legal provisions); probate activities (that is, handling probate matters for clients); notarial activities (that is work governed by the Public Notaries Act 1801) and the administration of oaths (that is taking oaths, swearing affidavits etc).[6]

The direction policy was taking created both problems and opportunities. The criticism of professionalism was not only directed at lawyers, but at all professionals as part of a pro-enterprise culture associated with economic liberalism, individual freedom, the sovereign consumer and the non-interventionist state (see Webley 2015). The concept of the professional having certain privileges (for example, market control and self-regulation) in return for occupational expertise, knowledge and competence, which Paterson (2012: 16, 53) refers to as a 'compact', was being challenged. 'Traditionally', Evetts (2015: 24) observes, 'despite having always had one foot in the market, a primary characteristic of professionals has been their claim that they operate according to a general ethics based on social solidarity and citizenship'. In Paterson's words: 'lawyers are expected to adhere to the core professional values of independence, loyalty, confidentiality, upholding the rule of law and their duties to the court—plumbers are not' (Paterson 2012: 13).[7]

This changing policy climate was accompanied by the gradual development of a 'discourse of enterprise' to be fitted alongside the language of professionalism, quality, customer service and care' (Evetts 2015: 34). At the same time as the LSA established a new regulatory framework for lawyers, initiating a managerial ethic into the provision of legal services (Boon 2010), the Ministry of Justice was 'embedding' management consultants in the department and beginning to refer to 'segmenting the market' for legal services and to

---

[6] Legal Services Act 2007, s 12 and Schedule 2.
[7] Paterson adds: 'The scandal of Enron and the devastation to the world economies triggered by greedy bankers do not make happy exemplars for the new business paradigm.'

legal service users as 'customers' instead of 'clients'. Changes in information technology stimulated new ways of advertising and offering information and advice, and more online solutions were predicted. As for family lawyers, while they were now more free to work in new and hopefully sustainable and productive ways, they were shocked by the sudden withdrawal of legal aid from significant areas of private law work and dispirited by the repeated but unsubstantiated negative policy messages about how they maximised hostility between clients and were eager to proceed to litigation.

II. NEW QUESTIONS

In this changed climate, it is important to try to discover how the new structure is affecting the market for legal services. Is, as Evetts (2015: 31) suggests, a reconciliation of the 'enterprise' and 'professional' paradigms possible, resulting in a kind of 'hybridity', and if so what does it look like in practice? Are solicitors still consulted at the time of relationship breakdown or other family change or crisis? In particular, are they consulted about divorce, which brings about legal change in many aspects of family life, not only of civil status but also regarding home ownership, mortgage and pension arrangements, division of assets, wills, and maintenance arrangements for a spouse or children? A solicitor may be needed simply to give information and advice regarding these issues, but may also be asked to help to obtain information from, or negotiate with, third parties, such as local authorities, pension providers, insurance companies or building societies. Beyond that, if dispute arises, they can be called on to negotiate an agreement, whether concerning financial matters or arrangements for children. If this is the case, the solicitor may need to help with verifying disclosure of assets, or seeking expert advice on tax, or child welfare, or checking a proposal agreed in mediation. The most likely outcome will be an agreement which may be put into the form of a Consent Order so as to make it enforceable as an order of court and avoid later court applications. In rare cases there may be adjudication in a contested final hearing in court.

If lawyers are being consulted, we need to know what kinds of services they are offering and how they are doing it. Do they still have extensive face-to-face client meetings, or is there greater use of phone and email? How is the work charged and paid for in the wake of the recession and LASPO? How extensively are fixed price offers used? How often do lawyers help clients to obtain loans which may be secured on property which may be part of the divorce settlement? Has pro bono work increased? How do the services provided by solicitors fit alongside the newly developing forms of advice and support now available either with or as a substitute for the traditional work of the lawyer? These include mediation, early neutral evaluation, arbitration, counselling, parenting education, forensic accountancy, tax advice, and also online services including web-based information or advice. The latter ranges from the general to the specific, with and without charge, and from simple document handling and checking in non-conflicted cases to more complex information and advice in more difficult cases.

III. THE CHANGING MARKET FOR DIVORCE-RELATED SERVICES

A. Demand

In our earlier research into the financial consequences of divorce (Eekelaar and Maclean 1986: 101) we found marked differences between the behaviour of divorcing parties who had children and those who did not. In a general population sample of 274 men and women who had divorced in England and Wales since 1981, 61 per cent of the childless had seen a lawyer, compared with 87 per cent of those with children. Only 9 per cent of the childless received legal aid, compared with 63 per cent of those with children. Court orders for continuing maintenance were made in 55 per cent of those involving children but only 10 per cent of childless divorces, and legal costs were generally under £200, including conveyancing. Ten years later, in a sample of 152 divorced parents screened out from the general population (that is, not a court-based sample), we found that 73 per cent had seen a lawyer (Maclean and Eekelaar 1997: 133). These figures are consistent with those found by Hazel Genn (1999: 115) where, from a sample of 165 individuals reporting a justiciable problem of a non-trivial nature related to divorce, 89 per cent had seen a lawyer. But by 2013 Barlow et al (2014), drawing on a general population sample which yielded 288 adults in England and Wales who had divorced since 1996, found that only 53 per cent had sought any legal advice.

We might ask whether this decline in the rate of consultation with lawyers was associated with increased use of alternative forms of dispute resolution, and in particular mediation, as government had long been encouraging. But Barlow et al's study found that only 48 people in their sample (16.6 per cent) had seen a mediator, and only one of these had done so without also seeing a lawyer. Perhaps levels of public satisfaction with legal services had fallen? We are not aware of evidence to support this view, and the level of satisfaction with legal help found by Barlow et al remained high (65 per cent), similar to that found by Genn (1999: 30–31)[8] compared to 41 per cent expressing satisfaction with mediation.[9]

---

[8] 53% found the advice helpful and 28% found it very helpful. Genn found that of those seeking advice in divorce and separation, 66% wanted to know their legal rights, 43% asked about procedures, 44% wanted advice on how to solve a problem and 43% sought advice on their financial position.

[9] See also Moloney et al (2011), which gives high satisfaction ratings for lawyers in Australia.

Another possible factor could be increased use of 'self-help' through the use of web-based advice services. These services are hard to define and rapidly developing, but a 2013 survey carried out by YouGov,[10] drawing on 866 adults aged over 25 from their online panel who had been involved in divorce proceedings over the last five years (that is mostly before the legal aid changes), found that 60 per cent consulted solicitors or law firms, and generally expressed satisfaction. 20 per cent had incurred legal fees below £1,000, 44 per cent under £2,000 and 28 per cent above £5,000. A quarter of the sample (but one-third of those aged 25–34) had arranged the divorce themselves, though only 30 per cent of these used a DIY website, of whom two-thirds sought free information and advice or to download documents. Only 11 per cent of the total divorcing sample had used those sites for free consultation or advice. 64 per cent had incurred legal fees below £500 and 30 per cent below £200. These were, however, in the lower age group (25–34 year olds) and were coping with simpler, less conflicted, divorces. Mediation services were reported as little used, and there was limited use of other support and advice agencies. Another factor is the effect of the recession. The Legal Services Board reported that between 2006/07 and 2010/11 there was a 46 per cent fall in residential property transactions, a 72 per cent fall in the number of approvals for re-mortgaging and a 30 per cent fall in applications for probate, and that the Legal Services Consumer Panel reported a drop in purchasing family law services (Pleasence, Balmer and Moorhead 2012: 2). Yet in the Legal Services Board's benchmarking survey of 4,017 individuals, published in 2012, 10 per cent of respondents reported facing legal needs around divorce in the preceding three years; 9 per cent of adults reported legal needs in respect of relationship breakdown, followed by 6 per cent facing children issues, and 6 per cent domestic violence. In all 4 per cent of the public had used legal services relating to family matters in that period, second only to conveyancing and will-writing (both 7 per cent). Of those seeking professional advice for a family problem, 82 per cent had used a solicitor. Fifty-eight per cent were face-to-face consultations, while 15 per cent were by telephone and 16 per cent online. Nearly three-quarters were satisfied with all aspects of the service, though only a little over a half thought it was good value for money (slightly below average for all classes of service) (Legal Services Board 2012: 9–11; The Law Society July 2013: 163–65, 167–8).

B. Supply

The previous chapter referred to evidence indicating an apparent decline in the provision of family law services after the legal aid changes of April 2013.

---

[10] (2013) 43 *Family Law* 1086. http://reports.yougov.com/sectors/legal/legal-uk/family-law-divorce/.

But reduction in legal aid payments and the new regulatory regime, with its emphasis on a business-like approach, changing fee structures, increased competition, changes to ownership rules and the introduction of new technologies, had started before then, particularly with the Legal Services Act 2007. The Law Society's Baseline Survey of solicitors' firms in 2007 (Pleasence, Balmer and Moorhead 2012) includes information on the cumulative effect of these changes, combined with the recession, on family law firms, and family law work in general firms even before the legal aid changes of 2013. The most common problems reported by the sample as a whole related to compliance with regulations, costs, obtaining finance, responding to competition, and adapting to the changes in legal aid; firms doing substantial criminal and family work were strongly affected by the latter (Ibid: 21). Thirty-two per cent of firms in existence in both 2007/08 and 2010/11 reported an increase in turnover during the period, while 41 per cent reported a decrease. The size of the firm was an important factor. The provision of legal services in family and children law is almost wholly comprised of small and medium firms, with the 10 highest earning firms having only a 7.1 per cent share of the market, well below the average of 19.3 per cent in other areas of law (see The Law Society July 2013: 161). Twenty-eight per cent of larger firms (with over 40 solicitors) had increased their turnover by 10 per cent or more over the previous three years, and only 6 per cent reported a decrease of 10 per cent or more, whereas only 19.6 per cent of smaller firms (2–5 solicitors) improved turnover by 10 per cent or more, while 30.3 per cent reported a decrease of 10 per cent or more.

Firms between these sizes presented a steadier picture, with about a quarter increasing their turnover by 10 per cent or more, and another quarter experiencing an equivalent decrease (Pleasence, Balmer and Moorhead 2012: 33 and Table 12). The results for firms for whom at least 25 per cent of their work was in family law were in line with the results generally, 16.6 per cent increasing turnover by 10 per cent or more and 27.7 per cent reporting an equivalent decrease (Ibid: 34 and Table 13). But firms with at least 50 per cent of their work in family law fared slightly better than the average in terms of turnover (Ibid: 34). So at this stage solicitors doing family law work were adapting to the changes in much the same way as others, although in 2010/11 firms of all sizes with a significant (more than 30 per cent) focus on family and children law generated less turnover per fee earner than the average for all firms (The Law Society July 2013: 162). With LASPO looming, as we observed in the previous chapter, '31 per cent of current legal aid firms were considering withdrawing from one or more areas of legal aid work in the next 3 years. This was most significant in the case of firms undertaking family legal aid' (Ibid: ii).

Further data from the Law Society (The Law Society 2014) tell a similar story of problems with competition for work, financing, legal aid changes and compliance with regulations. But the outlook varies by type of firm.

While 35 per cent of the larger firms (here defined as comprising 26 or more partners) reported problems in competition for business, only 14 per cent of small (1–4 partners) and 19 per cent of medium (5–25 partners) did so. However, small and medium firms were much more likely to report problems in regulatory compliance and regarding legal aid. Only 8 per cent of the larger firms reported problems concerning legal aid compared with 24 per cent of small firms and 29 per cent of medium-sized firms (Ibid: 5).

Our discussions with practitioners indicated that the small firms are trying to meet these challenges by cutting staff costs through hiring more legal assistants and fewer assistant solicitors. The differences in levels of skill between the two may be decreasing as law graduates are increasingly turning to the Chartered Institute of Legal Executives (CILEx), now registered as an approved regulator, for training to begin a legal career. Single practitioners and small firms are forming networks, or 'pods', sharing expertise and office space, often only using this for initial interviews, thereafter working by phone or email from home to keep costs down. These networks can provide quality assurance and wider specialist coverage, and also share the risk in setting fixed fees. Specialist help can increase web visibility via various search engines, Twitter and firms' pages on Facebook and LinkedIn networks. As we will explore further later, some solicitors are training as mediators in order to be able offer this as an additional service either in a legal or non-legal setting.

A Law Society Report on the Legal Services Industry in March 2013 (The Law Society, March 2013: 97) noted the division of solicitors into two sectors, the top 200 firms and small and medium firms. The latter group (comprising 98 per cent of all firms) compete for just one third of the total income of solicitors' firms in England and Wales. They had fared less well than the top 200 during the recession and were facing serious competition not just from local and national firms of solicitors but also from 'other regulated, non-solicitor providers of retail services, unregulated providers and household brands offering retail services on a large scale and fixed prices (regulated and otherwise)'. They were facing both reduced legal aid income and changes to civil litigation funding, both of which were expected to reduce case volumes. The report concluded that 'business models geared towards lowering costs (that is, cheaper and fewer staff) may be the only way to make some government fixed fees viable' and that 'a significant proportion of the small and medium firm sector is thought to lack the finance necessary to invest in order to adapt to competition by, for example, using IT to reduce costs of back-office operation or to develop the service delivery and client acquisition'. But it also remarked that innovation and adaptation is possible without substantial financial investment, and 'unbundling' of services could be just one of many ways in which small and medium firms provide affordable services while generating viable income. Desire to form an ABS remained low, with only 6 per cent of firms expressing an interest (Ibid: 46).

Looking at the available information as a whole, and accounts of our discussions with practitioners, it seems that the high-street firms with local clients are experiencing the greatest difficulty. The specialist or niche firms were doing relatively well, but legal aid work is likely to become restricted to a much smaller number of firms and geographical coverage is threatened. These pressures have led to a general move among law firms towards developing a more business-like approach to marketing, pricing, and making the running of the business as cost-effective as possible. In one interview with a key practitioner with offices in London and the north of England, we were told about the firm's interest in developing international business, and in making links with firms of accountants and financial advisers, which could lead to multi-disciplinary practice or even an ABS. We have also been told by a young energetic former practitioner, now business consultant, about the growing recognition of the need to use business advice, to inform marketing strategy through more effective analysis of where work is coming from, to attract work through clear pricing, free initial interviews and fixed-price packages, taking on carefully defined elements of a case (unbundling) and to trim costs, perhaps by using well-trained legal executives, or by outsourcing activities.

Richard Susskind has long advocated what he calls 'decomposition' of various tasks so they can be performed in the most efficient way, and better use of IT by lawyers. In *Tomorrow's Lawyers* (Susskind 2013: 31) he describes how even document reading can be outsourced. The 2012 Baseline Survey (Pleasence, Balmer and Moorhead 2012: 5) reported that firms, especially in the commercial client sector, were relying on greater outsourcing of work, 'be it "back office" work such as accounting or computing services, or fee earning work such as due diligence (over and above traditional outsourcing of advocacy and agency work)', but found that, while outsourcing IT increased productivity, outsourcing finance/accounting or other services made little difference to productivity (Ibid: 29–30). New dispute resolution services are being developed and offered by law firms, including mediation, arbitration, collaborative law (whereby lawyers for both parties meet and negotiate face to face but promise to withdraw from the case if the matter cannot settle and court proceedings are expected), and also specialist financial planning services such as forensic accountancy, tax management and financial planning for divorce. The latter may include help with arranging finance for the divorce process, and using the proceeds of a settlement to underwrite a loan for the cost of the case, though this may breach the exclusion of family matters from the permitted range of conditional fee arrangements. We were also told of payments to existing clients in recognition of their help in recommending friends and colleagues to use the firm. There is no rule against this, though it seems to sit closer to the world of business than the traditional ethics of the legal profession.

Some firms, few so far, are making more formal moves towards working as ABSs as permitted under LSA 2007, forming companies and working with related professionals and experts. However, our discussions suggested that many of the more commercially astute firms are itemising elements of their work and making sure that each is carried out by the most cost-effective members of staff, moving away from the traditional all-round personal client care tradition which is now referred to as 'full legal' service. Some firms, where lawyers are working with members of the Bar, accountants, tax specialists and financial advisers, may present the firm as primarily providing financial services, with family law as a subsidiary service. In addition, high-street 'names' are becoming involved in family law work, the best known being the Co-operative Society, which set up Co-operative Legal Services in 2006, an early ABS. This is discussed further below.

C. Pro Bono Work

With a long tradition of legal aid funding for family matters, there has been less incentive in the UK for widespread pro bono work than in, for example, the US, but this too may change. In chapter 1 we referred to examples of limited pro bono assistance for litigants in person (LIPs).[11] As regards solicitors, from our initial meetings with practitioners it seemed that it is the large 'Magic Circle' firms who now offer the bulk of such pro bono help as there is, as the high-street firms are unable to afford this kind of subsidy, concentrating instead on offering low-cost work hoping for higher case volumes. The Law Society's Practising Certificate Holder Survey on pro bono work published in 2013[12] found that 44 per cent of certificate holders had undertaken at least one hour of pro bono work in the 12-month period prior to the survey, a slight increase on the 40 per cent of PC holders providing pro bono services in 2012. The largest source was solicitors in private practice, but the proportion of government and in-house solicitors providing pro bono work had increased five percentage points respectively since 2012. The average number of pro bono hours (using the mean) worked by PC holders over the past year was 45 hours, representing a slight decrease on the 47 hours reported in 2012. The Law Society's own pro bono service, LawWorks, is popular and of high quality, but appears to be heavily oversubscribed.[13] Citizens Advice Bureaux (CABs) have traditionally referred potential clients to legal aid practitioners rather than directly offering a service.

---

[11] See pp 22–23.
[12] www.lawsociety.org.uk/policy-campaigns/research-trends/research-publications/pro-bono-work-pc-holder-survey-2013/ (accessed 9 February 2015).
[13] A response to a telephone inquiry in February 2014 quoted a six-week wait for an appointment.

IV. WHAT ARE FAMILY LAW SOLICITORS OFFERING
TO PROSPECTIVE CLIENTS?

To find further detail on innovative ways of working with family cases, we carried out a small survey of the websites used by a sample of one in four firms who attended the Resolution Conference in 2013, who, as members of Resolution, may be expected to represent those actively seeking to develop their work and to accept a non-adversarial collaborative approach to practice. We have analysed the content and developed a typology of firms based on the solicitors' own description of new ways of working and how far these might meet current need for information, advice and support for those experiencing divorce and separation.

The sample yielded 31 family practitioner websites. The first and essential message included on a website is to indicate the core business of the firm, and these could be divided into five groups by content. All the firms were offering family work, but not all had this as their main activity. Our first group comprised larger commercial international legal and financial businesses, mainly in central London, offering help with family matters to existing clients, sometimes described as 'high net worth individuals'. Second we found a group of law firms which offered the full range of legal services and included family law work in their portfolio. The third group were specialist family firms offering help with the full range of family work, including child-protection cases. Some of these were based in a single large office, others were local with three or four High Street branches in a particular area serving middle-income clients, and in some cases offering legal aid work. Our fourth group were the 'niche' firms, small, but with a national or even international reputation in a particular area of family work, such as child abduction or 'big money' divorce cases. Lastly we identified a group of innovative, often newly established, firms which were moving away from traditional forms of practice and developing networks, embracing additional forms of service including ADR, sometimes describing their way of working as 'holistic' and non-adversarial, offering not only mediation and collaborative law but life-counselling and parenting classes. This is a rather different profile from the traditional high-street family solicitor. Looking at the website information on the firms grouped in this way, we try to identify which firms were offering legal information, advice and support, whether this was free or subsidised, their charging practices, and the degree of innovation being developed for the different segments of the market.

Group 1: Commercial firms and corporate internationals (n=9) (firms 1, 5, 6, 7, 11, 12, 18, 20, 28)

These websites aimed first to establish the 'high net worth' of the clients they worked for, and the international and entrepreneurial nature of their work, proclaiming, for example, 'Company, commercial and planning ... linking family work with tax and trusts. We are an entrepreneurial business' (11);

'high-value disputes and international arbitration' (18); 'corporate, employment and real estate' (20). Another gave an annual fee income of £32.5 million (7), and another boasted a professional staff of 175 (1). Some had high-profile family law practitioners on board, and there is no reason to think that they were not offering an excellent service for an appropriate fee in complex financial family matters, whether disputed or simply needing careful planning. The websites were essentially designed to encourage the potential client to join the elite group served by the firm, and there was little legal information offered, nor any mention of additional services such as mediation, and little information on charging. There was no apparent indication of any modification of practice to safeguard or increase business. Even though recession may have prevented them from doing particularly well, there was no indication of serious problems.

Group 2: General legal firms (n=7) (firms 3, 4, 8, 9, 14, 15, 17)

These firms offered a full range of legal services in mainly civil matters, including help with family-related matters such as trusts, property and probate. One firm (9) offered help with child protection, and five firms offered personal injury compensation work. Among these firms there was less emphasis on the assets to be managed or distributed and more on the need for good information and accessible advice. Two firms (14, 17) referred to dealing with large estates, and another (4) stressed that they worked with a wide range of clients including 'big money' divorces. But three (3, 8, 9) offered particularly clear legal information, and one (3) specifically offered to 'prepare, support and protect' family clients. Another (15) had developed an online document 'shop' where clients could download forms and have them checked by a solicitor for a small fee, while another (17) had developed their own less complex version of the official Form E which requires parties seeking a financial order from the court to set out their assets and expenditure in daunting detail. Firm 9 offered leaflets on domestic violence. There was little mention of alternative dispute resolution services, but three firms gave a considerable amount of detail on charging, the level of fixed fees, and exact descriptions of what was included in the price. Only one (8) gave a free service of an initial first half hour. But another (9) gave an estimate of the final cost after a first meeting, and fixed-fee divorce if uncontested for £300 plus VAT and the court fee. Firm 17 stated the cost of a mediation information and assessment meeting (MIAM) as £100 to £300. Again there was variation within the group, but overall less reference to the wealth of the clients and more emphasis on giving good clear information and clear instructions on costs.

Group 3: Specialist family firms, some with local branches (n=6) (firms 16, 22, 23, 25, 26, 31)

All these firms offered a free first meeting and one held a free Legal Clinic twice a month at a local office specialising in child protection work. Two of the firms (23, 31) offered a moderately priced fixed-fee scheme, and one (16) a Legal Advice and Relationship Clinic at a cost of £190 for those not sure what stage they had reached with their problem. The rural sole practitioner offered home visits and another solicitor gave out high-quality fact sheets without charge. Only one of these firms (26), a practice run by two female partners who did not give information on costs but promised 'discretion and sensitivity', seemed to be targeting clients with above-average incomes. All the firms mentioned collaborative law and mediation and the focus overall was on the provision of affordable information and advice.

Group 4: Niche family firms (n=2) (firms 2, 29)

These two firms had quite simple websites, perhaps reflecting their confidence in their international reputations, and the lack of any need to advertise. The first (2) specialises in international child abduction, forced marriage, and abandoned spouses. They offered information about the countries in which they had worked, and the range of languages available. They offered little specialist legal information or free service. They appeared to deal with cases at many levels of client income or wealth. But a key element in the website was the provision of emergency numbers which a parent could use to access help at any time in the event of an abduction incident. The second (29) specialised in children work, both private and public law, in the East End of London. It offered a range of services and a provided a detailed description of the staff. Charging ranged from the traditional hourly rate of £280 for advice on children cases to fixed fees, and they had developed a DIY package whereby a parent could access the necessary forms and help with filling them in for £150. Both firms appeared busy and confident.

Group 5: The innovators (n=8) (firms 10, 13, 19, 21, 24, 27, 30)

Finally we identified a group of firms where we saw evidence of marked changes to traditional ways of working by offering new packages of services, new charging practices, and in some cases a new orientation to family law services. These were designed to maintain quality and cut costs, not necessarily reaching the former legal aid client group, but providing a good service at high-street rates. One sole practitioner (13) had begun to work as a consultant to another local firm, offering an hour-long initial meeting for £75. A second firm (21) had entered into an agreement with another firm to produce a total staff of 350, offering good legal information on the website plus an hour's free meeting. They offered 'early neutral evaluation', whereby both parties, accompanied by their solicitors, could be heard by a barrister who would give a view on the likely outcome if the case were to go to court. In addition they had identified a large potential client group in the staff and families employed by the local city council to which they were offering a special rate. Another firm (27), with two women partners, had formed a network of services, guaranteeing quality service across different areas of work at high-street prices, including collaborative law, mediation and advocacy by a barrister member of the network. They gave prominence on their website to their definition of the term 'partner' as referring to a 'shareholder or director of their company or person with equivalent standing and qualification' and gave their trading name as regulated by the SRA. Firm 10 offered a fixed-fee divorce for £500, plus disbursements and court fees, and a further £100 for representation in court if needed. This firm had also developed a fixed fee for resolving financial issues where the assets exceeded £300,000. This innovative organisation of work and charging was grounded in a new approach to family legal services whereby this firm also offered life coaching and parenting classes. The firm described itself as offering a holistic approach to family law. The senior partner came from a background in counselling and social work and saw family law as having moved away from 'fighting'. The firm aimed to provide a premium service at high-street rates.

This account of the rich variety of legal services on offer indicates the need for a better understanding of the term 'family lawyer' and the work being carried out. Even an apparently simple classification such as 'sole practitioner' covers a wide range of approach and practice. The two sole practitioner firms (31 and 24) whose websites we looked at sit at opposite ends of the tradition/innovation spectrum, but were nevertheless remarkably similar in their commitment to clients and their efforts to meet their needs. The first was a middle-aged man who had served his rural community for many years, as his father had done before him. He offered a free phone call or a drop-in office visit, as well as being willing to make home visits to help local people with divorce and conveyancing. The second was a young woman in a university town offering all the new and exciting forms of service, collaborative law, round table meetings, an informative website, fixed fees and negotiated hourly rates, again seeking to provide a quality service at a moderate cost.

V. ONLINE DIVORCE SERVICES: EXTENDING THE BOUNDARIES OF LAWYERS' SERVICES?

The most innovative developments we observed take us beyond the websites of legal firms to the specialist websites advertising online divorce services, which offer a complex, varied, though largely unregulated, response to the need for low-cost divorce services. There has been considerable interest in this development, which appears ready to use new technology both to provide for those who wish to take control of their affairs and are computer literate and able to do so, but also to try to fill the gap left by the removal of public support for legal help in divorce or separation for those unable to compete on the open market for legal help. For example, in July 2013 a

Good Housekeeping investigation of divorce packs offered on line declared Co-operative Legal Services to be the clear leader in the field, as their work is carefully marketed, of high quality and carried out by lawyers regulated by the SRA (see above). We referred above to the YouGov report of 2013 which stated that in the five years before the legal aid changes, 30 per cent of respondents who had arranged their own divorces without external help had used a DIY website, of whom two-thirds sought free information or to download documents. Only 11 per cent used those sites for free consultation or advice.[14]

In this context, there is room for confusion about the status of those providing information or advice, or carrying out activities. Only 'reserved legal activities' described earlier[15] fall within the ambit of regulation by the approved regulator and should therefore be undertaken only by qualified professionals accredited as members of the Bar or holding a practising certificate from the Law Society as a solicitor. It is therefore clear that giving legal information or advice, and even the handling of much documentation, falls outside the regulation and need not be performed by solicitors, barristers or legal executives. As Lisa Webley (2015) points out, there appears to be nothing to stop individuals who do such tasks from calling themselves 'lawyers', presumably providing that they do not mislead people into thinking that they have qualifications which they do not have. Nevertheless, Webley remarks that 'all non-reserved forms of legal work are open to anyone, legally qualified or otherwise and so much family law work is not "law" at all for the purposes of regulatory or disciplinary oversight' (Ibid: 314). The problems which may arise for a user of digital services where the source of the information or advice being given is unclear is that were they to receive poor-quality advice or incorrect information and suffer some detriment, they would have no recourse to compensation for any loss if they were helped by a non-accredited 'lawyer' who has no professional indemnity insurance. In the context of divorce-related financial matters, this could have serious consequences as there are few grounds upon which orders about property division can be set aside once made, and courts are very reluctant to do so where someone has acted on bad or negligent legal advice.[16]

A. The Survey

What, then, are these new services offering and what part is being played by the legal profession? To try to answer this question, in May 2013 we carried out a small survey of the divorce information and advice legal websites, using five search terms: DIY Divorce, Divorce Advice, Divorce Petition

---

[14]   Above, note 10.
[15]   See p 26.
[16]   *Harris v Manahan* [1997] 1 FLR 205.

Forms, Divorce Papers and Divorce Online. We looked carefully at the 41 sites which came up on the first Google page, rejecting two press divorce stories, 11 duplicate sites and one that was not yet contactable. This left us with 28 sites, of which the largest group of services were 10 solicitors' firms, essentially extending their marketing through this new dimension, including Co-operative Legal Services. There were also four independent advice sites (the CAB, the peer group support networks Netmums and Mumsnet and the Independent Money Service), three non-legal practitioners (counsellors and mediators), three commercial sites (Moneysupermarket, Lawpack and WH Smith) and two government websites. But the second largest group was made up of six sites which we have called New Specialist Providers of online services. We repeated the survey in June 2014 and, although there were some changes to the headlines posted, the actual services offered remained largely the same.

The overall array of digital services looks impressive. They range from money advice to family counselling, from the peer support of Mumsnet and Netmums to 'fast facts and reference, answers now!' from Divorce Rights, to low-cost forms from WH Smith (£12) or free forms from the government. Is this emerging array of specialist services offering a new freedom of choice in the absence of legal aid? Or is the first-time user who may be under stress able to make informed and safe choices without guidance or quality assurance? For example, when first viewed, Divorce Online appeared with the tag 'official' and a phone number urging the reader to 'get started today!' But beside this there was an advertisement for the not-for-profit organisation Wikivorce who were offering free divorce advice and fixed-price solicitor divorce for £179 saying: 'Online Divorce … are you sure? Why risk it? Our solicitor managed divorce costs less than a divorce on line!'

B. New Specialist Providers

Looking in detail at the new specialist services, our first concern was to establish who was providing the service, that is, whether a site is offering the advice of an accredited and insured lawyer, or a paralegal, or anyone with some legal knowledge. When we asked in follow-up phone calls whether providers were lawyers, the answers ranged from 'Yes, er, no' and 'Yes we are lawyers but not working as lawyers' to the clearer 'We are legal executives, we can handle non-contested matters'. Wikivorce intriguingly told us that a firm of solicitors 'does our legal work for us'. In some cases what had looked at first sight like a new specialist provider turned out to be a legal firm, for example Divorce Rights, Law Shop, and Alternative Family Law. Later we were to meet a solicitor who had set up a specialist website within his legal practice. On the other hand, Divorce Aid Solicitors sounded like a firm of solicitors, but on closer examination was a service which helps the client to find a solicitor. We look here at four examples of the organisations which, while using solicitors, are run by others: Quickie Divorce, Managed Divorce, Wikivorce and Divorce Online.

Quickie Divorce offered to start the divorce process for £37, or to 'have all the divorce forms you'll need to send to the court completed for you for just £67'. Court fees were not mentioned. An 0800 free telephone advice line is offered where 'our teams of experts can give guidance on all matters relating to divorce processes, and can also help you choose which service is right for you'. No claim is made to be offering legal advice, or to advise on issues, but only about the divorce process and which service to use. They also offer a 'Personal Plus Service which includes all the benefits of our Personal Service plus a Clean Break Agreement and Lifetime Will (worth a total of £195) all for £135'. The Clean Break Agreement is described as a Consent Order. 'Enjoy the security of knowing that a panel solicitor is overseeing your case from start to finish and that all the necessary forms will be completed for you from issuing the petition until your decree absolute is in your hand'. In response to a phone call, the response was quick, friendly, but brief, and insistent that they could only deal with cases where there was no dispute. Information on court fees, then £340 on filing and £45 for decree, was given, but it was stated that there would be no court appearances or solicitors' fees for court attendance: 'We're not a solicitors' firm.' When asked about the reference to panel solicitors, we were told that when making the Clean Break Order, the forms would be sent out to an external solicitor to check. In sum, Quickie Divorce offers a no-frills document management service for non-contentious divorce, without in-house lawyers. It could be useful to those seeking a quick and affordable divorce where there are no issues. But it would be less helpful to those where issues arise during the course of proceedings.

Managed Divorce claims to have been used by 20,000 people in 2012–13, about 8 per cent of the divorcing population in England and Wales.[17] On a single webpage this service offered a premium 24-hour service initiated by a free phone call for £97. The process is described as follows:

> A quick chat to one of our divorce specialists—no forms or questionnaires to fill in; get your email, print and sign the documents, it really is as simple as that! Hand all the documents and attachments to the courier when he calls at your door.

In response to our phone call we were told that this was not a firm of solicitors: 'We are an online company, we manage documents for you.' Managed Divorce appears to offer a minimal document-handling service, with no reference to working with lawyers.

---

[17] There were 118,140 divorces in England and Wales in 2012 (Office of National Statistics, Divorces in England and Wales 2012): www.ons.gov.uk/ons/rel/vsob1/divorces-in-england-and-wales/2012/stb-divorces-2012.html (accessed 6 August 2015).

Wikivorce claims to offer free support, information and advice to help 50,000 people a year through divorce, about a fifth of the divorcing population in England and Wales. The organisation is run by volunteers and is government sponsored and charity funded. The website information is clear, accurate and accessible, giving advice on avoiding conflict, staged information and guidance on how to help yourself, and offering clearly defined packages of divorce services for divorce only (£179), financial settlement (£139) or both (£279), in each case 'managed' by a solicitor. They help with access to mediation, divorce support groups and provide a divorce calculator which works out a fair estimate of a financial settlement for ancillary relief in England and Wales based on individual circumstances. In response to our phone call asking for detail on what was meant by a solicitor-managed divorce, we were told that a local legal firm provides help,[18] and also that no Wikivorce matter is dealt with other than by a lawyer, though by lawyers at different grades. We have noted earlier the indeterminate nature of this description. For example, divorce forms would be filled in by a paralegal. The calculator provides a quick and easy way of working out the probable financial outcome based on the income of both parties, and their household needs, categorised as essential, child care costs and lifestyle costs, and finally a statement of assets and liabilities. The process requires computer literacy and collecting the necessary information, but is commendably user-friendly, and is likely to be making a positive contribution to informed access to negotiating a fair outcome. Finally they offer a price comparison table, giving fixed prices and a website link for managed divorce in 30 legal firms. The most expensive price quoted was £870 and the lowest £179 from Wikivorce.

The last of the new specialist providers was divorce-online.co.uk. This website offered a range of services from £45 for all the forms and a guide to completing them, plus sample letters to the court, through £189 for a managed divorce with £299 to include a clean break, to £385 for a solicitor-managed divorce. The website offered a link to the Bar Pro Bono Unit and the *Handbook for Litigants in Person*. It was difficult to judge from the website whether the service offered was more than document handling, but in response to our phone call it was made clear that this was not a legal firm, but 'paralegals, qualified to take two people who are willing through the divorce process. We deal with amicable divorce.'

The message from all these four services is clearly that disputes cost money, whichever route is taken, and that amicable change of status costs less, at least at the point of delivery. Where there is conflict, it seems that qualified lawyers (solicitors) will be involved to some degree. We should therefore consider how these specialist digital services compare with other

---

[18] Further detail on this arrangement follows in the next chapter, p 64.

attempts by legal firms to offer a low-cost divorce service. For example, Simpson Millar, a large firm with a turnover of £13 million and offices in 10 cities, developed a pay-as-you-go legal advice service restricted to those who would have been eligible for legal aid prior to the LASPO changes. They then charged £75 per hour plus VAT, with early estimates of the total likely cost and the possibility of buying future time credits.

Finally there is a great deal of interest in the development of family work by Co-operative Legal Services, an ABS fully staffed by lawyers, which had plans to employ 3,000 lawyers nationwide, but is still largely working in London, with offices in Manchester and Bristol. The service has an informative website, offering a wide range of packages. These include a basic DIY divorce with forms, guide to completion, information about the issues to consider, instructions on how to file and examples of draft letters for £99 for each party, plus court fees and VAT, coming to a total of just over £500 per couple; a fixed-price non-contested 'divorce petitioner service' (currently priced at £570, including VAT) and a 'divorce petitioner plus' service 'if you feel you may need a high level of contact with or support from your lawyer as your proceedings progress or you may need assistance with issues which are not covered by our divorce petitioner service but which are not serious enough for you to need extensive negotiations' (currently priced at £900, including VAT).[19] There is a range of other options, such as a 'negotiations service' on financial matters (£1,620 including VAT for up to three months), on children (£900 including VAT for up to three months), help including mediation (£1,140 including VAT for finances and children) and many others.[20]

If the internet surfer looks for free rather than low-cost advice, the options are more limited. Many of the options which come up are not free and do not constitute advice. For example, Expert Answers asks what the answer to your question is worth to you and says that the higher the sum you are willing to pay the quicker you will receive an answer. Onespace.org, advertising help for lone parents, offers free legal advice, but on ticking the box for concerns about domestic violence, we were advised to see a solicitor and pay. Perhaps the last word on specialist online services should go to Rocket Lawyer, which aims to deliver legal services via a 'freemium model', using an online interactive interview process to create straightforward legal documents. But it does not yet fully cover family law. Or there is always SOS, the government information website for Sorting Out Separation with information relating to children and finance. The app is now up and running but carries strong government messages about shared parenting, little legal advice or information and is difficult to use (Albeson 2014).

---

[19] Costs as at 9 February 2015. These do not include court fees then of £410.
[20] Further detail on CLS follows at p 65.

C. What can Web-based Services Offer?

Our conclusion is that effective use of IT can help law firms and individual lawyers at various levels to improve their marketing, streamline their administration and management, and develop or become associated with new ways of providing services which are directly web-based. But it appears that the web-based services with no or minimal lawyer involvement are able to offer little more than low-cost document handling in non-contested matters. This is of course of value to those with no disputes and able to work online. But they come nowhere near providing the kind of information, advice and support that we saw in our observations of solicitors some 15 years ago (Eekelaar, Maclean and Beinart 2000), and for the more vulnerable parties, choosing such a service carries risks. There is interest in developing regulation for these services, but so far with little success. As soon as conflict emerges, evidence has to be tested, negotiations conducted, and a web-based service has to ally itself with legal staff, and costs increase.

Web-based work has developed in other jurisdictions (see Smith and Paterson 2013), notably in the Netherlands, which has good internet access and where the net is widely used. The best-known service is the Rechtwijser, which offers a simple child support maintenance calculator. It is highly regarded as interactive and user-friendly. But when we asked about what happened when one party raised questions about the statements of the other about their income or assets, Bregde Dijksterhuis, who is researching the process,[21] said parties who do not agree cannot use the service. There is research in England and Wales which supports this view of the effective but limited scope of web-based information and advice. In an experimental study of the use of a high quality interactive website by a sample of young computer-literate people presented with a legal problem, Catrina Denvir (2014) found that they could access legal information and even limited advice easily, but when it came to making decisions about the next step to take, they turned to trusted advisers for help, often their parents.

It seems that the web can offer so much but no more, so far. Information for those who can access it at low cost or without charge is of great value. But when advice and support is needed the web-based services appear to need to work with existing legal services and costs rise accordingly. The lawyers clearly continue to have a part to play. In the next chapter we move on from describing what they are promising and how they are experimenting to comment on what we observed in their day-to-day work for divorcing and separating clients.

---

[21] Bregde Dijksterhuis, 'Users Opinion about online self help tools on alimony payment', Paper to Legal Profession Group Meeting of the Research Committee on the Sociology of Law, International Sociological Association, Frauenchiemsee, July 2014.

3

What Solicitors are Doing

T HIS CHAPTER MOVES from consideration of the structural changes
affecting the delivery of family law services and the way in which
lawyers are presenting themselves and advertising their services to an
account of the reality of the way they work as observed in visits to lawyers
in 17 legal practices. The speed and breadth of change suggests a need to
offer an updated and empirically based picture of this work. There is a popular optical illusion set in a double image which the viewer perceives either
as a beautiful maiden or an ugly witch. Once a view has been chosen, it is
difficult to alter the perception. We were particularly interested to see how
far the image we perceived in our earlier research (Eekelaar, Maclean and
Beinart 2000) of the family law solicitor as a helpful professional, offering
a necessary service to clients during a difficult period of transition in family life, can still be seen, or whether the alternative image of the lawyer as
profiting from private troubles is now more evident.

I. THE STUDY METHODOLOGY: OBSERVING SOLICITORS

In our first study of 15 years ago, the key distinction in both large and small
firms was between those with high- and those with low-income clients; in
effect, those with private clients and those doing legally aided work. In that
study we sat for a working day with 10 solicitors who had been approached
through personal contacts. In addition we interviewed a sample of 40 solicitors selected by using a fixed interval and random start number from the
Law Society Regional Directories, of whom 28 did legal aid work.

For the present study, however, conducted from January 2014 to March
2015, we realised that we would need a more flexible approach. Working practices have developed to include greater use of telephone and email,
not all solicitors used offices on a daily basis, and more legal assistants but
fewer secretarial and administrative staff were employed. Also, the kinds
of work carried out have expanded to include forms of alternative dispute
resolution, including mediation and arbitration, early neutral evaluation,
and collaborative law. We wished to explore how practice had changed over
the past decade, and so began by following up our original sample, of whom
three were still practising. We then went on to seek examples of the different

kinds of practice we had seen advertised on the websites described in chapter 2, maintaining wide geographical coverage in England and Wales, and adding a group of young practitioners beginning their careers. The result is therefore not a representative but a purposive sample, chosen with the aim of carrying out an exploratory study of a rapidly changing situation which will raise questions rather than provide firm explanations. We are most grateful to the solicitors who welcomed us back after 10 years, and to those who were willing to share their working day with us for the first time.

Our final sample was made up of 24 solicitors working in 17 practices, 14 of whom were qualified mediators (though less than half were active), and two were qualified arbitrators, one of whom offered Med Arb whereby clients would agree to mediate and at the same time agree to arbitration by the same practitioner for outstanding issues. A small group of three had trained as collaborative lawyers, but none had had more than a handful of clients. A further group were working in new settings, including the Co-operative Legal Service (an ABS) and the Resolution Divorce Matters pilot scheme attempting to contribute to meeting the shortfall in publicly funded legal provision after LASPO,[1] while others were working in digital services or offering business advice to practitioners.

At the time of our first study it was relatively easy to say that 'the researcher simply sat in the office and observed (and recorded) all that happened', and that we interviewed solicitors by asking them to 'talk us through' a pre-selected case 'from its inception to its current position', 'explaining the progress of the case' (Eekelaar, Maclean and Beinart 2000: 31). This time, it was not so easy to do this as although all were practising solicitors, their range of activities had widened, as can be seen from their description in the previous paragraph. In some cases we spent a working day with a solicitor who was not seeing clients, or not using an office; in others we observed meetings with clients in the traditional office setting or by phone. For these reasons, and also because of the growing practice of 'unbundling', where the lawyer is involved only in a specific aspect, or specific aspects, of a case, talking us through a case file to see how the case progressed would not necessarily capture important aspects of the solicitor's activities. Our data therefore takes the form sometimes of descriptions of meetings between lawyers and clients, and sometimes of accounts given by the lawyers of the way they were working.

For analytical purposes we have divided the sample into four groups which are closely linked to the groups emerging from the website analysis in the preceding chapter. As in the website data, the activity observation data also yielded a group of legal firms (Group 1) with commercial expertise and international experience dealing with high net worth clients offering family work among other services. But the next two website groups

---

[1] See above pp 16–20.

(2 and 3), which were clearly differentiated in their website marketing according to whether or not they offered a range of work (Group 2) or only family law (Group 3), looked different when their activities were observed. The reasons for these differences were strongly related to the firm's economic position. The family-only practices (Group 3) were far more vulnerable to the impact of legal aid cuts and unable to cross-subsidise from more profitable work, and client income profiles were a key determinant of the way the practitioners were able to work. We did not visit the niche firms (Group 4) for observation. But the final group (Group 5), identified from the website material as Innovators, were clearly present and of great interest in the observation sample data. They revealed different ways of using professional experience in advising, teaching and working with digital services, and, in the Co-operative Legal Service, attempting to develop a viable affordable service through an ABS.

In the ensuing discussion we give examples from each group except Group 4, since we did not interview any of the niche firms at this stage of the project as their work appears to be largely unaffected by recent changes. We also saw a solicitor who had recently stopped working as a solicitor and now operated solely as a mediator, who will be discussed in chapter 5, and five solicitors who were no longer practising but were working solely in mediation or training, who are discussed in chapter 6.

Group 1: Family solicitors working in commercial and international firms, with high net worth clients (n = 3) [Condition: stable]

We asked the lawyers we met about how their practice had changed over the past two to three years, whether they were busy and secure financially, how they saw the future, and also whether we might sit with them for a day. We interviewed one solicitor (L1.1) and sat with two (L1.2, L1.3) in this group. Their working methods for family clients were by far the most stable over time of all the groups. All reported feeling reasonably secure in long-established firms with enough work. All had high-value international work with 'high net worth individuals'. One was in the process of setting up an office in Europe with venture capital. All offered financial services, and property and estate management. Offices were in prime locations, elegant, welcoming, and well provided with support staff. Two of the solicitors had trained as mediators and in collaborative law, and would like to work in these ways, but had few clients. Unbundling was mentioned, and was undertaken at the request of clients who not only wanted to save money but to keep control of their affairs, though the lawyers found it unnerving to be in the position of not knowing what they did not know about the client's situation. Clients were reported as now requesting greater clarity about costs, and practitioners were providing help in arranging finance for the case. None had done any legal aid work, but one did offer a free clinic, only partly as a marketing device. Referrals came by personal recommendation or through the internet.

But all three were still providing what is coming to be known as 'the full legal', that is, the traditional form of total client care throughout a case which was the expected form of service 15 years ago.

Group 2: Family solicitors in general firms with a strong family department backed up by other services: middle income clients (n = 6)
[Condition: challenged but coping]

The second group, defined in the website analysis as general firms dealing with civil and criminal work and including family matters, was characterised in this part of our study as feeling the strain of rising costs and falling private client demand, but rising to the challenge. We met six solicitors (L2.1, L2.2, L2.3, and L2.4 with two assistants, L2.5 and L2.6) in three firms in this group who were responding to pressure in various ways. They were coping reasonably well, particularly the firms offering family work who also had other more profitable departments, such as conveyancing, despite the ending of the monopoly. Others had a profitable specialism such as international child abduction, or had developed an innovative approach to pricing and marketing. One firm (L.2.4) described seeking to establish trust and confidence by offering high-quality work at low cost by reducing overheads through using smaller premises and reducing support staff. Others (for example L2.2) were careful to allocate work to the appropriate level of staff, making greater use of legal executives who were often bright law graduates who had been unable to find a traditional training contract. All three were setting fixed pricing mechanisms with care, paying attention to marketing, using websites and social media, and outsourcing their IT. The impact of austerity was leading to talk of firms merging in the interests of economies of scale and reduced costs for premises, but they expected to survive by offering value for money on a wide range of services. Two had trained as mediators but one was not practising and the second would like to but had no clients.

Group 3: Family specialist firms with a strong legal aid tradition and low-income clients (n = 4) [Condition: struggling]

This group of four was in the greatest financial difficulty. One reported how her firm had given up the full range of family work and was concentrating on child protection work for which the legal aid funding continues. This was not her area of work, and so she had taken early retirement (L3.1). Another (L3.4) had stopped being a partner in a firm and become a 'locum', taking temporary jobs filling in for solicitors on sickness or maternity leave. For the first three years he had done well, but in the six months before the interview he had only had six weeks of paid employment as firms were managing without locum support to cut their costs. Others (L3.2 and assistant L3.3) were actively seeking to join with other firms and add new services to their practice, training as mediators and offering the service within their legal practice. L3.2 was developing a new service which combined legal help and mediation, even taking their own DNA swabs when needed and cutting costs with effective use of IT for making appointments, dictating and emailing notes and summaries by phone, and using templates for many documents.

Group 5: The innovators (n = 10) [Condition: enthusiastic but unproven]

This group of lawyers had turned to radically new ways of using their legal skills. One (L5.1) had identified the need for legal practice to benefit from business and marketing advice, and had set up a successful consultancy. Two others (L5.2 and L5.3) were working for a new pilot service developed by Resolution and funded by the Department of Work and Pensions, expecting to work as mediators, but being drawn into crisis situations often with vulnerable clients needing legal and other kinds of help. Two solicitors had become involved directly in setting up (L5.4) or entering into a business arrangement with digital services (L5.5). Another (L5.9) had set up a service seeking to combine legal practice with mediation and arbitration. The final group of three solicitors (L5.6, L5.7 and L5.8) all worked for the Co-operative Legal Service, which provides high-quality digital and packaged help with a modular approach allowing clients to progress easily, at rates charged according to the service provided, to more individual help, mediation, or representation if their matter becomes more complicated. This business began with a great deal of publicity and an ambitious programme for expansion, but has been adversely affected by the difficulties encountered by the Co-operative, particularly its banking business, and also by the difficulty of offering high-quality service at low cost and remaining profitable.

II. THE OBSERVATIONAL DATA

We now turn to our data on the actual working practice of members of these groups of solicitors.

Group 1 (Working with high net worth clients)

Beginning with the solicitors working with above-average-income clients, we describe two days, the first with an experienced practitioner who is also a trained mediator and collaborative lawyer (L1.3). The subject matter included an international finance case, and also a child and finance case which followed a failed mediation. Next we visited another firm where we spoke to an early career practitioner who is not a mediator, who set out how she handles a first meeting with a divorce client.

L1.3 has practised family law for over 30 years, and took part in our earlier study. She is well known for offering a good service, often beginning with a reality check session for women seeking divorce or separation which she acknowledges is not cheap but which she expects to potentially offer all the help that they will need. She is a trained mediator and collaborative lawyer, but finds little demand for these services. Clients include difficult divorce cases where resources exist, but are tied up in complex family trusts and settlements. She finds 'unbundling' difficult, as it requires her to start a case without the first session 'where you get the nature of the beast … it's hard to see what lies around and behind requests' and also less interesting than the traditional 'full legal'. She finds that clients are now seeking more face-to-face time in their desire to be understood. She enjoys and would like to do more mediation: 'it's magic … satisfying …', but is also involved in legal support for mediation carried out by others. She is enthusiastic about mediation by trained lawyers, but commented that non-lawyers can sometimes produce 'ridiculous memorandums of understanding (MOUs) with figures that do not add up and plans that don't work with the given figures' which she cannot easily turn into Consent Orders. She worries about mediation clients who are advised to seek legal advice and do not, either because they cannot afford it or do not understand the need. She says that mediation is not cheap any longer, and that clients have multiple needs for mediation, accounting and financial help as well as legal advice.

The central London office is built around a central area, which facilitates frequent and helpful internal communication. Two cases were observed on the first visit. The first was a limited case, not the 'full legal'. L1.3 was acting for the wife. A phone call had been booked for 10 am, and the researcher was able to read the file in advance and listen in to the call. The husband was not from the UK but ran a business here. The wife has no address for him. He has debts, and makes no financial contribution for her or the children. He meets the teenage children regularly but in public places, and they deliver his mail to him. The wife runs her own business and pays the mortgage, though the house is in his name. The assets outside this jurisdiction are unknown, but thought by the wife to be considerable. She has asked L1.3 to advise on a Consent Order, and this call is to finalise the draft. She wants him to remove his business and possessions from the family home, and to transfer his interest in it to her. She wishes to release him from the mortgage, will make no claim on any other of his assets here or elsewhere, will relinquish any claim to further financial provision, pension sharing or property adjustment, and make no further applications to the court. L1.3 assures her that this would result in the house being in her sole name. The wife remains anxious, and asks what would happen if the bailiffs come after the house for his debts. L1.3 tells her that the house will be in her name only. The wife remains anxious, and L1.3 continues to reassure.

L1.3 then raises the question of what would happen if the case came to an argument and says that she is a little anxious that the wife might have to go to court as a litigant in person, and suggests rehearsing what might be said there. 'He is saying, in effect, that he can run up debts and you would have to deal with them … but, shall we think about what might be said about you?'

She wishes to prepare the wife to respond as a LIP if evidence were to be tested in court. The wife is anxious about not having an address for him, but L1.3 confirms that the order as drafted would require him to give an address. But she urges the wife not to give ground on the mortgage, saying: 'The parts the court can enforce are the easy bits, it's when third parties are involved; you can't let him loose on the mortgage.' She also asks where his passport is, and suggests that, to protect the children: 'Don't tell them about the £1 a month (nominal child support)—it would be upsetting. If he gives them something from time to time, we can live with that? He needs to do a Form A. Yours is in the Petition, I think the CO (Consent Order) will be all right.' When the wife says that he is being difficult again, L1.3 responds: 'He's just having a flounce, a "You can't tell me what to do" moment. I'm not worried, I think it will work.'

L1.3 is warm, supportive, confident and authoritative, and several times refers to what might help the children. She continues the conversation, saying that the information supplied looks better than it did last week on the dates, his projections and the mortgage. She says she can now send the draft order the wife has approved out to both but checks: 'Or would you like to see it again first? It's cheaper if I send them out to you both at the same time.' The wife suggests that if he remains unwilling to let her have an address, a member of his church could hold his address, and L1.3 agrees that this would be 'better than me; I'm too involved'.

She then sets out the next steps, sending the D81 form, which sets out background information the court needs when seeking a Consent Order: 'You both have to sign twice and serve it on the mortgage lender. I will have to get rid of the best endeavours term so that the mortgage lender will agree to the statement of truth.' The call ends. The draft order will now go to both parties to agree before being sent to court. L1.3 reminds the researcher that if she had been mediating she would not have been able to go to third parties, including the mortgage lender, and a solicitor would have had to come in to 'finish the job'.

The second case that day involved L1.3 working on the papers in a file in a case where both parties had been advised to seek legal advice following mediation. The wife had come to L1.3 seeking a draft Consent Order. The non-lawyer mediator, whom L1.3 described as financially unskilled, had included proposals in the MOU that he had drawn up about using the existing mortgage to fund new arrangements, but did not appear to understand that mortgage requirements had changed and that a parent or former partner would not necessarily be accepted as guarantor. Because there was an MOU the mediator would have seen this as a successful mediation, but L1.3 regarded the MOU as so defective that she referred to this as a 'failed mediation'. The couple had a disabled child, and both wanted to care for him, but it was unlikely that they would receive grants to convert two homes. The father would not be able to continue to care for the child unless he could rent a place with suitable access.

L1.3 commented that if she had been mediating the case, she would have called a lawyer in for one session. Referring to the case, she said: 'The couple just can't afford what they want, which is two homes suitable for a disabled child. The mediator was good to keep an eye on the care package being offered by the local authority, but mediators drafting their own Consent Orders is not on.' L1.3 identified four options: to keep the house with dad to guarantee the mortgage, to sell it and share the proceeds, to sell later, or to sell and buy new properties. The open financial statement was available.

This case prompted her to comment, as an enthusiast for mediation, on the differences between the work of mediators and solicitors. She said that mediators are 'stuck in a bubble'. They work 'in the room', there is little discussion with colleagues, they cannot approach third parties about, for example, a mortgage, and they often have limited financial acumen but nevertheless make suggestions. L1.3 noted that the cost for mediation in this case was £120 an hour each, and in total could reach £4,000. She added that the solicitor meets the client one-to-one, but there are also other meetings, phone calls, and general support. Suggestions are made, additional questions are raised by the lawyer to avoid future conflict, and the solicitor can work with third parties and verify documents. The background information document for the D81 form sent with a draft Consent Order will not have been verified by the mediator, so the solicitor may or may not go on to verify it, but can check if he or she feels the need, and can give a good estimate of the total cost of the case. In this case L1.3 estimates her input will add £3,000 to the total cost, and the solicitor for the husband will add £1,500 for doing much less of the work. The researcher asked what would have happened if the solicitor had been the only professional intervention. L1.3 replied that this couple had needed mediation first as they had been too conflicted to settle. If they had gone straight to court as LIPs the costs would have been lower but the outcome perhaps less nuanced.

L1.3 works a 40-hour billable week, and two complex cases with full legal service are taking half her time. She plans to spend one-sixth of her time on mediation or collaborative law, but at present does not have sufficient clients. The remainder of her time is spent on unbundled work. As we finished our conversation, the finance administrator came in to update accounts. L1.3 handed over a cheque, and is owed a great deal more, but was not concerned about whether clients will pay, only with the timing. She likes to warn them before they get a monthly reminder from the firm. She is a panel member for Novitas, who arrange loans to the client through a solicitor who they have accepted onto their panel, and who draws down as required. She commented that clients are better informed than they were 10 years ago, that nearly two-thirds of her work has an international element, and that her clients come from the ends of the income scale, those in the middle doing more of the work for themselves. She commented, however, that even this highly respected firm would like more business.

The second day's observation with this group was with L1.2, a solicitor at an early stage in her career in a specialist central London firm which has taken over the general suburban firm where she began her career. She has not trained as a mediator, and does not wish to do so, expressing reservations about what she sees as pressure from Resolution, and regrets that some solicitors may be jumping on the mediation bandwagon and may not all be interested or suitable.

While waiting for her first client who was coming in for a first appointment, L1.2 took the opportunity to explain in detail how she conducts these meetings, in effect giving the researcher a first interview and setting out the options. She described how she begins by 'chatting to settle the client; then I ask what has been happening and if there is any chance of reconciliation and give the names of counsellors who might help'. She then explains the divorce petition and checks whether timing is important. She gave the example of a recent client whose husband was about to move abroad and therefore it was important to act before he left this jurisdiction. She says that things come up in discussion, but when grounds are being decided she suggests that these should be as low key as possible 'to avoid upset and progress the matter'. She will then ask for details about the children, explain parental responsibility, residence, and contact (now child arrangements) and the no order principle. She would ask: 'What are your thoughts ... will it be agreed?' She would explain that the aim is not to go to court, and to use lawyers only to facilitate agreement unless the other parent is very unreasonable. On finance, she asks for a snapshot of the situation, and then gives four options for taking things forward:

1. Collaborative law: 'I think the pros are that it can leave you happier, more empowered, able to choose what suits you, a made-to-measure outcome. The cons are that you can't issue proceedings, and the costs are front-loaded. Or you can do round tables, which are not quite collab but are more practical, if you are afraid of the cost of collab ... You can't estimate the cost of collab.'
2. Mediation: The pros were that the client may have already been to a session (and begun to work on the financial information or practical arrangements for children). 'I say it's helping to reach agreement, empowering, not in the legal arena, and it is easier to talk if you can without the cost of lawyers. The cons are that if it doesn't work then you are a step behind and the lawyers have to work very hard to get constructive and amicable agreement. For mediation (in house) we must give an idea of the outcome, ask for thoughts, look at boundaries (that is, what a court would do), what can be offset, manoeuvred ... so I give timescales, costs, charge out rates and next steps processing.'

3. Voluntary disclosure:[2] 'Or I say you can use lawyers but with voluntary disclosure and no court proceedings.[3] You can exchange information, use the same cause letter, but no issue of proceedings. I would diarise every month to check progress and would issue to get things going. Matters can go on for years. I once had a case for six years and everybody was happy but it is expensive. I don't charge for refreshing my memory, but every time you open a file it costs. My charge is £296 an hour plus administration and disbursements, barrister's fee, court fee etc … A voluntary disclosure case could take three months, and if it's not working you can go to court.'

4. Court: 'Then I talk about process, court, and Final Hearing. The pros of court? Very few. And now there are terrible delays. I can give a timetable. FDR (financial dispute resolution) is usually with a sensible judge. The cost of a Final Hearing is high and the judge may make an order you don't like, it's a lottery. One judge has a high settlement rate because no one will risk his judgment. But courts will focus minds and I can give cost estimates for each stage. I have a chart of average costs based on my actual costs.'

L1.2 explains that she then gives the client a Form E, the financial questionnaire used in court proceedings, which will identify what needs to be valued. She would explain how the divorce and the finance work run alongside, understanding that the weaker party may want to hold up the divorce until the finance side is complete, for example until a joint tenancy is severed. She would explain rights and restriction on the matrimonial home, occupation orders, the need for new wills and so on. She says to clients that they must look at capital, spousal and child maintenance, duration, and any trade-offs of capital against income. She comments that people find it hard to be realistic when filling in Form E, making current and projected estimates of expenditure. She says: 'I always give a D81 to the client to complete when working towards a Consent Order. It's a summary of finances and when drafting a consent order the solicitor should always check. It may go to a client meeting, or the client may take it to a mediator and then back to me. If we take the voluntary disclosure route I write to the other side and set up a timetable.'

Regarding costs, L1.2 advises that for the Court Route, average costs would be £15,000–£20,000 to first appointment; £30,000–£40,000 to FDR, and at least £80,000 for a Final Hearing plus counsel's fees and court fees.

---

[2] This option appears to correspond to the definition of lawyer-led negotiation used by Barlow et al (2014). There the screening question used asks if the respondent has heard of 'solicitor negotiation in which solicitors engage in a process of correspondence and discussion to broker a solution on behalf of their clients without going to court'.

[3] It is also possible to make an application to court for disclosure as part of a financial matter which may be resolved by negotiation without a hearing.

The timescale would be six months to FDR, and nine months to a Final Hearing or perhaps longer given recent changes to staffing and the shortage of judges. The voluntary disclosure route would cost £15,000 and take three months. Simply drawing up a Consent Order costs £5,000. These estimates can be refined when she knows what the other side's position is, or what their style is like. She is not enthusiastic about unbundling, repeating L1.3's concern that 'you don't know what you don't know'.

Overall, the picture of working practice presented is recognisably close to the picture we observed 15 years ago, in that the lawyers are dealing with complex cases, offering information about legal and practical issues and possible outcomes, setting the options but offering advice, and providing support and practical help in dealing with third parties. There is no indication of an aggressive approach, or of any reluctance to co-operate with other forms of dispute resolution, though there is a preference for mediation carried out by trained lawyers. New kinds of service are available, some popular with clients if not with practitioners, such as unbundling, and some popular with practitioners but not in demand from clients, such as mediation and collaborative law. But overall the picture is of a relatively stable position for this kind of firm, conscious of marketing, but continuing to work within traditional professional parameters. A good but expensive service is on offer, now available only to those with access to substantial resources.

Group 2 (General practice)

L2.1, who took part in our original study, had a small legal aid practice in the Midlands which had proved unsustainable following LASPO, so she had joined a larger firm with a busy and profitable wider practice and a number of branches. She focuses on public law children work, for which legal aid is still available, and contributes to Hague Convention cases as a Law Society accredited Children Panel specialist. This work is profitable, a recent abduction case having incurred £18,000 in costs in one month. She highlighted the problems when a children case lies on the boundary between public and private law. She currently has a case where child protection issues had arisen in a contact and residence matter, and the local authority required a finding of fact on allegations against the father who is seeking the return of the children to him from foster care in which they had been placed when they could no longer live with the mother, who still has a Residence Order. The costs involved included £8,000 for an assessment from the NHS-run Family Assessment and Safeguarding Service, and a meeting with experts costs £126 an hour, plus £756 for updating and writing the report. The firm's family law department had previously done half publicly funded and half privately funded work, but the ratio had changed to 80:20 in favour of private client work. The firm has done a few collaborative law cases, but the senior partner (L2.2) observed that he was uneasy about the outcome as men appeared to do better in collaborative law because if a settlement is proposed which is only just outside what a lawyer would regard as reasonable, the lawyer can only advise in this setting, but cannot proceed with an application to a court.

The enviable level of stability and increasing business in the firm as a whole requires stringent cost control. A junior partner (L2.3) who handled legally aided child protection cases described the increasing pressure on family solicitors. 'Until 2007 we had an hourly rate, then fixed fee, then tendering, then another cut. But overheads are not changing. We recruit at lower salaries and then have no increase in earnings for five years. We have to make the same fees. This firm is brilliant, switched on, but other firms struggle. Government doesn't want to think about the future of the profession. Training takes time. We charge £90 an hour for a trainee but the private client doesn't want a trainee. In care cases, if I do a £2,000 fixed fee, I won't make a living: I can run two cases a year. I carry on, but I don't see young people at court any more.'[4] He commented that CILEx had been astute in 'upping the quality' of their training seven years ago. 'The Law Society on the other hand underestimates what has been happening. The training contract offers a low salary for two years. So we took on secretaries, funded CILEx exams for people on a low salary who had aptitude, they study for two years, get a Fellowship of CILEx, and use the time to do a Legal Practice Course and become a solicitor. But McKenzie Friends![5] £200 for a one-day training course, then £50 an hour. I would do better to set up as a McKenzie ... no overheads!'

A second firm we visited with middle (and some high) income clients in a rural area in Central England advertises as a specialist family firm but also offers trusts, tax and pensions, including offshore trusts and corporate structures. The firm was set up in the south of England within the last 10 years by a former commercial litigation solicitor (L2.4) with experience of setting up family departments in commercial firms to provide non-legal aid services. Her business strategy was to provide a high-quality service but keep charges low and to counter negative attitudes towards the legal profession by working with others, including mediators, and offering a free half

---

[4] A QC working mainly in the High Court can run over 60 cases a year.
[5] Guidance from the President's Office: Where proceedings are held in open court and a party is not represented, the litigant has the right to have reasonable assistance from a layperson sometimes known as a McKenzie Friend who may take notes, help with case papers, quietly give advice on points of law, procedure, issues a litigant may wish to raise, questions the litigant may wish to ask witnesses, but has no right to act on behalf of a LIP, nor address court nor question witnesses, may not attend closed court without permission from the court, may not act as the agent of the LIP nor manage the case outside court eg by signing documents. www.google.co.uk/url?url=https://www.judiciary.gov.uk/wp-content/uploads/JCO/Documents/Guidance/pfd-guidance-mckenzie-friends.pdf&rct=j&frm=1&q=&esrc=s&sa=U&ei=vjRLVdT1AqOp7AaIrYGwAQ&ved=0CCoQFjAA&usg=AFQjCNFG-Ee-b_81CTT2LIRqY3oE_DVJgQ (accessed 7 May 2015).

hour (often longer) of initial advice. Her charges are in the region of £1,000 for divorce, including court fees, and £3000–£5,000 if there are financial issues. The business has grown and now has three assistant solicitors. They are not affected by LASPO, but are feeling the impact of delays in getting court hearing dates, and the reduction in court staff. Bundles have to be delivered by hand, often after waiting in a long queue. They also described having been involved in more litigation recently with LIPs on the other side who are not able to negotiate.

L2.4 is a qualified mediator but had only one client last year. She charges £220 for both parties to attend one session, co-mediating with a male mediator with social work experience, each being paid £100 per hour with £20 for administration costs. She is used to dealing with clients who come in after a failed mediation, and feels that the National Family Mediation (NFM) training on finance is not adequate. But for children matters she said: 'It isn't legal, it's the acknowledgement, to say to each other, you are a good parent.' She said that with a good mediator she can draft a Consent Order from the MOU 'when they are experienced family lawyers. Failed mediations are coming in to me, they are bitter, they go all the way (to a contested final hearing).' 'I worry about the disclosure. It is more efficient to disclose first and then go to mediation for resolution, it's cost-effective.' She actively promotes mediation, and would like to do more. But she also had a realistic and robust approach to advising women in a vulnerable position. 'I say: "If he says you don't need a lawyer he's already got one". I say: "Don't leave the house with the children in it, you won't get it back". If the house is on the market I say: "Steady, don't put the cart before the horse".' The initial free advice helps to attract business, and build up trust in the local community, though she also said: 'Some exploit you, go off and do DIY or try something from the Internet. One came with something from New South Wales. It's an uphill struggle. LIPs come here when they are stuck, and go round patching bits and pieces together from different free interviews. We could be sued! People get distressed, there are mental health issues. I call it the shadow syndrome, our clients are not mad enough to be diagnosed but they are madder than the general population ... normal people are sorting themselves out.' 'I think just mediation, no lawyer, is OK about children, but not about money. You need discussion with a lawyer, then mediation, then a Consent Order. A client is complaining about me because I refused to turn his MOU into a Consent Order, but it contained open-ended undertakings. I couldn't sign it off.'

The firm refers 50 per cent of their cases to mediation with lawyer mediators, and estimate that half reach agreement. L2.4 says she has seen cases with 10 sessions with a non-lawyer mediator and no disclosure. 'We need better stepping arrangements between law and mediation.'

This group of family practitioners with middle income clients is facing the challenges of austerity but coping by refocusing on child protection work where legal aid continues, by cross-subsidy from other branches of their business or through rigorous cost-cutting and skilful marketing. Some are trained mediators, and the service is offered within their practice, but little used. There is more work to be had in sorting out the aftermath of mediation, whether or not agreement has been reached. But, while supporting mediation by lawyers, these practitioners, like those in our first group with high net worth clients, were critical of the work of non-lawyer mediators in financial cases.

Group 3 (Family work under pressure)

As in Groups 1 and 2, we began our observations by meeting a member of our earlier sample, L3.1, who had then been an active member of a firm in the West Midlands doing legal aid and mental health work. Her own practice in private law has now disappeared and she is taking early retirement, deeply frustrated and distressed by her inability to continue helping her clients after LASPO. One of her former clients had called asking for help when her partner who had a Contact Order had failed to return their two-year-old son after a visit. All L3.1 could do was tell her which form to use, C100, and that she would try to help her fill it in over the phone. Her firm could no longer offer free advice. They may not even be able to afford office space for much longer, and may try to continue working from home. They offer a fixed-fee first interview for £72 and £70 an hour thereafter. But these are heavy bills for clients on benefit. Even though legal aid continues for public law matters, there is no help when a private law case, like this one, looks like becoming a public law case, at consequently far greater public expense.

Another legal aid practitioner in the north of England (L3.4) told how he had given up his partnership in a legal aid practice three years ago, and set up independently as a locum practitioner. He had done well at first, earning more than he had drawn in partnership. But since LASPO, work had dwindled and during the six months before we met he had only had six weeks' work, charging £25 per hour. He commented that he had always found that his legal aid clients needed more help than was paid for, and were not 'the brightest on the block, needing a lot of help in understanding what was happening'. He found that private client firms were not picking up much work through free introductory sessions, and were advising people 'just get the forms, self-refer to mediation and then start yourself off on First Directions hearings, saving your money for later in case things get difficult'. He had found a few people helped by mediation, but thought that many are not suitable, and by and large people did not want it. He did not want to train as a mediator himself. He did think that money had been wasted in the legal aid sector, but that any reforms should have kept a proper merits test, that maybe mediation could be made more robust and lead to an order, and that 'heads should be knocked together'. In the Magistrates' Courts 'you would have a 3.30 appointment and still be waiting around at 4.30'.

In the north-west we spent several days in a small firm with a strong legal aid background with three branches, two of which offered other services, including crime. It is now struggling to stay in business. The senior partner (L3.2) and her assistant were interviewed and observed over three days. Faced with the possibility of closing down, the senior partner worked with great energy and determination to develop a way of continuing to do what they had always done, helping low-income families with family matters. To achieve this involved a range of strategies. They included charging low fees, training and practising as mediators, combining in a group with other local practices in six neighbouring towns, cutting overheads by using IT to make appointments, and dictating notes to an iPhone which then prints or emails. In addition they had set up a new process which enables clients to attend a free assessment and information meeting to discuss mediation on legal aid. They offered free initial advice and a variety of fixed-price packages, including pay-as-you-go fixed-fee advice, fixed-fee Family Court representation, proactive tailored advice and representation, fixed-fee document checking and preparation, fixed-fee mediation with the associated mediation service, collaborative law, and next step planning. L3.2 would like more mediation work, but is finding it hard to attract, even though she is willing to work as a mediator and solicitor in the same office on the same day.

Here we will describe a working day in her modest local office, close to a station, with one large shared office and one small office and consultation room. Despite the lack of amenities, the office has a warm and welcoming atmosphere, and would not be intimidating to low-income clients. We observed client appointments from 9.30 to 4.30 without breaks. L3.2 commented that there are fewer face-to-face meetings now, more being done by email and phone, but nevertheless there is still a 40 per cent no-show rate for appointments (for both legal advice and mediation).

The day began with an urgent and complex phone call about a case of the assistant where a local authority had misunderstood information about an MOU which referred to domestic violence issues as a request for action. At 10 am the first client, Mr X, arrived for his second appointment about his divorce, saying 'I hate papers'. Mr X was from Cyprus with some language problems, but L3.2 was able to both explain and engage him in the process with charm and humour. She repeated the cost of her work (estimated £700) to deal with his divorce. No aspect of the matter was straightforward. She asked about properties, none of which were in his wife's name, and a business property which was funded by informal loans from business associates. L3.2 ascertained that the wife was not willing to divorce as she believed that she would not then be able to stay in the UK. There were four teenage children. There was no will, and Mr X found it hard to understand that if there was no will and he died while married, his wife would inherit, not his son. His wife, he said, did not speak English, but their eldest son would help her. L3.2 had to explain that the court would need proof that the wife had received papers, and this might involve using a private detective to hand them to her. Even the spelling of his name and the date of birth on the marriage certificate were in question, as Mr X had been born in a village where births were not registered, and had to have his age confirmed by medical tests before marriage and had disagreed with the estimate. Choosing which of the facts on which to base the divorce was also complex, as Mr X was not familiar with the no fault concept. Eventually he explained: 'Fighting, arguing ... love finish, respect finish.' L3.2 replied that the judge would decide if that was enough, and if not they would have to show two years' separation with the wife's consent, and five years without it. She explained that they would have to establish the value of the house, that there was no pension or life insurance, and his self-employed status. Mr X was anxious for the commercial partner to help with these matters which he did not associate with the divorce process, even though L3.2 had warned him more than once that his wife would have a claim on part of the property even though she did not own it. L3.2 said that she would copy everything to the eldest son, as go-between, and the papers would go to the court the following week. Mr X left, and L3.2 commented that her approach had been very like mediation, not giving advice, just intimating: 'This is the law, and what are your instructions and plan of action?' If it had been a mediation session she would have called in an immigration lawyer and an interpreter, but the wife is not her client.

The next client arrived at 11, a girl needing a DNA test as part of legally aided care proceedings. L3.2 has been trained to take swabs, which she gives to her colleague in a laboratory across town for analysis. She took the swab and talked carefully to the girl about the forthcoming criminal proceedings she was facing concerning the injuries to her child and the likelihood of a custodial sentence. She would endeavour to arrange a final contact before this began.

While waiting for the 12 noon appointment L3.2 caught up on calls, remarking that it can take up to six calls to set up a mediation session, since a time must be agreed with both parties, at least one of whom may be reluctant. If she is working in the office, waiting time can be used, but this is more difficult if she is at an outreach site. This can be particularly frustrating in view of the 40 per cent 'no show' rate.

The next appointment arrives. Mrs Y is a divorce private client seeking an unbundled service to keep her costs down. She has limited income and is a full-time carer for her disabled twins aged 14. The husband has a progressive medical condition and is currently on holiday abroad. He refuses mediation. L3.2 had advised Mrs Y to go to court and ask for half the total costs against Mr Y, and she had returned with the order and is delighted. Sadly, when L3.2 looks at the form, it is only for half the costs excluding the disbursements, that is, court fees. L3.2 checks the husband's pension position and the amount left on the mortgage, and suggests that Mrs Y should follow this up with her assistant for a lower rate (L3.2 charges £185 an hour). They have the house and a flat where he is living. Mrs Y has not sought any part of his pension, hoping to set this off against a larger share in the house, which is adapted for the twins. Mrs Y has been paying the mortgage on the house, and the loan on the flat. L3.2 says: 'You have been enabling him to have additional money to spend on his legal bills. He could be more reasonable or he could ask for maintenance pending suit. Are you under strain?' Mrs Y replies that she lives from one month to the next. The children's money is totally used for him, and she must educate them to manage their own money at 16. She hopes that the children will be able to lead independent lives. L3.2 says: 'The question for the court is how long will the children be dependent on you: another four years?' Mrs Y replies that she will always need ground floor accommodation for her son, but hopes her daughter may go to college. L3.2 says: 'We need to look at special needs for those under 18 and levels of dependency. We might need a report, that might cost, but it might say a home is sacrosanct for x years.' Mrs Y says that if the house is sold now she would have to repay the cost of the alterations. L3.2 says she needs to sit down and pull it all together and put all the information in an asset schedule: 'Do a draft Form E.' She says they need to put off the decree absolute, and be aware that the other side are litigious. 'Whichever approach you take, be careful, you have cut your cloth ... you have used the children's money to subsidise him. For Form E I want you to look at outgoings, itemise it! Food, household, petrol, electric, gas. You have altered your lifestyle, so make it clear what you were doing. Don't underestimate. Leisure?' Mrs Y says: 'Swimming.' L3.2 replies she had a lady who spent £90 a month on make-up and slimming products. She tells Mrs Y to remember car service, tyres, MOT. 'Look at the cost of three-bedroom bungalows, get the evidence, the cost of replacing the car and washing machine, fridge. Your income looks a lot but it's the kids' money. A lot of it will stop when they are 18. The benefit is high because the expenses are high.'

Mrs Y says that Disability Living Allowance stops at 16, and Family Allowance and Tax Credit at 18, and she will be on £1,000 a month. L3.2 advises her to show what she was earning as a foster carer. She says: 'Show your tax returns are now zero.' Mrs Y says she has sorted out her father's will and will have a quarter of the value of the bungalow which she could use to pay the husband off later. 'He is spending his inheritance and after that he will have nothing. I will pay the loan on the caravan but not the site rental any longer.' L3.2 sums up, identifying actions for Mrs Y: update outgoings, do projections of future income, write to the caravan site manager, cc his solicitors. She asks if she would like a bill from her, or a standing order, as sometimes regular outgoings are helpful. She will do the summary. She exclaims: 'It would have been SO much easier to go mediation. Any questions?' Mrs Y leaves.

At 1.50 Mr D arrives for an Assessment and Information Meeting (AIM). He looks dishevelled and undernourished, but has always had his children for the weekend and now his ex-wife has stopped this arrangement without explanation. Mr D says he has been to mediation before, and it worked. L3.2 notes he has been a client of the firm before and asks what for: 'A bit of a fight' is the reply. L3.2 then makes an appointment for him by telephone to see a mediator in another firm, and asks if it was helpful coming today, and he replies: 'Better I come here, not go there and start kicking off.' He leaves, satisfied in the expectation of mediation.

The rest of the afternoon was spent on L3.2's description of the state of the business. She has 25 referrals a month for mediation and needs much more to keep her four full-time staff who were taken on in the expectation of an increase in mediation after LASPO and the Children and Families Act 2014. But this has not happened. She feels that judges have not been sufficiently helpful and that CAFCASS may be training their own mediators, a further source of competition for scarce business.

The outlook for these former legal aid practices is depressing.

Group 5 (Innovations)

All the lawyers described so far were making some innovative changes to their ways of working in response to austerity measures in the public sphere and recession in private client work. In Group 1, L1.3 was seeking new work in continental Europe. In Group 2, L2.4 was lowering the cost of high-quality work in an attempt to rebuild public trust in the profession, and in Group 3, L3.2 was bringing together a number of small legal aid practices to share overheads and developing a wide range of services from unbundling to packaging, mediation and even DNA testing. But our final group (Group 5) of 10 lawyers, all qualified solicitors, had taken up the challenge with an even greater degree of innovation in their work as described below. One was applying her legal training to provide business advice to legal firms (L5.1), another was training mediators in family law (L5.9) and two were providing crisis services (L5.2 and L5.3). Another had combined mediation with arbitration (L5.10). Two were working closely with digital services, one in a contractual relationship (L5.5) and one as a direct provider (L5.4). Finally we observed the family work of Co-operative Legal Services (L5.6, L5.7 and L5.8), the first large ABS.

Business consultancy: L5.1 had formerly worked in both high and low client income family firms, and trained as a mediator. She became interested in the potential for any firm to improve performance by thinking about marketing, streamlining administrative practices, and making effective use of social media to raise their profile. She offers help with website design, maximising Google visibility by packing key words, writes blogs and teaches effective use of Twitter, Facebook (especially for international work) and LinkedIn. She helps to improve the public space for a firm, and staff interpersonal skills. She discusses use of paralegals, noting how able law graduates are now seeking this route into a legal career in the absence of training contracts. She described how firms are encouraging clients through the door for a first meeting to establish a relationship and working thereafter by phone and email, sometimes renting a serviced office for meetings but working from home, and choosing their preferred working hours. Fixed-price packages are being developed after careful analysis of what cases cost for particular pieces of work, such as non-conflicted divorce. Some solicitors protect themselves by joining a network with fixed fees, to spread any loss.

Legal training for mediators: On finding it no longer economically viable to work full-time as a family solicitor, L5.9 trained as a mediator and began to train mediators in family law on foundation courses which included explaining the fine line between advice and information. She teaches: 'If you don't know, get legal advice yourself from your colleagues or our legal consultation service, or advise a client to see a lawyer.' Most NFM mediators work in mediation services and can speak to colleagues, but sole practitioners have varying degrees of legal knowledge and still no requirement to update. She was confident that lawyers can be trained to mediate, but that they tend to be more cautious than non-lawyer mediators, who ask clients for more information, such as local house prices. The pressure from the Legal Aid Agency to complete a mediation means that some sessions last all day. This also happens for family mediation in privately funded practice as well as commercial cases, and she mentioned a complex financial mediation which had lasted over 12 hours, cost £8,000 and failed to resolve the matter. As a lawyer she sees solicitor-to-solicitor negotiation as a non-court route to dispute resolution, and would tick the box saying that this had been attempted as required on the MIAM form. She advises mediators when sending a client to see a lawyer to type up the information held, and the question to be asked, and she would like to see Legal Help come earlier in the process. She is also concerned that, following LASPO, mediators are doing more than they are trained to do as there is no one else for clients to turn to. For example, she found mediators helping with an S8 form and others with C100s, both of which include questions about domestic abuse in the context of contact and residence.

Combining arbitration with mediation: L5.10 is a practising family solicitor, qualified as a mediator and arbitrator, who sought a way to enable the process of dispute resolution to be completed in the context of mediation. She offers MedArb, whereby when signing the agreement to mediate the parties also sign an agreement for the mediator to arbitrate on matters left unresolved. The advantages of a 'one-stop shop' are clear, but there might be concerns about one individual acting in both roles. Take-up has been very limited so far.

Crisis legal help: L5.2 is a qualified solicitor and mediator working in a law firm but employed by a pilot project[6] developed by Resolution and funded by the Department of Work and Pensions in the aftermath of LASPO. This aims to help separating parents to get through the breakup in a way which will cause as little disruption to the children as possible, and to access the information and help that best meets their needs. The staff are described as 'guides' who will use their skills and expert understanding of the law and legal system 'to help you work through the issues you are dealing with'. All are qualified as lawyers and mediators. L5.2 described the project as 'intended to work in a similar way to the Australian Family Relationship Centres, and to meet the needs arising post LASPO'. Clients are found by networking locally in Children's Centres and the law firm where it is based when clients are told legal aid is no longer available. The service is free for those earning the minimum wage or on benefit.

A mediation model is used, respecting the autonomy of the clients and not intervening when they are in agreement. When we asked whether the service sees itself as family support or dispute resolution, L5.2 replied that she cannot give individual advice, but might give legal information to a couple together. When we first spoke with L5.2 at the beginning of her work, it seemed that she might largely be acting as an agent for putting distressed clients with complex behavioural problems in touch with relevant services, and be frustrated by not being able to use her legal expertise. When we spent a day observing her work some six months later, it was clear that the work had developed into a mainly legal crisis service to those now excluded from legal aid. For example, a girl with mental health issues had stopped taking her medication, and needed support to be able to apply to the court to re-establish contact with her child. L5.2 commented that she had a number of clients with mental health issues and social services involvement. Another client that day was an illiterate disabled man who had been taking care of his three children, but the mother had appeared and taken them. He needed urgent legal help. L5.2 said that the courts do not have a crisis model, but 'I don't do social work. It's good to have a legal person as first contact ... Mediation takes too long to set up ... I do active listening about what is the issue. Social work is for the most needy, and I can do signposting, but there is always a legal element. There is no legal aid, the forms are intimidating and there are no counter staff. For example poor families in council housing can only get rehoused if there is domestic violence. What we do is what CAFCASS did at the beginning. What can I do? I have two autistic parents with a baby and dad is having overnight care; in another case the babies were born after a relationship lasting an hour, and dad is wanting contact after 10 years away. Our original plan was for one meeting to give legal information. But we are taking the cases mediation rejects. We are often the

---

6 Family Matters: www.resolution.org.uk/familymatters/.

go-between, very time-consuming, predominantly for clients with mental health issues needing a crisis service.' This project is an interesting non-commercial model and is being monitored. The approach is law-centred, but takes a law-plus-welfare approach with elements close to social work and family support, and the desire to see both parties as in mediation.

A new and successful combination of sensitive legal services and the Internet: L5.5 heads the family department of a general firm in the West Midlands which deals with middle-income clients and has doubled its volume of work over the last two years. She takes pride in leading an emotionally sensitive group of lawyers. They employ a counsellor and offer a short course for older ladies called 'Moving On' which includes a session on the grief cycle, communication and building a life after divorce, during which the ladies can go out to a restaurant together with their new friends in the same position and enjoy a public function without a male escort. The key to this business model is a firm belief in the difference between straightforward and complex divorce. Of the 1,000 files the firm opens each year, L5.5 believes that 80 per cent are straightforward and can be helped by online services offering DIY advice, plus help with documents, and packages of service marketed as solicitor-managed divorce. She has contracted with a digital not-for-profit service to support the legal information and packages offered online, and where more legal help is needed, her firm steps in to provide for specific individual needs. She is working on how to make it possible for those who have bought into a basic package to smoothly upgrade the level of help they buy.

She understands that the Legal Services Agency is interested in consumer response and keen to make sure that cases are looked at by experienced lawyers. But people have different priorities. Some need speed, and others to limit costs. It may be possible to achieve separation online, and then pay for speeding up financial settlement. She says that in family work it is important to understand the different needs clients have, and how hard it is for them to know what they need, unlike in conveyancing or commercial work where there is no emotion involved. She is developing workshops on how to write a budget, how to deal with wills in blended families and other difficult decision-making processes. The clients tend to have sufficient resources to meet the cost of their case, but are attracted by the independence and control of using a web-based service. The firm does not offer in-house mediation but does assessment post-MOU work preparing Consent Orders. She comments on the 'weird agreements' they see, which they deal with by putting in recitals such as 'the parties say this … are doing that …'. They handle 80 Consent Orders a month. They have a team of 22 on the digital side. Overall this productive partnership between traditional legal service and an independent web-based service is attracting a high volume of work, helping the family law solicitors to remain profitable and still offer a high-quality, reasonably priced product.

An alternative way of working with a digital service was developed by L5.4, who works part-time as a consultant from a serviced office in central London and has set up an in-house digital service. Clients using this can handle a non-contentious divorce for a small fee, and if they need further help, can become clients of the firm buying the full legal service. The site was developed with a professional IT colleague and is user-friendly and comprehensive, handling about 20 clients at a time, some of whom may become full clients.

Alternative business structures: the Co-operative Legal Service (CLS)

The Co-op was not the first ABS approved by the SRA to offer the family services formerly only offered by solicitors. That honour belongs to Tracey Miller of Liverpool, who set up a mobile service, promising to visit clients seven days a week (The Law Society March 2013: 158); but the CLS came second, launching its family law service in May 2012 with 500 employees in Bristol and 20 in London aiming to offer a full range of fixed-price family services as well as a range of options including face-to-face work. The service offers free initial telephone advice, fixed-fee services for child protection, a DIY or lawyer-managed service for undefended divorce, finance and parenting arrangements, mediation in arrangement with NFM and arbitration. The phone lines are open 8 till 8, the website is user-friendly with a 'hide screen' function to protect user privacy—especially necessary where there are domestic abuse issues. The service prides itself on being sensitive and jargon-free. The information packs and forms are well designed and cover a wide range of family matters including house purchase for cohabiting couples, negotiating post-separation contact for £250 and an initial consultation on finance for £175 plus £250 for further negotiation. The charge for all issues mediation is £714, and is £570 for finance only (all fees as at July 2014). Further legal advice and information is available, chargeable by work done. The service was launched with a strong publicity campaign in the run-up to LASPO, and was described by *The Guardian* as 'the Wapping moment for family law'[7] and by the Co-op as 'fixed fees with no nasty surprises'. There was talk of jobs for 3,000 lawyers. Sadly, achieving profitability involved a 'nasty surprise' for the service, which made a pre-tax profit of only £26,000 in 2012 (The Law Society March 2013: 158).

We spent two days in the London office of the service, both before and after the move to the new offices near the Old Bailey. We first observed and interviewed policy and administrative staff and lawyers one year after the launch. The London offices were open-plan, with 30 enthusiastic young newly qualified SRA-regulated solicitors, supported by legal professionals accredited by the Chartered Institute of Legal Executives (CILEx). They hold

---

[7] *The Guardian*, 10 November 2011. This refers to a notorious industrial dispute in 1986 which resulted in failure for the strikers, with the implication that a monopoly had been broken.

a contract for telephone advice from the Legal Services Board. They offer DIY packaged services and there is a team for complex cases. There are few face-to-face interviews because the service attracts users from throughout the country. The first high-profile director of policy, Christina Blacklaws, worked effectively to raise awareness, and was elected Lawyer of the Year at the Modern Law Review Awards in 2013. A £2 million publicity campaign ran in London raising brand awareness from 1.6 per cent of the population to 6 per cent in the first year.

There were inevitably constraints associated with being part of a big organisation and these were exacerbated when the Co-op experienced serious difficulties with its banking business and general management. But the CLS itself was carefully managed, beginning by employing only solicitors, with a view to establishing credibility, and then going on to train paralegals to take phone calls, taking care to enable them to recognise more complex cases. The legal profession was critical, saying the CLS would damage high-street practice. The CLS response was that it was LASPO, not they, who were causing problems, and that they were simply trying offer a quality but innovative and affordable service. For example they offered a domestic violence medical certification service whereby a nurse took the story by phone and signed the form for a fee paid by the CLS (£50–£90) who could than take on the now legally aided client. But the Civil Legal Aid Procedure Regulations 2012, s 33 (as amended by the Civil Legal Aid (Procedure) (Amendment) Regulations 2014) ended this by requiring the assessment to be carried out in person. There were attempts to make the website more interactive, but this has limitations where matters are in dispute.[8] The aim was always to provide a high-quality service for those with incomes just above the legal aid limit. The user is not locked into any package, and upgrading is easy when needed. But concerns grew about the impact of the Co-op's problems. The CLS had always taken a position between a subsidised service and full profitability, in line with the Co-op's ethical stance,[9] but was under pressure to increase profitability. The head of legal services, a family solicitor with 15 years' experience, described the Legal Aid Authority audit as demanding. The NFM contract was quiet, but there was a new contract with the National Centre for Domestic Violence (NCDV) for work in domestic abuse cases.

Sitting with a Solicitor Senior Family Caseworker, L5.7, in her paper-free work station, we observed her work on screen with a contact case preparing for a hearing the following day in the County Court, where she would be

---

[8] Bregde Dijksterhuis, 'Users' Opinion about online self help tools on alimony payment', Paper to Legal Profession Group Meeting of the Research Committee on the Sociology of Law, International Sociological Association, Frauenchiemsee, July 2014.

[9] See   www.co-operative.coop/corporate/press/press-releases/headline-news/Join-The-Revolution/.

doing the client's advocacy. She described how the system is modular. A client can build on the help received so far, but the service stresses clarity and will give the information which the client needs in order to choose further help. The basic Divorce Pack still costs £25, and DIY divorce with document checking and help online or by post is £99, and very popular. The pack includes pre-paid envelopes, or email. Each document is checked only once, the most common mistake parties make being the location of their marriage.

There are 40 solicitors hot-desking in the office. Phone advice is based in one corner. Another corner has child protection and private law cases; difficult legal aid work is in another, and then work on finance and children. Eight lawyers were in court on the morning of our visit. The packs are sent out from the Bristol office, which takes the initial information and narrative, which on return is allocated by a Team Leader after a conflict check to make sure the other side is not a client. L5.7 had 50 files open currently. Most of the DIY cases need further help with finance. The case she is working on now came via the National Centre for Domestic Violence. She has obtained a non-molestation and occupation order for the client but there are also children issues, as mum says dad has threatened to remove them. The evidence for eligibility for legal aid is now so tight that she had to get the non-molestation order first and can then apply for legal aid for the children in two stages. She says there is never a single issue in these cases: 'We prepare the papers for both (domestic violence and child) matters at the same time for court and issue first for the injunction and then when we have the order we issue on the children matter. We got her a residence and prohibited steps order. Dad cross-applied for a non-molestation order so it went back to court. They agreed basic undertakings and now it's the contact issues. They had agreed some contact but the elder child alleged chastisement. Social services are involved and recommended no direct contact while investigating. I don't have their report (it was due two weeks ago) and the hearing is tomorrow, a first hearing for directions. Mum is now not agreeing the contact.' She breaks off as the report comes in by email as we are talking. L5.7 comments: 'It says little, the social worker has had a supervised contact session and says the children are happy to see their father, there is a bond, but nothing about whether there should be unsupervised contact.' Tomorrow she expects to need to speak to the client, and the court will ask for a section 7 report and further statements. She says: 'I get paid £80 for the whole morning and will do the advocacy. I haven't met the client yet, I took over the case from a colleague on maternity leave. Often I don't meet the clients because they are not local. Some clients really need a face-to-face contact; this service is not the best for them. I had a disabled woman last week. But most people find this way of working easier. Everybody has email on their phone, so don't need to take time off work.'

When asked how clients choose the service and package, L5.7 replied: 'They get a service letter and an agreement which sets out exactly what is covered and what is not. About children, if people can agree they don't need anything from us, but generally need an order for finance. Or they may need small help. With a package they can have add-ons, a one-off meeting, or full legal. They can dip in and out. We don't charge by the phone call, but a consultation fee about a hearing, what happened, what to do next is £175. Based on most cases we get a good idea of what is likely to happen and what to do next.' L5.7 charges £150 an hour; a senior solicitor costs £175. 'We say this is the work needed, this is the best fit, if the client says it's too expensive, we advise, they choose.' Of all the innovations the CLS was the largest in scale and aspiration. It has, however, not proved easy to achieve financial viability.

III. CONCLUSION

Lawyers are now less visible in government departments. The diminished role of the Lord Chancellor has removed their champion from Cabinet, and for the first time there have been two Lord Chancellors and Secretaries of State for Justice who were not lawyers. And in other jurisdictions, Ministries of Justice have been renamed as the Ministry for Security and Justice in the Netherlands, and for Justice and Consumer Affairs in Germany. Nevertheless, family lawyers remain the first port of call for the majority of those seeking help with family matters. Their work appears relatively unchanged for high-income clients, but seems to be changing to a more limited specific activity for middle-income clients combined with other services, and under threat and undergoing complex but energetic change for the client group without the resources to purchase legal help in the market place. Twenty-five years ago solicitors charged on average (without legal aid) £75–£100 for a simple divorce without contested finance or children issues, and in 1979 earned on average £2,205 a year (Zander 1980: 27). They might be surprised to see free DIY on Wikivorce, or legal costs of reputedly £8 million for *Radmacher* (a very high-profile case), and a gap in provision in the middle ground which CLS has made a brave attempt to fill. Resolution is campaigning for a family justice system which provides support throughout relationship breakdown, puts children first, helps parents to work together in their children's interests, provides fair and lasting outcomes, and protects all those at risk of harm and sufferers of abuse.[10] Sadly greater autonomy and choice in a complex marketised legal world also carries undeniable risks for vulnerable parties who lack purchasing power or the essential skills and resilience to navigate their way through the tangled market and legal complexities and emotional pressures of family breakdown.

---

[10] Resolution, *Manifesto for Family Law*, February 2015: www.resolution.org.uk/familylawmanifesto/.

4

The Organisation and Aims of Mediation in England and Wales

I. ORGANISATION

THE DEVELOPMENT OF government interest in the promotion of mediation as the primary service for separating couples in place of legal negotiation was discussed earlier. While the government's motives may have been initially inspired by financial concerns, much emphasis was also placed on perceived differences in the way lawyers and mediators worked. This perception, in our view, arose from largely inaccurate beliefs about legal practice, as explained earlier, and the next chapter will suggest that the differences between the two may have become exaggerated. However, the ethos and structural environment within which mediators have operated have been different from those of lawyers. Individuals who practise mediation come from a range of disciplinary backgrounds and, as will be seen, have worked in a variety of institutional settings. Compared with lawyers, mediators work within a tighter context of meetings with the participants, with less involvement outside the meeting, do not usually work with third parties,[1] and have generally less infrastructure to support them. Some of the difficulties associated with understanding the new profession for the general public as well as the policy maker arise from the variation in the organisation, aims and codes of practice among the different groups of mediators who pioneered the rapid and effective establishment of their profession. This chapter therefore looks at the move towards the development of a more coherent framework for the practice and organisation of

---

[1] See T Whatling, Letter (2015) 45 *Family Law* 609, questioning the appropriateness in mediation of 'external' consultations by the mediator. There is some involvement with third parties, for example a non-lawyer mediator when sending clients for legal advice told us that she sought legal advice from a third lawyer to use in the following session. This was paid for by the service. Other mediators mentioned the practice of sending MOUs to be read by lawyers for conformity with law and current practice. Roberts (2014: 116–17) accepts that where expertise beyond the knowledge of the participants is required this may be introduced into the process in two main ways, either via the mediator or via a consultant either to the mediator or to the parties outside the process, adding that research confirms that the occasional presence of a legal consultant causes no difficulty to clients and nor does it disrupt the flow of negotiations.

mediation, including training, accreditation and regulation, before turning in the following chapter to discussion of mediation by lawyers and non-lawyers in practice.

In England and Wales mediation (then usually called 'conciliation') began to develop after its endorsement by the Finer Committee on One-Parent Families in 1974.[2] When mediation first received public funding in 1996 the then Legal Aid Board had introduced a requirement for mediators undertaking legal aid work to pass a competence assessment and follow a statutory code of practice. In response to this need for professional oversight the Family Mediators Association (FMA) (representing individual practitioners) and National Family Mediation (NFM) (representing not-for-profit services) and Family Mediation Scotland set up the UK College of Family Mediators which they hoped would provide this, but this organisation faced a difficult task (see Roberts 2005). Membership gradually dwindled until the College closed in this form in 2007, though it remained (as the College of Mediators) as a voluntary membership body open to practitioners in all areas of mediation (see Lester 2014: Part 1). The College of Family Mediators was followed by the Family Mediation Council (FMC), established in 2007 to provide some co-ordination between bodies carrying out family mediation in England and Wales. Member organisations were Resolution, the FMA, NFM, the Law Society, the College of Mediators, and Alternative Dispute Resolution Group (ADRg). The Family Justice Review (2012: para 4.104), while generally supportive of mediation, was critical of the functioning of the FMC, whose Board comprised one representative of each member organisation, plus three independents (though two of these were vacant for long periods: McEldowney 2012: para 63). It stipulated that 'a clear plan must be developed to maintain and reinforce standards of competence and to ensure the effective regulation of mediation as numbers of mediators increase' (Family Justice Review 2011: para 4.102). It also said that government should 'closely watch and review the progress of the FMC to assess its effectiveness in maintaining and reinforcing high standards' and that, if necessary, the FMC should be replaced by an independent regulator (Ibid: para 4.104 and Executive Summary para 122).

It is hardly surprising that a young profession, which had developed so rapidly in different ways from different starting points, should have concentrated on getting the services under way rather than on developing unified codes of practice, training and accreditation and regulation. Indeed the world of mediation was well known to be complex, divided and at times disorganised, but full of energy and commitment to providing a better service for separating families. In response to the Family Justice Review, the FMC

---

[2] For more details, see Manchester and Whetton (1974); Dingwall and Eekelaar (1988: ch 1); Roberts (2014: 35–38; 51–56); T Whatling, Letter (2015) 45 *Family Law* 609.

commissioned a review from Professor John McEldowney into the practice of its member organisations and the role of the FMC.

When the McEldowney Report was published in 2012 (McEldowney 2012), the six member organisations of the Council were carrying out family mediation in England and Wales from a variety of starting points and varying standards and codes of practice. According to the report, ADRg was a commercial organisation undertaking all forms of civil mediation, with the trading name of IDR Europe Ltd and ADR Net Ltd. It had a registered company office in Bristol, and had been involved in family mediation since 2000. It was reported as having 72 mediators on its register, and had adopted the FMC Code of Practice (McEldowney 2012: paras 48–49). The College of Mediators, the successor to the UK College of Family Mediators (see above) had a register of 104 family mediators 'from a range of professional backgrounds'. It operated its own Code of Practice (Ibid: paras 45–47). The FMA was established in 1988, and at that time had 495 mediators from 'a wide range of professional backgrounds', which would have included both solicitors and therapists, on its register. By the time of the Review it had adopted the FMC Code of Practice (Ibid: paras 36–38). The Law Society is the national body accrediting solicitors in England and Wales. It has a Protocol for accredited family solicitors, and also family mediators, then numbering about 155, with three different routes to membership, and used its own Code of Practice for solicitor mediators (Ibid: paras 42–44). NFM was founded in 1982 'as an umbrella organisation with a network of affiliated member services in England and Wales'. It then had a register of 311 mediators 'employed by its services', who might have worked in sessions for more than one service. It operated the FMC Code of Practice (Ibid: paras 33–35). It was concerned to make mediation available across the country, and therefore collected information about service locations rather than numbers of mediators, who often work in more than one place and are not usually from a legal background. Members of Resolution, now numbering some 6,500, are mostly specialist family lawyers who subscribe to the organisation's non-combative approach to family lawyering. At the time of the Review, 606 were also mediators (Ibid: paras 39–41). It had its own system of accreditation for Resolution mediators (Ibid: para 39), and followed the Law Society Code for Mediators. All solicitors practising family law are covered by the Law Society's Family Law Protocol (currently in its third edition, 2010) which lays down guidelines for good practice in handling family law cases. The Protocol now 'endorses' the Resolution Code of Practice,[3] which spells out its 'constructive and non-confrontational' approach and requires Resolution's members to 'abide by' Resolution's comprehensive Guides to Good Practice. Resolution's Guide to Good

---

[3] Law Society Family Law Protocol (2010), para 1.2.1.

Practice on Mediation was last revised in 2015. This group may overlap with the Law Society registered mediators.

According to these figures, the total number of family mediators appears not to exceed 1,743, though there is likely to be double counting as individuals may be affiliated to more than one body. The Final Report of the Voice of the Child Dispute Resolution Advisory Group (2015: paras 28, 29) estimated that there were 1,535 mediators registered with the FMC, of whom three-quarters were also lawyers, leaving around 400 non-lawyer mediators, though these figures are necessarily approximations.[4] The group has always been numerically small compared with the number of family solicitors. For example, in 1997, 25 per cent (14,300: 9,900 men and 4,400 women) of all enrolled solicitors were doing some family work,[5] of whom about 28 per cent (3,900: 2,600 women and 1,300 men) were family law specialists spending not less than half their time on family work.[6] Specialism decreased with age and increased with the size of firm. So there were 3,900 specialist family solicitors in 1997 and 5,000 members of the Solicitors' Family Law Association (now Resolution), which would have included most, perhaps all, of the 3,900 specialists. By 2012 the total number of solicitors identifying themselves as practising family law had fallen to 13,685 (The Law Society, July 2013: 158), but this figure must be seen in the light of the information that 31 per cent of legal aid firms have indicated that they may not be doing legal aid work in three years' time (Pleasence, Balmer and Moorhead 2012: ii).

The number of mediations carried out is difficult to assess as different organisations are collecting data for different purposes. Regarding publicly funded mediation, there was an average of 13,378 mediations a year from 2006–07 to 2013–14 (which includes a significant fall from 15,357 in 2011–12 to 8,432 in 2013–14) (Ministry of Justice and Legal Aid Agency September 2014: Table 7.2). There are no comprehensive data for non-publicly funded mediation, which has traditionally been more common in more affluent parts of the country (the south rather than the north-east, for example) and less dependent on solicitors for referral. National Family Mediation (2014) gives a figure of 29,000 MIAMs (that is, mediation information and assessment *meetings*, including meetings with both parties separately or just one party) conducted by NFM member services in 2013, of which 16,000 (55 per cent) were legally aided and 13,000 (45 per cent) privately funded. But only 6,200 (21 per cent) led to mediation starting, of which one or both participants were legally aided in 3,500 (56 per cent) of

---

[4] The recent FMC database is designed to provide each mediator with a unique reference number, so that they are not counted twice. At present many mediators are members of more than one organisation, and are counted by their memberships.

[5] By 2012 the total number of solicitors identifying themselves as practising family law had fallen to 13,685: The Law Society (July 2013: 158).

[6] Maclean, Sidaway and Beinart (1998) using data from the Law Society Omnibus Survey.

cases, leaving 2,700 privately funded. If we add this (2,700) to the 8,432 publicly funded mediations recorded by the Legal Aid Agency over much the same period, this gives a total of 11,132 mediations. On the basis of a total of about 1,535 FMC mediators, thus would provide an average of 7.2 mediations a year for all FMC mediators on 2013–14 figures, though of course they would hold many more mediation assessment meetings.[7]

The McEldowney Report (2012: para 87) noted that there was then no accurate number or identification of all the family mediators practising in England and Wales, and that there was duplication of membership between member organisations. Furthermore, there was no common code of practice, no common method of training or accreditation 'and therefore no single transparent system in place for sorting out competent from incompetent mediators', although 'the establishment of a single accreditation scheme now represents work in progress' (Ibid: para 88). The review was frank about the current problems, observing (Ibid: para 14):

> Family mediators encounter difficult and troubled families, including victims of violence and abuse. The expertise of family mediators is often taken for granted or misunderstood. The mediator's skill set is drawn from many disciplinary skills ranging from financial and legal to the social and psychological. There is a general wish, if not claim, amongst many mediators that they ought to be accorded the full respect due to their professional status. Consequently the professional role of mediators is not always easy to discern … There is some distrust between legally and non-legally qualified mediators which may lead to disparagement or professional tensions. Family mediation may be the loser in any professional rivalry … Publicly funded mediators are subject to the LSA's Quality Mark Standards for Mediation as a pre-condition for contract. Private mediation is also a thriving business but there is no national register and miscellaneous providers.

Among the major recommendations of the McEldowney Report were that the FMC should be 'strengthened to develop, with governmental assistance, a regulatory framework that will develop and maintain family mediation practised to a high standard' (Ibid: Recommendations, para 3), that there should be a 'single and generally accepted accreditation system resulting in a common practising certificate' (Ibid: para 89 and Recommendations, para 10) and that members should comply with the FMC Code of Practice (Ibid: Recommendations, para 1). The FMC responded positively to the Report, and supported by the Ministry of Justice, commissioned Dr Stan Lester to develop professional standards and regulatory practices (see Lester 2014: Part 2 and Part 3). Lester found that 'four sets of competence standards or assessment criteria (were) being used in family mediation, none of which could be described as adequate for use as general professional

---

[7] This is inevitably a rather broad-brush calculation, and an unknown (but probably small) number of mediations are conducted by non-FMC mediators, but gives a sense of the wider picture.

standards' and proposed changes to the governance of the FMC, suggesting a Professional Standards and Accreditation Board (PSAB) separate from the main council, and common competence standards, training, monitoring and development, assessment and accreditation, leading to a single qualified-to-practise status (FMCA: FMC Accredited Family Mediator). Under this compromise scheme, the FMC remains a representative body, but the PSAB has some independence from it:

> while ensuring that its family mediator members do not all come from the same Member Organisation, professional background or type of practice; it is also envisaged that its members will include both practising family mediators and some from outside the immediate family mediation community, for instance from adjacent professions and from mediation or family law academics. This model provides the PSAB with greater independence than a typical professional standards committee in a self-regulating professional body, a measure considered necessary due to the nature of the FMC as an umbrella organisation, but it avoids setting up a separate organisation along the lines of those in law and architecture.

It should be added that, outside this framework, the website of the marriage guidance organisation 'Relate', while mostly offering counselling services, also offers mediation.[8] In response to our inquiry about what Codes of Practice its mediators followed, and whether these were accessible, an email message simply read: 'Please contact your local Relate centre for these details as they may vary from centre to centre.' According to their website, 13 centres offer mediation, and further enquiries elicited varying information about the status of mediators in such centres. Two centres offered publicly funded mediation. This underscores the range of services on offer to the public if they wish to have resort to mediation (see also Webley: in press). The Bar also holds a 'Mediation Directory' of barristers who offer mediation, though only about ten offered family mediation and had undergone appropriate training.

II. QUALIFICATIONS AND TRAINING

A. Qualifications

As regards qualification to practise, while it is proposed that all new and existing members of the FMC should hold the FMCA status, this will not be a legal requirement except for the conduct of publicly funded mediation or MIAMs under the Children and Families Act 2014. Hence unaccredited mediators could still operate outside the scope of the FMC. The proposals concerning the common qualified-to-practise status (FMCA) began to be

---

[8] www.relate.org.uk/relationship-help/help-separation-and-divorce/mediation   (accessed 13 July 2015).

implemented in stages as from 1 January 2015, with various transitional arrangements for holders of existing forms of accreditation (Family Mediation Council 2014). From that date there are to be three categories of FMC mediator:

(1) **FMCA mediator:** All mediators who have been competence assessed via the FMC route and mediators who have successfully completed the Law Society route to professional competence;

(2) **FMCA mediator (cannot undertake legally aided work):** Resolution and FMA accredited mediators in good standing with their organisations who have been passported through to FMCA status on 1 January 2015;

(3) **FMCR registered mediator:** all mediators who have successfully completed the foundation training, are in good standing with their organisations, and are working towards achieving FMCA status.

Also an interim PSAB was planned to be instituted from that date.

The details of the requirements for training and FMC accreditation in order to achieve this qualification are set out in the FMC *Manual of Professional Standards and Self-Regulatory Framework* (Family Mediation Council 2014). To acquire FMC accreditation (FMCA), the mediator must have passed the assessments on an FMC-approved initial training course, completed the post-training requirements, and passed the final assessment of professional competence.

The minimum requirements for the initial training course should cover the 'principles, knowledge, techniques and skills stated or implied' in the Standards of Professional Competence set out in Appendix 2 of the Manual, including applying them in a simulated environment, and cover knowledge of children and property/finance aspects. 'Each participant must play the role of the mediator several times over the duration of the course and be provided with adequate feedback, such that s/he has a fair and adequate opportunity to demonstrate the relevant learning outcomes.' There must be at least 60 hours of contact time, spread over a minimum of eight days with sufficient intervening periods to enable reflection, private study and preparation for assessment.

Having successfully completed the initial course, before starting to mediate alone, the prospective mediator must begin the process of accreditation[9] by acquiring a supervisor (known as a professional practice consultant or PPC), and either have observed or co-mediated in a mediation session conducted by an FMCA mediator, and produced an evaluative account of the session. There is no requirement that a mediator must have conducted an observed mediation before beginning to mediate on their own but the mediator must have a pre-case discussion with their PPC before starting to mediate their first case and also hold a post-case review with their PPC.

---

[9] These and the following requirements are set out in section 2.1 of the FMC Manual.

In order to acquire FMC accreditation, a wide range of further requirements must be fulfilled, including at least 10 hours' one-to-one, principally face-to-face support from the PPC, with sessions recorded in a log countersigned by the PPC; at least one mediation session observed by the PPC (which must not be a session co-mediated with the PPC) and a minimum of three cases taken through to completion. These will need to be written up for assessment, together with a reflective account of working of up to 2,000 words, and answers given to a set of practice-based questions. This must be done within two years of completing initial training. Award of FMCA status is made following an assessment of a portfolio of work assembled from the period between completion of training and application, the contents of which are set out in detail (Family Mediation Council 2014: Appendix 1).[10]

B. Training

In order to acquire a better understanding of the approach to mediation imparted by this process, we obtained direct experience over two days, the first being the second day of an eight-day Resolution FMC compliant foundation course given by three trainers (all practising mediators, two with legal backgrounds) with a group of 20 young lawyers on working with children cases, and a second day specifically on how to how to carry out a MIAM. The fee for the eight-day course is £2,600). We were also very fortunate in having access to a recently successfully completed portfolio compiled for the accreditation process, and to have been able to discuss the process with the lawyer-mediator who had prepared it.

A MIAM training day

The training on providing MIAMs began with instruction on how to get parties to 'think in a mediation way', to be clear, but also 'to remember you are selling a service, so think offer, acceptance, purchase'. There was discussion among the group about whether the purpose of the meeting was 'selling' mediation, or should there be careful presentation of the options. Some thought the time in the MIAM should be used to prepare for the first mediation session (that is a lawyer's approach to accepting a client to work with them over time, rather than the traditional mediation approach to taking on a dispute which is presented as the task in hand). The skills and

---

[10] The portfolio must contain a personal training and development plan, CV, foundation course certificates, an assessment signed by the mediators and the PPC and testimony from the PPC of readiness to practise alone, commentaries on three main cases with an MOU for each and a full set of notes for one case, a reflective practice essay, responses to case study set questions and a completed competences grid.

techniques needed were summarised as 'managing the process, acknowledging and normalising the clients' experience, clarifying and summarising the position, giving neutral and mutualised information, and leaving time for effective closing and setting out the next step'. Trainers advised participants to dig for key issues but not too deeply. There was some reluctance to carry out the legal aid assessment as this is not therapeutic. On the question of screening for safety, the legally qualified trainer stressed the need for appropriate careful screening, and offering information about other processes for resolving financial disputes, including solicitor negotiation, information about children and parenting when parents live apart, information about legal process and being a LIP, and signposting to other services. The trainer ended by talking about active listening, advising practitioners to 'pay attention, look at the speaker, use your body language to show attention, listen with your eyes ... use silence ... and remember the need for safeguarding'. On being asked: 'What do I do if there is a question of child abuse?' the trainer replies: 'Stay calm, be clear about your duties, listen, reflect back, check details, explain what you intend to do ... you only need a next step. Sometimes you have to report to a third party.' The group was advised of the new CAFCASS pilot schemes which aim to help mediators identify concerns. Finally the trainer advised the group to plan how they would deliver information on MIAM charges, administration, support staff and colleagues, build professional networks, and assess financial eligibility.

A foundation training session on children

The children day consisted of short talks interspersed with role play in small groups, with students playing the parts of parents and mediators in turn and discussing the process amongst themselves and with the trainers assessing them. These ranged from a high anger role play concerning a mother having an affair with her disabled child's carer, to a more routine role play about telling the children about the separation, and screening a presentation from Christina McGhee from Texas on 'How to divorce without screwing up your children'. All this was useful information, and the role plays helped to develop the lawyers' emotional understanding of the process from a number of points of view.

The training gave information about the experience of children at separation, the statistical background, the work of the Family Justice Council Young People's Board, the factors which can be damaging for children, including high unresolved conflict, the absence of a parent, economic effects, and further family breakdown. Guidance was given on how to advise parents to tell children about separation, accept bad behaviour around that time, seek stability and continuity where possible, give loving permission and support for the child to spend time with the other parent, and to remember that parents are not bad people, they are just in a bad place. Strong emphasis was placed on making efforts to see the situation from the child's perspective and how to communicate this to the parents, helping them support their children through transition, and using clear language as a mediator. On finance, the trainer said: 'Remember, as lawyers you do the work, as mediators the clients do it ... focus on asking questions ... solicitors make plans and it is easy to get people to agree, but it is better in principle to help them make their own.' If parties are unable to make progress, the group was told: 'It is OK to say, are there other options? I wonder whether ...'.

C. Accreditation

A portfolio prepared for accreditation

As stated above, it is a requirement for acquiring FMC accreditation that the mediator compiles a portfolio which includes an account of a minimum of three cases taken through to completion under the guidance of the PPC, and the mediator's reflections on them. We could not experience accreditation directly but were able to discuss her portfolio with one mediator who, reflecting on her training, said: 'We were told to ask "What do you want to achieve?" and in a children case to say "Tell me about the children?" and then they agree, and relate as parents.' She believed in a holistic and client-focused approach. She would like to see what she called a 'community arbitration service' to integrate with mediation for the things which cannot be agreed. 'Create something around the families. Lawyers are not good as mediators because they have a right answer in mind.' The portfolio is a complex and demanding assignment of over 80 pages including a personal development and training plan, a recent CV, certificates of training taken, witness testimony (sic) from your PCC (in this case referring to 58 hours of face-to-face mediation). The PCC felt that this mediator had worked to convert her approach in her previous role of legal adviser to that of information giver rather than legal adviser, whilst building on her knowledge base, and that she carries out the disclosure process properly.

The portfolio includes a readiness to practise assessment covering four elements: (1) to prepare and set up mediation; (2) to stage the process; (3) to manage the process and (4) to evaluate and develop their own work. This is signed by the candidate and the PCC. In addition there are three case commentaries about five pages in length, each with outcome statements, an MOU for each case, two open financial statements (OFSs), and a full set of case notes for one case, a reflective account of up to 2,000 words, responses to case study questions, and a completed FMC competences grid showing where assessors may find evidence.

In the first case, where one client had become upset and left the room, the mediator described regret at not having been able to foresee and avoid this, but was able to prepare the OFS and MOU, which were attached. In the second case, which was about contact, the mediator explains why her technique of asking parties what they sought from mediation had worked well, in that there was a clear dispute about what would happen on a change of school, though she states that it would not work so well when conflict is less well defined or parties (sic: not participants or clients) are less confident. She also found her supervisor's technique of asking the parents what the child wanted from them worked less well in this case, sensing that they were reluctant to say something which they perceived might go against them in the litigation. The supervisor tried to get them to slow down and consider issues rather than react too quickly. Contact arrangements were agreed, but conflict continued about the specific issue of the child's medication.

The third case had started with a query from one party about being refused legal aid, which led the mediator to worry about the parties' confidence in the process. But the financial side began with considering what would be required from both of them in order to satisfy the service and solicitors about the veracity of their disclosure. She said that in her interventions she 'showed that I was asking questions that any solicitor would ask of them at a later stage, and therefore attempting to save costs and promote efficiency for them both' and that this approach kept him engaged. This was clearly a difficult mediation, and the mediator reveals that although the financial decisions were within what a court would order, she suspected that the wife might have been able to achieve a better settlement through contested proceedings 'but in the debrief she and her co-mediator agreed that the wife had made the agreement within the principles of mediation and this should be respected'.

The reflective account describes the mediator's background experience of mediation as a solicitor who had been advising clients to use it, her surprise at the gentleness of mediation and her appreciation of supervision, and gives three examples of learning experiences in practice. These comments were far more nuanced than the responses to the fairly blunt questions set in the written responses to the case studies section which included whether it was possible to mediate in the family home, or what to do if a party is deaf or smelling of alcohol. The portfolio appeared both knowledgeable and sensitive to the differences between ways of working in mediation and legal practice. The overall assessment of this portfolio was surprisingly critical, but the document provides an excellent starting point for further consideration of the relationship between legal practice and mediation.

III. CODES OF PRACTICE

As regards the various Codes of Practice used by FMC Member Organisations, by 2012 ADRg, NFM and FMA were already using the FMC Code of Practice which dates from September 2010.[11] The College of Mediators has its own code dating from 2008. In December 2012 the Law Society agreed to replace its former Code of Practice for Family Mediation with the FMC Code 'in full' because it was confusing to have two codes.[12] Resolution in effect has its own code in its comprehensive Guides to Good Practice of 2012 which cover legal practice and mediation. The revised Guide to Good Practice on Mediation of June 2015 (Resolution 2015: 2) refers to the FMC's Manual of Professional Standards and Self-Regulatory Framework referred to above and states that all mediators must adhere to its requirements and the requirements for time spent annually with their PPC 'as set out by the Family Mediation Council Standards' (Ibid: 8). It also states that 'the requirements in regard to impartiality and conflicts of interest are set out in the Mediation Council Code of Practice (of which Resolution is a signatory)' but goes on to set them out in its own language (Ibid: 10).

While moves to produce a common code could be presented as being no more than a matter of tidying up, the implications for practice, on paper at least, of the differences between codes are not minimal. For example, the Law Society Code stated that 'parties *should* be informed if their proposal lay outside what a court might order',[13] while the College's Code[14] positively discourages it by saying that mediators 'must not predict the outcome of court or formal proceedings in such a way as to indicate or influence the participants towards the outcome preferred by the mediators'. The FMC Code adopts an intermediate position, saying[15] that mediators *may* inform participants if a proposal falls outside what a court would accept only if the parties consent, while adding that they 'must not seek to impose their preferred outcome on the participants or to influence them to adopt it, whether by attempting to predict the outcome of court proceedings or otherwise'. It is difficult to envisage how this guidance deals with a situation where one party agrees to hearing the information but the other does not, especially where there may be a power imbalance. The Resolution Guide informs its mediators that they '*have a responsibility* ... to inform clients if they consider that the outcome/s they are considering might or would fall outside that which a court might approve or order' (Resolution 2015: 11, our emphasis). We will return to this issue below. The Resolution Guide also contains extensive guidance on the preparation of documentation and record keeping

---

[11] www.familymediationcouncil.org.uk/us/code-practice/.
[12] www.lawsociety.org.uk/support-services/accreditation/family-mediation/law-society-family-mediation-scheme-developments/.
[13] Law Society Code, section 5.10 (our emphasis).
[14] Section 6.9.
[15] Section 5.3 (our emphasis).

by mediators[16] which has no equivalent in the FMC or College codes. Other differences will be considered in the following discussion.

A further dimension has been added by the provision of criteria according to which family mediation may be publicly funded. The Legal Aid Agency (LAA)'s *Family Mediation Guidance Manual* (Version 4.0, March 2015: para 2.2) states that:

> In order for a matter to fall within the scope and remit of publicly funded mediation there must be a **legal dispute** present. It is not sufficient for there simply to be a dispute between the parties that if left unresolved could lead to a legal dispute and the potential for family proceedings being issued.

'Legal dispute' is understood by considering the question: 'Are these disputes over legal issues, rights or duties, ie capable of giving rise to family proceedings?' The document smuggles in an additional criterion of 'significance' by continuing (para 2.4):

> If there are no significant legal family issues in dispute and the role of the mediation is simply to improve communication and the relationship between the parties then this will not fall within the scope of public funding. Public funded mediation will not cover therapeutic types of support provided via mediation which solely focus on trying to define issues and concerns, improve relationships and communication between family members and any other party to the mediation, such as a Local Authority.

While it seems clear that the LAA is seeking to exclude from funding therapeutic processes designed solely to improve relationships, it also excludes processes where the participants may not be in overt dispute, but are merely seeking to find out 'where they stand' and what is the best way to take things forward. We therefore need to consider whether mediation covers those types of situations as well.

IV. DOES MEDIATION ONLY DEAL WITH DISPUTES?

In their book, *Mediation: Principles, Process, Practice*, which is not confined to family mediation, Boulle and Nesic (2001: 3–7) comment on the extreme difficulty in defining what mediation is. They suggest two

---

[16] See, eg, Resolution Guide 2015: 27: 'Any written record undertaken by the mediator as part of the mediation process is open to the clients' scrutiny. Mediators should explain this to clients and, if note-taking, should keep such notes to the bare minimum of facts, tasks yet to be undertaken and any other information that assists both clients and mediator to progress the mediation. Mediators may wish to consider whether they should send clients a brief and balanced summary of discussions and tasks to be undertaken between meetings as part of client service. Any summary provided should be one document sent to both clients, separately if they prefer. Mediators who choose to do so should also ensure that their fee information reflects this, or that any such correspondence is costed into their overall fee.'

approaches: a conceptual one, which focuses on ideals, and a descriptive one, which focuses on what happens. For themselves, they see the core feature of mediation as being an emphasis on decision making rather than dispute resolution. That gives mediation a role in conflict prevention as well as conflict resolution (Ibid: 13). Family mediation in England, however, has given predominant attention to dispute resolution. This is evident in the title of Marian Roberts's book, *Mediation in Family Disputes: Principles and Practice* and throughout its text (Roberts 2014). The website of Resolution proclaims: 'Mediation begins with parties *to a dispute* agreeing to mediate, setting ground rules and selecting a mediator.'[17] In the 2014 edition of her book *Family Mediation*, Lisa Parkinson (2014: 7) describes mediation as offering 'a means of managing and resolving conflict', though later she adds as an objective '(to) work out agreed arrangements'. Section 2 of Resolution's Guide to Good Practice on Mediation (2015: 9) also begins with a broader perspective and refers to decision making:

> Family mediation is a process in which those whose relationship is ending or has ended, regardless of whether they are a couple or other family members, appoint an impartial third person to assist them to communicate better with one another and to reach their own agreed and informed decisions concerning some or all of the issues relating to their separation, divorce, children, finance or property by negotiation.

But it then proceeds: 'Family mediation is a principled and structured process of family dispute resolution.'

We have seen the condition set by the LAA that there should be a 'legal dispute' if public funding is to be provided. It is natural to imagine mediation as dealing always, or almost always, with disputes. However, as Boulle and Nesic (2001) make clear, this is not always true of mediation. It is possible for people to fail to agree, yet not be in dispute. In a classic paper, Felstiner, Abel and Sarat (1980–81) sought to focus more attention on the way disputes emerged, and proposed that this occurred in four stages: first, recognition that they have suffered an 'injurious experience' ('naming'); second, attributing responsibility for the harm ('blaming'); then seeking redress for the harm ('claiming') and finally rejection of the claim.[18] So two people lost in a wood may have a problem in that they are not able to agree which route to take if their path splits into two, not because they are in dispute, but because neither knows what to do. If a couple part, neither may know what is the best thing to do either for themselves individually or for both of

---

[17] http://expert-evidence.com/mediation/?gclid=CIHNyeTtpcQCFYrLtAodwzUAAA (accessed 13 March 2014) (our emphasis).
[18] Felstiner et al (1980–81) consider only private law disputes. But disputes in public law contexts can be analysed in the same way with minor modification. For example, a child protection agency may perceive a child to have suffered harm ('naming'), attributed the harm to someone ('blaming'), and proposed remedial measures ('claiming') which were rejected.

them. All the elements of a dispute articulated by Felstiner, Abel and Sarat may not be present. They may, as one of our interviewees put it, each have a problem, and may need to reach a decision, but 'we all have problems, but that does not necessarily mean that those problems should lead to conflict or a dispute'. With appropriate assistance, that can be avoided.

In fact, the FMC Code does not insist on the presence of a dispute, giving two objectives of mediation:

> 2.1 Mediation aims to assist participants to reach the decisions they consider appropriate to their own particular circumstances.
> 2.2 Mediation also aims to assist participants to communicate with one another now and in the future and to reduce the scope or intensity of dispute and conflict within the family.

Roberts (2014: 70, emphasis in original) makes the same point when she writes that mediation practitioners (across all fields of mediation) are united in the 'common view' that mediation 'provides an *opportunity for the parties* to achieve what *they* want to achieve, whether it be the settlement of a dispute or some less specific purpose such as an improvement in personal communication'.

So there can be two separate aims, resolving or reducing conflict and (simply) reaching agreement on a way forward where there may be no conflict. Both may be pursued together, but not necessarily so. This is recognised by Parkinson's addition of the objective (to) 'work out agreed arrangements' referred to above.

The matter may seem of small importance, but it is central to the strategy of LASPO that, outside the excepted cases, public funding should not be available for legal help in private law family matters. Since legal help will often take the form of providing guidance if there is no dispute, or before one emerges, and a limited amount of money remains available for mediation, it is important to the strategy that this money is not given if mediation is providing the same service as legal help. The distinction is maintained in two ways: first by insisting that public funding is available only if mediation is dealing with a legal dispute; and second, by adhering to the principle that mediators impart only legal information, and not legal advice. It will be an important part of our investigation to examine how far these assumptions can be supported.

V. INFORMATION AND ADVICE

Section 5.3 of the 2010 FMC Code states:

> 5.3 Neutrality
>
> Mediators must remain neutral on the outcome of a mediation at all times. Mediators must not seek to impose their preferred outcome on the participants or to

influence them to adopt it, whether by attempting to predict the outcome of court proceedings or otherwise. However, if the participants consent, they may inform them that they consider that the resolution they are considering might fall outside the parameters which a court might approve or order. They may inform participants of possible courses of action, their legal or other implications, and assist them to explore these, but must make it clear that they are not giving advice.

While the prohibition against '*imposing*' outcomes is obvious (mediators have no power to do this anyway), the statement goes further in stating that (mediators) 'may inform participants of possible courses of action, their legal or other implications, and assist them to explore these, but must make it clear that they are not giving advice'. The Law Society Code stated, in its Introduction, that 'the concept of not giving advice to the parties, individually or collectively, when acting as a mediator permeates this entire code'. The College of Mediators Code states this in peremptory fashion: '(Mediators) must not give legal or other advice' (section 6.9). Roberts (2014: 175) also insists on the distinction between providing information and advice, adding that advice involves 'recommending strategic courses of action or the making of tactical suggestions in the light of the law, decisions of the court and the particular circumstances. The giving of information, on the other hand, aims to be neutral, involving an explanation or clarification only of rights, resources, terms and so on.'[19] Parkinson (2014: 25–26: see also 256) also makes the distinction, though with less prominence, citing section 5.3 of the FMC Code (set out above) which she interprets as allowing mediators to 'assist participants to reach their own decisions without advising them or steering them towards a particular outcome'. The FMC *Manual of Professional Standards and Self-Regulatory Framework of 2014* (Appendix 2, C5) requires 'maintaining (and explaining to the participant) the distinction between information and advice' as part of mediation practice.

But is this distinction realistic? It is accepted that, in the words of Roberts (2014: 155): 'It is the task of the mediator to understand and manage this negotiation process between the parties' and that '(t)he mediator's main function is to facilitate the negotiating process between the parties (Ibid: 165)'. It is difficult to see how a mediator could 'manage' or 'facilitate' the negotiation without giving advice at least on matters of process. Indeed, the Code of the College of Mediators expressly *requires* mediators to 'seek to reach agreement upon (sic) them' (section 6.3). So advice on *process* (as distinct from advice on outcome) must be allowed, although the distinction is nowhere made. But this distinction is problematic because process can affect outcome. Further, while providing information is not *necessarily* the same

---

[19] See also Roberts (2014: 111) saying that legal advice 'includes evaluation and recommendation of a particular course (or courses) of action: "This is what you ought to do".' Legal information 'involves setting out information as a resource without recommending which course of action or which option to choose'.

as giving advice, whether they amount to the same depends on context. If A sees B about to enter a field and informs B that the field is inhabited by poisonous snakes, the effect is of advice not to enter it. But a notice on a secure enclosure that the snakes inside are poisonous could simply be information for the viewing public. Information is more likely to amount to advice where people are in an interactive setting.

Roberts (2014: 111) acknowledges that the distinction is 'more complex than it sounds', and this is illustrated by an example given in her *Developing the Craft of Mediation: Reflections on Theory and Practice* (Roberts 2007: 136) where Roberts sets out an extract from a mediator's description of a moment in a mediation. The mediator had said of a recent case: 'That was one situation where I actually thought the legal situation was important. So I said: "Look, the legal position *is this*. It is no good you waving your papers and saying you are going to law because there is nothing for you to gain. So can we put all that to one side and get on with the actual issues that we can agree or disagree about".' Roberts comments that this 'illustrates the clear but fine line that mediation draws between the giving of legal advice, which is inseparable from a partisan relationship of representation and is, therefore, not appropriate, and the giving of information, setting out information as an impartial resource to both parties, which is appropriate in mediation'. Roberts apparently presents this as a case of giving information rather than advice. Yet the mediator quoted does not *simply* impart information. She says: '*It is no good*' the parties talking about going to law. Indeed, the mediator becomes highly directive: 'So can we put all that to one side and get on with …'. She is saying: 'Don't do it!' It is different from standard legal advice in that it is offered to (indeed foisted on) *both* parties, whereas advice given by a lawyer is provided to one party only. But it is advice (and legal advice) nonetheless: 'Because you will gain nothing by going to law, don't do it.'

So context is everything, as Boulle and Nesic (2001: 172–73) recognise when they say the distinction 'will not always be easy to sustain and disputing parties might be forgiven for mistaking the former (information) for the latter (advice)'. A mediator might outline a range of options, indicating the implications of each, without urging any particular one on the parties. Roberts (2014: 200) recognises that making 'new suggestions', which 'potentially presents the most creative opportunities for the mediator', also holds 'serious risks' because it threatens mediation's tenet that 'party authority is central to mediation'. If the presentation of the information suggests or implies that any option might be better or worse for the person or persons receiving it than another, or if essentially only one outcome is put forward, this is surely an attempt to 'influence' the outcome, and can be seen as advice about outcome. This point was made in a report to the Scottish Executive by Myers and Wasoff (2011) who compared the responses of mediators and solicitors when presented with the same fictitious scenarios. They concluded that:

arguably, while mediators do not explicitly indicate a preferred course of action, their role in generating options, and the use of references to the law and authority of the courts, although described as 'information-giving', from the parties' point of view may function in a similar way to solicitors' 'advice' (Ibid: 7; see also 100).

It is true that either or both participants will be free to reject any suggested outcome, and the mediator may emphasise that, but that is true of any advice, including advice from a lawyer. Our earlier study of solicitors produced many examples of solicitors doing that, summarised by the solicitor who said:

> You don't say 'We're going to do it this way.' It's up to them to give you instructions. You give them the information and hope they understand it (Eekelaar, Maclean and Beinart 2000: 98).

There is a further difficulty regarding the effects of providing information. Section 5.3 of the FMC Code contemplates that, with the participants' consent, mediators may inform them that 'the resolution they are considering might fall outside the parameters which a court might approve or order'. This is despite the statement in the same section that they must not 'predict the outcome of court proceedings or otherwise'. But it is hard to see why a participant should not want this information to be provided unless they feared it would be to their disadvantage. So a mediator who withholds such information in such circumstances appears to be supporting that position. Yet it seems clear that providing the information would 'influence' the participants, and not simply for or against reaching agreement, but for or against a particular outcome, which 5.3 disallows. In contrast, as noted earlier, the Resolution Guide places on its mediators the 'responsibility' to provide this information (Resolution 2015: 11), which can only be seen as intended to have some influence on the eventual outcome.

It is true that section 6.15 of the Code states: 'Mediators must inform participants of the advantages of seeking independent legal or other appropriate advice whenever this appears desirable during the course of the mediation. They must advise participants that it is in their own interests to seek independent legal advice before reaching any final agreement and warn them of the risks and disadvantages if they do not do so.' But this does not remove the fact that the information already supplied, or (perhaps as significantly) not supplied, by the mediator could have strongly influenced the participants towards or against a particular outcome, which the opening sentence of 5.3 disallows. It is a form of legal advice.

Resolution (2015: 11) reiterates, along with the other codes, that 'mediators must remain neutral as to the outcome of any mediation. This requires that mediators monitor their practice at all times to ensure that they are not seeking to impose their own preferred outcome or to influence either or both clients towards an outcome not of their choosing.' It proceeds: 'Mediators may also provide legal and other information designed to assist clients in a mediation process to make informed decisions, but must make it clear that they do not provide partial advice of any kind. Information should be provided as neutral and mutual, and not "individualised" to either client', later insisting that the mediator only provides information on general principles and not 'advice or information on how it may affect the client's individual circumstances' (Ibid: 12).

We will see how far this approach can be sustained in practice. It is possible that the reference to the exclusion of *partial* advice provides a hint that the underlying objection is not to the provision of advice in itself (leading to insistence on the provision of information only) but to treating either participant as an individual client. Indeed, a distinction might be drawn between neutrality and impartiality. *Neutrality* suggests that the mediator has no concern in the outcome, and the injunctions against attempts to influence outcomes are consistent with this. But *impartiality* does not necessarily suggest lack of concern about outcome, but only that the mediator should not favour one participant over the other.[20] We will consider later whether this could allow advice about outcome to be given where this is directed, impartially, at the participants' common interests.

VI. CHILDREN

The Family Justice Review (2011: Executive Summary para 1.21) states, boldly: 'All mediation should be centred on the best interests of the child.' This echoes, if it does not quite repeat, the well-known provision in section 1(1) of the Children Act 1989 which is worded:

> When a court determines any question with respect to (a) the upbringing of a child; or (b) the administration of a child's property or the application of any income arising from it, the child's welfare shall be the court's paramount consideration.

Article 3(1) of the UN Convention on the Rights of the Child proclaims:

> In all actions concerning children, whether undertaken by public or private social welfare institutions, courts of law, administrative authorities or legislative bodies, the best interests of the child shall be a primary consideration.

Both these statements place a duty on (in the first case) the courts, and (in the second) other institutions, including 'private social welfare institutions', which would include mediators, that when 'questions' or 'actions' concerning children are decided or undertaken, the child's 'welfare' or 'best interests' are given 'paramount' or 'primary' consideration. How far do the mediation codes achieve this?

---

[20] This distinction emerged following discussions with Lisa Webley.

Sections 5.7.1 and 5.7.2 of the FMC Code state that:

> At all times mediators must have special regard to the welfare of any children of the family. They should encourage parties to focus on the needs and interests of the child as well as on their own.

> Mediators must encourage participants to consider the children's wishes and feelings. If appropriate they may discuss with them whether and to what extent it is proper to consult the children directly in order to ascertain their wishes and feelings.

There are provisions for mediators to withdraw from the mediation and inform the appropriate authorities if they think a child is likely to be seriously harmed. There are also provisions for direct consultation with children if the participants and the mediator agree and the child consents. The child must be offered confidentiality, and the consultation must be carried out by a specifically trained, and CRB (Criminal Records Bureau) cleared person (section 5.7.3–4). This will not usually be the person working with the parents.

Similarly, the Law Society Code (section 8.2) stated: 'In working with the parties, the mediator should also have regard to the needs and interests of the children of the family.' The College of Mediators' Code has provisions almost identical to those in the FMC Code on this matter (but refers to mediators having a special 'concern' rather than 'regard' for the children's welfare (section 4.7)), except for the requirement to offer the child confidentiality. By comparison, Resolution (2015: 14–15) states:

> Mediators have a special responsibility in regard to the welfare of any child of the family and should encourage and assist client parents to focus on the needs and interests of their children and their future parenting. Mediators must consider the wishes and feelings of any children of the family and encourage parents to consider the ways in which they may consider their children's views, wishes and feelings.

The Resolution Guide also goes further, for example in the provision that:

> Mediators should, however, be alert to parental concerns about their child's behaviour that is clearly outside that which might be considered normal—eg self-harming, eating disorder, risk taking behaviour, drugs, alcohol abuse etc—and for which parents should be provided with information and links to specialised services of assistance (Ibid: 25).

A requirement to have regard to or concern for a child's welfare seems to fall well short of a duty to ensure that the child's welfare is the paramount or a primary consideration. But Resolution's reference to having a 'responsibility' regarding a child's welfare suggests an obligation on the mediator, and not only on the parents, to try to ensure an outcome that is consistent with the child's welfare. So, while in all cases mediators must encourage parents to focus on the children's needs, interests, wishes and feelings, the FMC and College codes appear to see that as the totality of the mediator's duty. The

Resolution Guide might be read in that way as well, but also could be seen as proclaiming a responsibility regarding the child's welfare that surpasses the requirement to encourage the parents to concentrate on their children's welfare. If that was the case, the mediator would be obliged at least to steer the parents to an agreement that the mediator considered best for the child.[21]

There is little doubt that the wording of the FMC Code represents the traditional orthodoxy, for it is consistent with the fundamental principle of mediation as being a process that assists the participants in reaching their agreement. Attempting to influence this in the direction of what the mediator considers to be best, or better, for the child would breach that principle. So Parkinson's (2014: 185) discussion of 'child-focused mediation' sets out much information about how children are affected by arrangements made when their parents separate, which mediators are encouraged to impart to parents. But mediation is presented as 'a forum in which parents can discuss their children's needs in constructive ways and work out arrangements in broad terms or in detail'. The emphasis therefore is on achieving parental agreement. To be sure, such agreement may be well-informed and the most beneficial available for the children. Mediators often emphasise that parents know more about their children than the professionals. But if achieving agreement rather than ascertaining what is best for the children becomes the primary objective, the welfare paramountcy principle of the Children Act is, as in any private ordering process, left 'outside the room'. This concern was well illustrated in a study of mediation in Sweden which found that mediations seldom in fact focused on the children's interests since the parties, and the mediators, become caught up in the overriding objective of achieving agreement.[22]

The 'absence' of the voice of the child in the mediation process was acknowledged as a concern by government in November 2014, and a Dispute Resolution Advisory Group set up to consider the matter reported in March 2015 (Voice of the Child Dispute Resolution Advisory Group 2015), recommended that there should be a 'non-legal' presumption that children over 10 should have the opportunity to have their voice heard in mediation if they wish. 'Child-inclusive mediation' of this kind was currently rarely undertaken, but the Committee thought it should become the normal starting-off point, subject to stringent quality control, safeguarding

---

[21] A similar discrepancy occurs in New Zealand, where section 4 of the Family Dispute Resolution Act 2013 states that one of the two purposes of FDR is 'ensuring that the parties' first and paramount consideration in reaching a resolution is the welfare and best interests of the children', but section 11 says that an FDR provider 'must make every endeavour to … assist the parties to reach an agreement on the resolution of those matters that best serves the welfare and best interests of all children involved in the dispute': see Atkin (2015: 195).

[22] Ryrstedt (2012).

procedures, and parental agreement (though this would not be necessary for a child deemed sufficiently mature). The Committee explained:

> Giving children and young people the right to be heard during mediation is not about conducting forensic interviews, nor making them a party to the case, nor taking evidence, nor expecting them to make decisions, nor ascertaining their wishes and feelings in any formal way. Nor is it about occasionally involving or consulting children in mediation when parents and/or the mediator decide that it might be helpful and of assistance to the mediation process. From a perspective which respects children's rights as envisaged in the UNCRC, child inclusive practice is about providing a child or young person with the right to be heard (Ibid: paras 17–18).

The Committee considered four models for implementing this: the adults' mediator talking to the children; a co-mediator talking to the children and reporting back; another professional talking to the children and reporting back; the children taking part in a workshop with other children and their views reported back. It suggested they should be tested in pilot studies (Ibid: para 64). Funding would be required, and the development of training and monitoring procedures would take some time.

The report is thoughtful and thorough. However, although it recognises that some parents might feel that child-inclusive approaches might be perceived as 'interference' in the parents' responsibility to make decisions in respect of their children's upbringing (Ibid: para 103) the report does not address the implications of such a development for the principle of neutrality which, as discussed above, is said to be so central to the practice of mediation (see Webley: in press). For if the mediator forms the view that the adults are paying insufficient attention to the child's views, or that the child's views indicate that the course agreed by them would not be beneficial for the child, is the mediator to attempt to influence the outcome? Is this likely to promote or hinder agreement? A small qualitative study in Australia found that fewer (5 of 14) parents who used child-inclusive mediation considered that the mediation had assisted in resolving some or all of the issues than those who had not used it (13 of 19).[23] A majority, however, felt that the inclusive process helped them understand their children's feelings better and that it was appreciated by the children, half thinking it had improved the relationship between them. But despite these benefits, there was disappointment that their expectations that it would help to resolve their issues were not realised. This suggests that drawing attention to children's perspectives could make agreement more difficult, indicating that giving primacy to achieving agreement risks giving less attention to those perspectives.

The difficult cases where children issues involve welfare considerations and social services involvement might be needed, highlighted by the Family

---

[23] Bell, Cashmore, Parkinson and Single (2013).

Justice Review and others,[24] have also attracted insufficient attention in the past, partly because these kinds of cases may have been less likely to come to mediation before LASPO. But safeguarding issues are becoming more prominent, and will need careful consideration if courts begin to accept the agreements recorded in a mediation MOU as a suitable basis for a Consent Order (Saunders 2014).[25] They are addressed in MIAM training, and the Resolution Guide to Good Practice on Mediation as revised in 2015 includes Appendix 2, 'Safeguarding Children and Young People—Duties and Responsibilities' drawing attention to government guidance on action to be taken when information is received raising concerns about the safety of children and vulnerable adults and making it clear that this overrides confidentiality and needs to be brought to the attention of appropriate authorities without awaiting verification. The Voice of the Child Report (2015) makes important recommendations about the substantial training needs for mediators who will work directly with children.

The current training for mediators regarding children issues is incorporated in the specifications for course content for the basic training set out in set out in the FMC *Manual of Professional Standards and Self-Regulatory Framework* referred to earlier. It is stated that 'courses must cover knowledge of children and property/finance aspects' and that 'participants must be adequately proficient in handling both children and property/finance matters to pass the course' (Family Mediation Council 2014: 26).

VII. WHAT FOLLOWS

It will not be surprising that, given the complex history of the development of mediation, there will be variations in its practice. Perhaps the greatest variation to be expected will be between non-lawyer mediators, with backgrounds in NFM, and lawyer-mediators, who will be influenced by the more legally structured nature of Resolution and its Guides to Good Practice. The data about practice which follows is therefore divided into that relating to non-lawyer mediators and that which relates to mediators who are, or were until recently, also lawyers. Once the data has been considered, we will attempt to assess not only what light it throws on the practice of mediation, but also on the relationship between mediation and legal practice.

---

[24] Family Justice Review (2012); Harding and Newnham (2014); Harding and Newnham (2015).

[25] The C100 application form for a Consent Order, like any order involving children, is seen by CAFCASS and will be subject to police and social services checks and CAFCASS will report back to the court and request any other investigation thought necessary. In making a Consent Order a judge is bound by the welfare paramountcy presumption, but is not required to use the welfare checklist.

5

The Practice of Family Mediators I: Non-Lawyers

W E NOW REPORT our conversations with lawyer and non-lawyer mediators and our observations of their activity. We make no claim to statistical validity for the data, or to the representative nature of the sample. This is a small qualitative study, seeking to explore the practice and present our reflections on it. We can only say that this is what we saw, and this is what we think. This is an area where further empirical work is urgently needed. We were invited to sit with a number of practitioners, and we are most grateful for their help. Where details are given of any case, some facts are altered to protect the anonymity of the practitioners and participants, in such a way as to maintain the essential character of the case while avoiding even jigsaw recognition.

We observed and/or interviewed 25 family mediators in 18 settings in order to describe their day-to-day activity. At the time when we were carrying out the study, mediation services were under great financial pressure owing to fixed costs and falling referrals following LASPO despite the fact that government had encouraged them to expand their services in the expectation of increased demand. In spite of these difficulties, we were given a great deal of help by members of the Family Mediation Council, National Family Mediation, Resolution and many others, to whom we are most grateful. We were able to develop a purposive sample, as we had done with the family solicitors, with participants in the north, north-west, north-east, west and south of England as well as in London, the Midlands and Wales. It was not possible to constitute a fully representative list of mediators to use as a sampling frame, as none existed at the time. But we worked with members of key organisations, and arranged to talk to or spend time with mediators from a range of backgrounds and organisational settings. The range of working practice observed, which we believe to be characteristic of mediation as a form of intervention, makes it difficult to categorise the work we saw. The mediators ranged from retired people from the voluntary sector with a wide range of experience in business as well as the helping professions seeking to offer help rather than build a second career, to young lawyers seeking to add a new way of working with separating families after the demise of legal aid for private family matters. Some worked in offices alongside other therapeutic or support services for families and children, others in outreach settings (premises temporarily hired by a service).

Some of the lawyer mediators continued with their legal practice, others did not. Some non-lawyer mediators worked in legal offices. It may therefore be more realistic to think in terms of a continuum of activity from ADR to legal services, rather than a single sharp division, a point we will develop further in chapter 7. So, while for presentational purposes we give the data on non-lawyer mediators in this chapter and on legally trained mediators in the next, we have subdivided the non-lawyer mediators into different elements reflecting this continuum. In view of our interest in the relationship between legal services and ADR we chose to present the data in the form of the distance between (at one end) non-lawyer mediators in a non-legal setting and (at the other) lawyer mediators who practise law and mediation from the same office on the same day, showing the intermediate stages of non-lawyers in legal settings and lawyer mediators who no longer practise law but mediate in both legal and non legal settings.

In these various settings we observed mediation in practice, including two training sessions, for periods ranging from half a day to three days, covering MIAMs, Separated Parents Information Programmes (SPIPs), all issues, finance-only and child-only sessions, some of which were initial sessions and others which were close to the ending of the process. Of the 13 non-lawyer mediators we saw, nine were working in mediation service premises or outreach premises and we were able to talk in depth to four of them about administration and running the service, and three were working in law offices. One was working as a trainer on a foundation course.

This chapter gives extensive summaries of meetings with members of both of these subgroups of non-lawyer mediators, and comments more generally on the group as a whole. Of the first group, non-lawyer mediators working in non-legal settings, we discuss in detail the work of M1, M2, M12, M3, M4, M5 and M6 and the comments of M10 and M11; of the second group, the non-lawyer mediators working in legal settings, we discuss M7 (with M8) and M9. We discussed a training session with M13 and LM11, who was in charge of the training, in Chapter 4. The next chapter considers the activities of the legally trained mediators.

I. GROUP 1: NON-LAWYER MEDIATORS WORKING IN NON-LEGAL SETTINGS

M1: A finance session

M1 described himself as a retired businessman with HR experience, working in a long-established mediation service with a legal aid contract which shares offices with other family services including a children's service. He works usually for two mornings a week for which he is paid £30 an hour.

This session, which he hopes may be the final session, is the third of an all-issues mediation between the husband (H), who is retired, and the wife (W), who is taking a course to qualify for a new job in the caring professions. It is held in a small room in the mediation service around a low table with a flip-chart. At the start of this session, which will focus on finance, M1 reviews the previous sessions and says to both participants together: 'Your proposal was simple: equal division,' to which W responds confirming that she thinks that this is a good starting point. It is now a question of how this will be carried out. M1 goes through a financial statement he has prepared for them based on the information they have provided so far (for which he asked for payment after the session). H suggests that some money for the children should be excluded. W then refers to money that came as a legacy from her family, and M1 asks: 'Should we take this out?' H suggests a sum, after which both mention other sums which might be excluded from the division. H says he doesn't want a lawyer 'going into all this'. M1 suggests they choose between a principle of equal shares of the value at a specific date, or 'a series of amounts'. However, H and W go on from talking of money for the children to mentioning specific sums they see as 'theirs'. M1 now takes them back to the central issue and refers to pensions, giving rough values, plus the value of the house. 'I want to give you some idea of the matrimonial pot. £650,000 each, how do you feel about that?' W responds by saying she has been trying to work out what her future finances would be like. If the only house available with those resources was not suitable for the children she would have to think again. M1 refers to child support, saying they were not obliged to follow the Department of Work and Pensions Child guidelines, but they could be used as a starting point. He then adds:

> Spousal support is different (from child support); there is no guideline, it can be varied, reviewable (your solicitor will tell you). It's important you get a nominal order so there is something to vary, keeps the door open. Doesn't mean you would win, but you can apply. People do this where their income is unpredictable like yours; you (W) just don't know, you are still a student and might need to reconvene (the mediation) after divorce and consider spousal support in the specific circumstances. If you share the pot you do have pensions sharing ... but it is important to be clear ... £1 of pension is different from £1 of property.

Until this point M1 had been putting forward various suggestions, while the couple kept referring to a variety of sums which they thought should be excluded from the equal division. But now he provides legal information about the possibility of a nominal maintenance order for W, adding the words 'It's important you get', plus information about possible consequences, relating it to her circumstances ('You are still a student') which reveal it as being in effect legal advice.

H responds by making clear that he wants only spousal fixed-term maintenance for W, who was taking an extended training course. H says: 'It's not my job to fund you through that course.' H and W appear to agree on fixed-term maintenance for the period of the extension of W's course, and M1 makes suggestions as to how they might go about settling the amount:

> You really need to look at the numbers. Look at costs, income from any source including state benefits, there is a quarter reduction in council tax for single parents. Then you can have a practical discussion, not just a theory.

Here M1 offers information, but is definitely also offering advice: 'You *need* to.' But it is advice about process, not outcome.

H now suggests setting aside some of the child support payments based on the child support calculator which could be drawn on later to meet 'large expenditure or sporting things, school trips'. M1 asks how W responds, and she details her monthly expenditure on the children, indicating that she would need the full child support amount to meet basic expenditure on food and clothing. M1 asks how H responds to that, and there is no reply. There follows further discussion of costs, especially regarding the children and servicing mortgages. H says he wants more discussion about the child support 'pot' idea, but W is against this, preferring allocating payment of specific costs between the two of them on an itemised basis as necessary. H says he wants to avoid 'who pays what' situations, but M1 gives him no support, and H gives in: 'I've made a suggestion which hasn't been understood, not worth pursuing.' M1 gives further advice on drawing up the list of costs: 'The more clear, the less need for the kind of conversation H is referring to.' In drawing up their respective lists, H suggests that they could share information about costs for housing and utilities, and M1 replies: 'Yes, but not for personal and leisure; that's personal taste.' M1 sums up the outcome: 'Two things happened today: you agreed that assets should be split 50/50. Child support and spousal support need to be discussed based on the facts. At the next meeting, with the information, we will be able to discuss both.' M1 then refers to sharing the contents of the home, saying: 'People often find contents easier than they expected,' and emphasising practicality: 'One house may be smaller than the other, smaller rooms …'. But the couple become irritated with one another and M1 brings the session to an end, asking them to work out an approach to contents and to bring figures about their sports club membership, which had been a source of contention, to the next meeting.

We have no information on how the couple had settled on a 50/50 asset split in previous sessions. But this session was largely taken up with determining how that was to be understood and implemented, and then how ongoing costs were to be dealt with. Although the wife did not press for a nominal maintenance order, as (in effect) advised by the mediator, the mediator clearly sided with her in supporting her wish for payment of the basic child maintenance in full rather than the husband's preference to pay part into a 'pot'. This may be partly because the mediator understood that the government calculations on child maintenance were intended to cover basic maintenance, not additional expenditure. He mentioned to the researcher afterwards that he had not pointed this out to the husband because he gives no information about legal parameters. But this seems an unexpected exercise of caution, given that the child maintenance calculations are explicitly based on simple percentages of gross income.

There were many occasions in this session where simmering disputes surfaced, whether it was over what sums might be excluded from the equal division of assets, or what maintenance payments were to cover. The mediator managed these by being firmly directive on matters of process, and was even prepared to attempt to influence outcome, on one occasion unsuccessfully (regarding nominal maintenance for the wife) and on the other, successfully (regarding child support payments not being in part diverted into a 'pot'). The distinction between legal information and advice was clearly difficult to maintain in the heat of the moment.

After the session described above, M2, Manager of this service, spoke at length with the researcher, providing copies of documents given to each participant in a National Family Mediation Financial Mediation Pack, which includes financial information sheets for recording monthly expenditure, assets and liabilities, pay slips, house valuation, mortgage details, savings and assets and pensions. This makes it possible to produce a concluding OFS and prepare the MOU which could be the basis for a Consent Order and the CAFCASS Parenting Plan. The service also provided a counselling service for adults and children, family support services, SPIPs and MIAMs, and had links with local firms of solicitors. Its caseload was shared equally between legally aided and private work, but referrals had fallen by 80 per cent since LASPO, and they were trying to build up their private work. All five mediators at the service work part-time, as do the three support staff who not only respond to enquiries, explaining the purpose and nature of mediation and encouraging participation, but also make appointments (which take time particularly when one party is reluctant) and handle a large number of calls from anxious participants during the process since mediators should not speak to them outside the session.

M12: A MIAM for the researcher

This senior non-lawyer mediator (M12) working in a mediation service in effect gave the researcher (R) a MIAM because the clients had cancelled the planned session observation. She also talked through two recent cases in depth. In the MIAM exercise she explained how mediation works and what it might be able to do, asked for an account of R's circumstances, whether she would be comfortable going into mediation and whether there were any safety issues. Mediation was described as 'an opportunity to sort out face-to-face all the practical and personal things directly but with the help of a mediator'. This did not appear to require the presence of a dispute.

'My job is to give you the opportunity to make good decisions.' M12 mentioned confidentiality and legal privilege. On costs, she said three to five meetings would probably be needed for finance and property, and two meetings for children. If not legally aided, the costs for persons with an income under £60,000 were £175 per person per meeting (usually 90 minutes). This comes to £1,225 plus VAT per person for seven meetings, compared with £200 an hour charged by solicitors plus items of service. Payment is required in advance and there is a cancellation fee. In response to questions about maintenance from R, M12 contrasted her position with that of a lawyer, saying that while a lawyer would 'encourage' a claim, 'We don't. But we say it's a claim you positively need to dismiss, not ignore.' She explained that they draw up a table of respective incomes, and look at various options including shares in assets. R asked about confidence in the financial disclosure. M12 replied: 'It's not just about numbers … there is evidence and you swap documents … you can ask anything, it's not for the mediator to ask but you can ask your lawyer to do it … you may both get legal advice. Make sure you understand it and bring it to the meeting and share and discuss.' She added: 'We will use the shadow of the court as a last resort. We don't start with rights and entitlements but you need to know how far what you are thinking of is in line with it.'

The reference to the 'shadow of the court' refers to a possible indication of what a court would decide, which the FMC Code allows, but only with the consent of both participants, although, as noted in chapter 4, the Resolution Guide to Good Practice on Mediation says that mediators 'have a responsibility … to inform clients if they consider that the outcome/s they are considering might or would fall outside that which a court might approve or order'. The distinction between 'encouraging' a maintenance claim and saying that it is a matter to be 'positively dismissed' and not ignored seems a very fine one, and later M12 said, in response to a question about how far mediators look ahead and plan for the future: 'It's harder to get women to look ahead, especially about pensions. We succeed in getting spousal maintenance and charge back when the children leave home and her income falls off a cliff.' If such an outcome is regarded as a 'success' it is hard to believe that the mediator makes no attempt to move towards it. Later she slips into saying: 'You can give better advice if you have information from both,' showing again, as with M above, that the distinction between giving information and advice in this context may be illusory.

M12 then went through a recent case involving expensive properties in which the couple had legal advice, where she had recognised the need for the parties to seek advice from a tax expert. She thought it would take six sessions to reach an MOU. She then referred to being asked by another service to read an MOU 'for sense and feasibility, fit with the law and common practice'. Some services ask a lawyer to do this. It does not constitute formal approval but comments are given, for a fee. A solicitor will then draft the

Consent Order. The wife in this case was eligible for legal help in support of mediation but had not taken it up. M12 thought the maintenance agreed left the wife £200 under what she needed, and the husband £670 over. M12 also commented on the pressures associated with legal aid work in that the Legal Aid Agency audit would examine 20 files, call for 100 if any problems were found, and could, if not satisfied, claw back fees paid.

Three mediators conducting five MIAMs: two service-based and three at outreach locations on child, finance and safety issues: what chance of conversion?

M4 conducted a MIAM with a young mother (M) in a busy office covering a large area which had taken on work from a service which had recently closed. M4 has no background information for this meeting. She asks M whether she had experienced mediation before, and is told that she had, but found it difficult being in the same room as the father of her child, her former cohabitant (F). M4 explains about confidentiality, and asks what the current conflict is. This turns out to be a contact issue, M claiming that F is using maintenance payments as a weapon in problems over contact, reducing it when he was dissatisfied. 'I need proper arrangements.' She wants to 'take control' of the situation. M4 explains how mediation works. '(We are) not sitting in judgment, just helping to manage difficult conversations.' 'I would make sure you are both able to say what you want to say and write up what you agree in a neutral setting, working towards the needs of the child.' She says they have a small office next door where a participant can withdraw if things become tense. In response to M4's query about domestic violence, M replies that it is 'more controlling behaviour' but she did once call the police to protect the child. M4 asks if mediation is still a possibility and M says she does not want to go back over old ground, and wants 'two-way flexibility'. Asked whether, if F refused mediation, she would go to court, M says she cannot afford a solicitor, whereupon M4 gives information about a new local service that helps LIPs, and explains that limited legal aid is available for the services of a lawyer alongside mediation. M4 says that M would need to bring in financial information for her to assess eligibility for legal aid, and finishes by considering where the best place for holding the mediation might be given that F lives several hours' drive away.

It is possible that mediation could ameliorate this conflict, but as F was in the stronger financial position there was little incentive for him to co-operate. If he failed to do so, M's only redress would be through the court, but bizarrely legal aid would only be available for her if F attended mediation. It seems unlikely that she could achieve her wish to resist F's controlling approach to his relationship with their daughter through mediation, but she had little alternative other than going to court as a LIP.

A second MIAM in the same office was carried out by M3, a more experienced mediator, who also manages the service. The client (H) had divorced some years ago, but continued living in the former matrimonial home, which was in joint names, paying the instalments on the joint mortgage. He had offered to buy out his former wife's (W's) share and wanted to live in it or rent it out, but she wanted to force a sale in the hope that this would lead to a better price. M3 described mediation and the availability of legal aid, for which he would need to produce information about his income. H asks what the position was if one participant proposed a figure and the other wanted everything: 'Will the mediator really not say something?' to which M3 replies: 'We would comment on what is realistic and what you both think is fair,' adding that it was confidential. H interjects: 'Not binding?' M3 agrees but says it could lead to a Consent Order. H says he just wants the house issue 'off his back'. M3 concludes that they may be able to resolve it in mediation, but if he did need to go to court he would at least have done his MIAM (which is now a legal pre-condition), at a cost of £42 administration fee, or £96 for an FM1 form for the court. Fees for mediation are on a sliding scale from £60 to £120 per hour per party. The next step for him to consider was for the service to contact his former wife, but as in the previous case, one party (here the former wife) was in a strong position since, being a joint owner, the only way the husband could achieve what he wanted was through an order under the matrimonial jurisdiction. Without that realistic threat, his former wife could maintain her position as long as she chose. The third mediator, M6, carried out a set of MIAMs in a rented outreach office, rather noisy and subject to phones ringing and people passing through. M6 is an experienced mediator, and carried out three MIAMs in the morning spent with her. M6 had little prior information about the participants. The first client was a husband (H) who had split from his wife two years ago. The session starts with an assessment for legal aid, M6 concluding that it was likely H would be eligible. 'That's done, thank goodness.' M6 points out that H wouldn't get legal aid for a solicitor except for a 'small pot of money if you mediate for advice on any agreements you make in mediation'. H explains that he is not being allowed to see his children, while the wife's (W's) new partner had moved into the house. 'I don't want someone in my house staying over.' There had been an argument leading to H being charged with criminal damage. He was on bail, with a condition of staying away from W. M6 asks if he would like to mediate. H says it is either that or communication by phone. W had suggested mediation but the cost had put him off: 'A mate had spent a lot on it and got nothing.' M6 says mediation can help. 'All the emotions are still there; park it; but you are parents for ever.' She explains that it is about learning how to work together. She encourages him to sometimes not argue back but to think of the effect on the children. H says he just wants someone impartial saying 'I can see them'. M6 advises him to forget the past and think how he can make things better for the children. Both of them will have to compromise. H said he was doing that already by taking lower wages so he could see the children more often.

But he 'can't look at her and can't communicate'. M6 says he can still ask her to come to mediation. She raises the issue of the safety of the meeting, and H asks if he could bring a friend. M6 says both could, with permission. There would have to be different arrival and departure times, and she would need to secure the permission of the court with regard to his bail conditions.

As in the previously reported MIAMs, the client wanted something the mediator could not give, a declaration supporting their position. But here the wife had herself suggested mediation and it is possible that the communication difficulties between the couple could be ameliorated by mediation. However, in the immediately following MIAM, the prospects of a mediation without the threat of court action looked bleaker. The father (F) said that for five years after he split with the mother (M) he saw his daughter frequently. Then six months ago M had moved with the child and suddenly would not allow any contact. M6 says that, for mediation, 'You need her to come', and if she did, perhaps the daughter could come as well. F thinks M wouldn't let her. M6 says the only other option is to go to court, and that she would sign the form (C100) saying he had been to see her. She says a judge would ask what the child wants. She rings her office, telling F he can download the C100 form and the office would send him a signed FM1 form. In this case it seems that only the immediate prospect of a court application could bring M to mediation, but it remains possible that if she attended, some solution might be found.

However, the last MIAM of the morning could not lead to mediation because of the absence of a second party. The client, who was looking after her sister's three children, needed a Residence Order with respect to one of them. This was agreed by all parties, including social services who had asked her to see the solicitor and were covering her costs, so there was no dispute, and no point in holding a MIAM other than to meet the requirement that a court application must be preceded by a MIAM.[1] M6 did, however, explore the issues with the client carefully, making sure that she understood why the form FM1 for court needed to be signed.

M6 is also paid £30 an hour, and the charges are £96 an hour per party. She works for 100 hours eight times a year in the service. She also acts as a professional practice consultant (involving supervision, monitoring and support of mediators), and arrangements are made privately for the cost of supervision. Hers range from £30 to £60 an hour.

This group of MIAMs make it clear why conversion of a MIAM to mediation is not simple: the other party had little incentive to take part in the first two, in the third there was a serious issue concerning domestic violence, the fourth mother appeared implacably hostile while in the last case there was no dispute.

---

[1] Children and Families Act 2014, s 10(1). See above p 15.

M7: *A child contact first session*

Prior to the mediation, the mediator (M7), who was not a lawyer but working four days a week in a legal office, carrying out mediation and training the lawyers who had previously done mainly legally aided family work, and one day in a mediation service, stressed to the researcher that she could not give legal advice, but that mediation was 'supported by legal advice', in the sense that she would indicate if she thought a court would not accept an outcome, and write it up not as an MOU but as proposals, with warning signals.

The mediation was preceded by a MIAM for each of the parties. M7 told them together that 'this is a solicitors' firm, but I don't give legal advice, but can point you in the right direction if you need it'. She then asks the father (F) to withdraw (giving him the agreement to mediate form to read) as he is nearest to the door, and begins the MIAM with the mother (M). M explains that they had separated eight years previously. Both had re-partnered. 'I want to talk to him. He won't.' He wanted her to communicate through a family member, but M found that difficult. M7 assesses M for legal aid and finds she is eligible. M says she does not communicate with F. He had initially seen the child (C) (now 10) no more than once a week, but this had now stopped. To M7's question: 'What do you hope for from this mediation?' M answers that she wants him to have a relationship with C. 'I just want a contact number' so that she can make arrangements and cope with any need to change arrangements at short notice. She is 'up for mediation'. Now F returns. M7 says he is not eligible for legal aid, and asks what he wants from mediation. F complains that 'everything has been done on (M)'s terms'. She had made false accusations to the police against him. He explains the intermittent contact as resulting from his being in and out of work. To the question why they have stopped communicating, F answers: 'I try to distance myself to avoid putting the baby in the middle. I want a third party.' When asked why he went to solicitors, he replies that he was hoping for something more structured, to which M7 responds that she thinks they both want that. She asks what they might disagree about. F agrees they want the same thing, but 'end up in a negative situation. It's serious.' M7 sums up by saying that they need to start communicating. 'You pretty much want the same thing, so it's about sorting out the detail.' The MIAM concludes and each sign the mediation agreement.

M7 then moves straight into the first session. The mediation starts by M asking F for a telephone number, which he had previously been unwilling to give. M7 suggests that they both buy cheap mobile phones to be used only for texting about arrangements for C. The couple respond positively to this idea and immediately agree to communicate by text message. The essence of the mediation that follows is assistance by M7 in getting the parents to talk about the details of contact arrangements. Contact had become sporadic and infrequent, with no overnight stays. F wants a weekend and a mid-week school pick-up and visit. M is willing. At one point, the question of C wanting to have the same name as his mum, the new partner and the step-sister arises, rather than F's name. M7 asks M: 'Is C feeling insecure?' M answers: 'Yes: he is seeing a psychiatrist.' F says: 'I didn't know. He says one thing to her; one thing to me.' M7 reassures them that that is what children do: 'Trying to please both parents.' M says that C's 'got so much in his head. He needs help', and M7 responds: 'You two can talk about this. You don't have to be best friends. What if you disagree?' M says they would have to sort it out and put C first. M7 says: 'Now that you will be communicating, what are you afraid of?' to which M replies, referring to F: 'Your wife, A.' F replies. 'Yes, I can't control her. Your S (new partner) is OK.' M7 says: 'What is important is that you can say all this.' There are further exchanges about contact arrangements, including overnights and holidays. M7 asks about money, to which M replies that she can't afford to bring up C on her own. F says he has a 'massive bill (from the Child Support Agency)' and he is struggling to pay it off. Now that he is self-employed, he needs to 'work it out'. M7 presses: 'I want to know what you think your responsibility is.' F replies: 'I need to set up a standing order as long as it's spent on him (C), but I see you going on holiday.' M suggests F just buys C things he needs, and F asks: 'If I give the CSA £100, do you get it? They don't tell me.' M replies: 'Yes, if you tell me what you give them I'll tell you what I get.' M7 says it is about building up trust. F says he doesn't get regular wages, but M7 says they should see what is achievable and fair now. F says: '£100 a month.' M says she is happy with that, but F says he wants receipts. M7 interjects: 'He (C) could eat more than that,' and F drops the idea of receipts. But M7 says to F: 'Maybe it would be nice for you to know where the money goes' and M says that if she buys something she will send him the receipt. After some more discussion of detail, M7 says she will write this up, and that she is impressed that they were putting C first. They both say they feel better.

This session demonstrated the strength of mediation in assisting in re-establishing communication between estranged parties. Since they both desired the same outcome, it is doubtful if there was a dispute between the couple other than over the details of arranging contact which arose largely through the inability to agree the means of communicating with each other and was fuelled by the hostility of F's new partner and M's mother. There certainly was no legal dispute over contact, though difficulties had arisen over the payment of child support. Clear progress was made in this single session, though it was surprising that the mediator did not follow up the reference made by the mother to the child seeing a psychiatrist and possibly needing help in the context of an immediate and substantial change in contact arrangements. Her concern was primarily that the parents should be able to talk about it. Nor did the mediator mention seeking the 10-year-old child's views.

Later that day the same mediator (M7) conducted a MIAM with a wife (W) on a financial matter. M7 began by explaining the process, referring to confidentiality, and saying she would be 'a guide, not a lawyer'. W asks if M7 has a legal background, to which the reply is: 'No, but I have legal knowledge and can make sure you have legal input when needed. I'm impartial but can help you communicate. Quite often people do need legal advice, go to a lawyer, and then come back.' W says she had tried to talk to her husband (H) but he wouldn't do it. They had been married 25 years. M7 asks what happened, and W replies: 'Lots of reasons. H is bad with money. There were debts. I lost respect for him.' Asked about conflict in the relationship, W says they argued, but he would just walk out. They both had new partners. There were two daughters aged 18 and 21. Since H withdraws from argument, M7 wondered if it would happen in mediation, to which W answers that it was possible.

M7 asks what is in dispute. W says: 'Property.' H was living in the former matrimonial home, which had been in her name because of his bankruptcy. It was worth £450,000, with a mortgage of £23,000, and 'he has offered me £15,000'. She had left the home and had now bought another house. He remained in the home with their younger daughter. M7 asks if they had a decree nisi or absolute,[2] explaining that for a full financial separation there needed to be full and frank disclosure so they could decide how to split the assets. M7 says that since they had not gone through a court, they were still 'financially connected', that 'if H won the lottery or went bankrupt it would have an effect on you both'. To separate financially it has to go through a court, and they have to disclose. 'So to start (mediation) with me, you would have to do that. We would send you a form to start on which you share. Disclosure is open. It's fact.' She asks if there are other properties, and W says the matrimonial home is 'one-third mine. I put in £40,000 and there is a £120,000 mortgage', and there was a holiday property in (a European country) for which £150,000 had been paid: 'It's a noose around my neck. I can't give it away.' M7 says they need valuations for each property. W asks: 'What about if he's never paid towards something and I bought after we were separated?' M7 replies: 'You are connected, but would have to look at what you think is fair. You don't have a lawyer?' W says she cannot afford one. If they can't agree 'he will have to take me to court'. She has asked

---

[2] The significance of this is not clear since, unless excluded by court order, an application for financial or property order may be made at or at any time after decree absolute. The court may make an order 'On granting a decree of divorce, a decree of nullity of marriage or a decree of judicial separation or at any time thereafter (whether, in the case of a decree of divorce or of nullity of marriage, before or after the decree is made absolute)': Matrimonial Causes Act 1973, s 23(1).

H for £40,000. M7 says she will send the form, and if W is willing to disclose 'you may agree', and if not 'and you need to go to a lawyer, you have done some of the work'. W says she is prepared to come down to £30,000, but does not think H will budge. She asks whether mediation would just be with H, or would there be a lawyer? M7 is non-committal, and asks: 'Will you give it a go?' W says she will, and agreed to an appointment in two months. It is not clear whether the couple are separated or divorced, with a decree nisi or absolute.

There was clearly a background dispute here, and W needed to know the strength of her legal position. The legal issues were not entirely straightforward, involving possible issues concerning shares in the equity of a house subject to mortgage, property acquired after separation, possible differences regarding property relations between married and unmarried people, and how the court might deal with the former home. It is not clear how helpful, or even legally accurate, M7's observations were on these matters. Since the house was in W's name, she may have been in a stronger position than M7 realised. But M7 did not offer legal advice, other than that W would need to go to a lawyer if there was no disclosure. W really needed a consultation with a professional lawyer, whether considered as the provision of advice or information. Two months after the session M7 commented that W had not returned. There really was little reason for her to do so.

The same law firm was also able to provide SPIPs, the Separated Parents Information Programme organised by CAFCASS. We were invited to observe. Two trainers were present, M7 and M8, both non-lawyer mediators who worked in mainly legal settings. This programme lasts four hours and began at 9.30 am in the law office.

Six mothers and two fathers were present, with the two trainers. All had been sent by the courts, but the courts no longer supply the court order or the CAFCASS report so the trainers have little background information and start from scratch. M8 gives a warm welcome and explains that the purpose is to think about what children need, not for experts to give instructions. Ice-breaking jokes and slides are well used. There is agreement that court is right for some people but not all. Group contracts are handed out dealing with agreement to take part, all sitting around a table.

Everyone is advised to speak only for themselves, and to say as much as they felt comfortable with but no more. The aims are 'to think about what children need from you as separated parents, how to manage conflict, to focus on moving forward and to begin by looking at your experience'. Then a DVD made by young people would be shown and after lunch the programme was to talk about the emotional side and communication.

M8 gives statistics on divorce. 'You and your children are not alone and children can be fine through separation; conflict is the problem.' She talks about the emotional aspects of parenting, being in the driving seat or wanting to get off the roller coaster. Everyone is asked to chat to the person next to them. Then M7 offers a 'Highway Code' for the journey: no fighting in front of the children, accepting children may have different feelings from yours, think about what you *can* do, what *has* worked, and be the best parent you can be. 'A' talks about taking his daughter on holiday and how she loved it, but how sad he was when she ran back to her mum. M8 says that a child can be happy with dad *and* cling to mum. She talks about taking small steps, taking care to have energy to help the children.

Then a 20-minute video is shown, followed by discussion about what the children in the film were feeling. Everyone is rather quiet after this, upset by the children in the film not being told what was happening, the 15-year-old trying to look after her parents, and the children's fear of being put in a home. 'B' says the message is that you should listen to the children, not argue in front of them. 'C' remembers when her parents split up and how her sister just refused to go to school: 'It was horrible.' M7 says children need information, to know it's not their fault and that it's OK to love both and have different family rules in different houses. 'Let the children develop at their own pace.' Everyone is invited to make suggestions about what to do in various circumstances. M7 says: 'Your ex can behave badly but you don't have to do the same.' 'What children don't need is badmouthing between parents ... they think of themselves as half mum and half dad; if you criticise your ex you criticise them. You can say you don't love each other any more, but you will always love them because it's a different kind of love.'

After lunch there is a session where the parents have to offer a positive thing about themselves and then think about what positive changes they would make. Next a vignette is used, in which a child sees dad every Saturday, mum has a job which starts at 1 pm, and dad is often late. The task is to work out in pairs what each person is thinking and feeling. M8 talks about the need to have more business-like conversations with the other parents about difficult issues. She says: 'You can't control your ex. Think about what you can control. Stay calm. Breathe slowly. There is a cycle of loss, from denial, anger, bargaining, to depression and acceptance. The leaver gets through it first.' 'A' says: 'I wish I had known this before.' 'B' says: 'I thought I was just mad.' M8 says: 'Think about hearing your child in 15 years talking about your separation; what would you not want to hear?'

At the end of the four hours, each parent tells of one small thing they are taking away: these include 'to be more open; to have more business-like conversations; to think about what my son needs, not me; to be aware that the child comes first; and to be more understanding of difference'.

M9: Continuing parental involvement

M9 is also a non-lawyer mediator working in a law firm offering mediation practice. We observed a first session (after a telephone conversation acting in effect as a MIAM with each participant) on a children issue (girls aged three and six) held in the law office. When the couple, who have separated (and have a decree nisi), arrive, looking stressed, M9 opens by asking if they had received the paperwork and signed the agreement to mediate. He explains that this is a 'child-centred forum to deal with children in a consensual way' and states his charges. He mentions legal privilege. Coffee is brought in and they sign. The charge is £250 an hour per person. M9 asks for more details about the family (and wider family) circumstances, and how much the girls understand of what is happening. Husband (H) explains the arrangements concerning the children's schooling and visits, that H is in the family home and that W has moved to a two-bed flat close by. Neither was brought up in the UK, and both are unfamiliar with English family law. M9 asks whether the couple think their separation is permanent. W says it is, and H agrees, though he says he was hoping it was not. M9 now asks each what they wish to achieve here. W replies: 'I would like the children full time; he wants the same.' H replies: 'Yes, to resolve what is best for the children' (actually rather a different answer).

M9 proceeds: 'I get the impression that you want some certainty.' He then gives legal information, first about parental responsibility, stating that 'you are responsible parents, you were before and you are now' and that there is an expectation that the parents will consult one another on major issues, and that the vast majority make their own decisions without court orders. He then moves on to the issue of where the children are living, saying to H: 'You told me the girls prefer to share the main home with you,' and adds: 'Have you read what works for children?' H replies: 'Some' and says his solicitor has mentioned '14-day cycles'. M9 responds: 'Let me share some information. There are a lot of ways of doing this. One home with 50/50 weekends and one night. Lots of ways.' He asks W if she has done any research, and she says not. M9 now says: 'H wants shared care.' (This appears to be his interpretation of 'You told me the girls prefer to share the main home with you'.) A little later he says: 'We have agreed.' It was not clear to the researcher how he reached this conclusion. M9 goes on to say: 'But look at the cycle of working days, not every other week-end. For shared care we must live in the same neighbourhood, near school. In my mind we have to build arrangements and have flexibility. Do you need to think about this?' W says: 'One week/one week?' M9 says: 'Research says what works is what you come up with.[3] It won't be perfect or as good as when you were together, there is a loss for both, but for the children, structure and stability. You are introducing a new home: you need to come up with something.'

---

[3] This may be a shorthand way of summarising the view that children do best when parents co-operate. But as stated it is misleading if it is intended to suggest that *anything* the parents agree on will be best for a child.

At this point both parents are in tears, and seem unable to make a suggestion. M9 now says: 'I introduce a suggestion. It's a tall order to come up with something by next week. With respect, I hope you don't know what is best now. Take a month and review. It will come from a spirit of exploration rather than "I must have".' This is obviously advice about process. There follows a tearful exchange between the couple, indicating that they would find agreement difficult. M9 is looking for a structure to take them through the next two weeks. He notes that H wants 'some form of shared care' and asks if they could agree that, to which W says she is not sure how it can work. After some probing about aspects of their parenting, M9 announces: 'Can we come up with a structure to get you through the next few weeks? You said one week on, one week off: there are other ways,' and, going to a flip-chart, mentions two days with one parent, then two with the other, and three with the first in one week, reversing the following week. That way, 'days don't divide': they can 'mix and match at weekends'. Commending this, he says that it avoids 'huge blocks of time' and gets the children used to seeing 'two homes: they can build two lots of everything in each, tooth brush, pyjamas, etc.' But: 'There is no magic here. It's down to your collaboration.' H responds by saying he wants to think about this a bit more, preferring 10 days with him, four or five with the wife. 'That would reflect the way it has been.' M9 asks W what her proposals are, but she is not able to make any. M9 then says: 'Where shall we start? Two days, two nights?', and details are discussed on this basis, M9 suggesting which days should be spent with which parent. H accepts: 'Just for this week'; M9 says: 'Suck it and see.' W suggests meeting again in two weeks, which H reluctantly accepts. They were asked to settle up on the way out: £225 each, plus VAT.

Although this is only an interim arrangement, it could prove a model for a longer-term settlement. The mediator seemed to see it in this way. Although he had observed that there were 'lots of ways' of doing this, he emphasised the model under which the children were divided each week equally between the parents in spite of clearly expressed opposition by the husband, who wanted to have the children for most of the two weeks. While M9 reiterated the need for the arrangement to be 'stable with flexibility', there was no evidence of any attempt to ascertain the perspective of the children (one of whom was aged six). Nor was there any discussion of the ability or willingness of the nanny, who carried out the daily care, to cope with this arrangement. The nature of the eventual outcome was certainly influenced by the mediator, almost moving beyond advice to something that looks as close to direction as a mediator could come. The parents were distressed, the mediator brisk and directive, reminding them to settle up on their way out. His comment to the researcher after the session referred to his many years of experience as a court welfare officer, that he had managed to avoid letting the parents criticise each other in the session, and had moved the matter forward.

III. GENERAL OBSERVATIONS

The non-lawyer mediators as a group appeared to have had a variety of training regimes, ranging from five to 15 core days, costing over £2,000 plus the ongoing costs of mentoring by their professional practice consultants ranging from £30 to £60 an hour. Those working in mediation services appeared often to work part-time, to be undertaking a second career, and to be paid in the order of £30 an hour for time in session plus half an hour for recording and pro rata for preparing formal documents (OFSs, mediation summary, proposals or MOUs and parenting plans). As we have seen, MIAMs do not always lead to mediation, and we could see how this could happen in cases where there was a clear disagreement between the parties, and the individual seeking the MIAM was looking for support rather than a more neutral facilitative role. The boundaries between information and advice were not always clear. The financial information given by mediators was not always clear or helpful. In children cases, there could be a primary focus on steering the adults to reach agreement rather than on the interests, needs or wishes and feelings of the children. There was an expectation that clients would also be seeking legal advice. The cost of mediation observed for the client ranged from £75 per person per hour to £250. The child cases observed comprised a single session, while three or more sessions were used in finance cases where issues became complex. For comparison, LM1[4] told us that where mediation is funded from legal aid, the rate (at the time of writing) is £482 each for two legally aided clients having a two-hour all-issues session, £232 for drafting an MOU, to a maximum total of £1,235 plus VAT.

The mediators working in services had less administrative support than those in legal offices, and perhaps less informal access to legal advice themselves though some clients also expected them to provide legal advice. The work is difficult and demanding, and sessions can be hard on participants and mediators, while the administrators also expressed anxiety over work flow and financial pressures. Our meeting with M11 gave a clear picture of the experience of a number of not-for-profit mediation agencies. She directs a large mediation service near a city centre sharing a building with domestic violence services and a contact centre. The service is not for profit and has independent offices. M11 echoed the comments on the financial difficulties experienced by other services, referrals having fallen in the first year after LASPO by 60 per cent, and the service had moved within months into deficit. Both private and publicly funded work had declined, as lack of legal aid ends a case. The proportion of legal aid work has fallen from 60 per cent to 40 per cent. Like others, the service may be forced to close. She said: 'We are dealing with people who are asset rich but cash poor. Conversion to

---

[4] See chapter 6.

mediation where one party is publicly funded and the other must pay £100 a session is not easy.' By LAA criteria, the service has a two-thirds conversion rate, of which 70 per cent have some success in the mediation.

The number of mediators working in the service had halved over the last year. But three of the five mediators were Law Society accredited. In her view mediation has lost focus and should work with general practitioners and Citizens Advice Bureaux. This service stressed involving children and had excellent recording systems. MOUs start with a summary of potential legal disputes (financial disclosure, how everyone is accommodated, periodic payments, pension sharing, residence and contact) and whether legal advice has been explained, taken, or may be taken, personal information and the rationale for the mediation. They conclude with a summary of proposals and remaining concerns, a timetable and means of implementation. But despite the high levels of skill and efficient office management, the service was facing great pressure and was unable to generate the volume of work necessary to maintain the current level of funding.

We turn now to the developing role of lawyers who have trained as mediators and who are now the numerically dominant group within the mediation profession.

6

The Practice of Family Mediators II: Legally Trained Mediators

O F THE 24 mediators we observed or interviewed, 12 had qualified as solicitors, and five were mediating in their own law practice while still offering legal services (LM1, LM2, LM3, LM4 and LM5). Of the other seven who had qualified as solicitors but were no longer practising, three (LM6, LM7 and LM8) were working as mediators from the offices of law firms where they did not practise as lawyers, and four were training or advising mediators (LM9, LM10, LM11 and LM12). Here we focus on the mediation work being carried out in law offices, their own and others, by mediators who have qualified as solicitors. The work of qualified lawyer mediators in other settings, including training, crisis legal work and arbitration, is discussed in chapter 3.

Of the legally qualified mediators who had held practising certificates but were no longer practising law (Group 3) we discuss in detail the work of LM6, LM7 and LM10. Of the five lawyer mediators operating in a legal setting (Group 4), we discuss in detail the work of LM4 and LM1. The mediation aspect of the work of the lawyer mediators LM3 and LM5, working in their own legal offices but interested in arbitration, has been described in chapter 3. The crisis intervention work of LM8 in family matters and the earlier work of LM10, formerly a mediator, now a business consultant for divorce services, and the training work of LM9, LM11 and LM12 were also discussed in chapter 3.

We start by describing those who were no longer practising law, then look at those who mediated within the context of their legal practice.

I. GROUP 3: MEDIATORS WHO WERE QUALIFIED SOLICITORS BUT WERE NO LONGER PRACTISING

LM6: A first session for parents

LM6 was a former family solicitor, now only working part-time doing mediation. The session we observed was preceded by an interesting comment from LM6 about the challenge of meeting a couple about whom she has no prior information. She said that sometimes she makes an effort to spot clients through the office window before they arrive so that she can gauge their levels of distress and ability to sit in the same room. The wife (W) comes in first and quickly explains that they were not divorcing, and that they might still reconcile even though she has had an affair. She is tearful, and LM6 is consoling, checks for domestic violence and establishes that W would feel safe in the same room with the husband (H). H now arrives and says he's hoping for reconciliation. LM6 explains about mediation and signing the agreement to mediate, and goes on: 'I am a solicitor but I practise now only as a mediator. We can work constructively and make your own agreements in real time. I can manage the discussion, not have dislocation with solicitors' letters going backwards and forwards.' She adds: 'I can offer information on the law, give you an indication if what you say is manifestly bonkers. There is an approach in law, and with a departure from it I try to bring you to the centre. If your ideas are outside the range, I will say so. I would be looking to get you to the middle.'

In response to H's query: 'So we have separate representation?' LM6 is silent. LM6 now asks about the children, and is told they are equally close to both parents. She finds out about the parents' employment, how they arrange child care and the attitude of their families. She elicits that both children have a medical problem, which is manageable but demands much medical attention. They are mainly in agreement about the children, but have different views about schooling, and this is discussed. LM6 explains that they both have parental responsibility and that the law expects them to make their own arrangements. H wonders what rights W's new partner would have concerning the children, and LM6 says he has none, and, as he has not met the children, LM6 strongly urges that this should not happen until this has been discussed here in mediation. She commends the parents on their concern for the children, and H becomes emotional, leaving the room. When he returns, LM6 goes through various options if they agree to separate, starting with the conditions that need to be satisfied to constitute the ground for divorce (apologising for their accusatorial nature) and indicates the types of things the local judge accepts as constituting unreasonable behaviour. H says he doesn't think they are going for divorce. W says: 'If we were, I don't mind adultery,' and LM6 says that in that case 'if you name him you would have to serve him with the petition'. LM6 goes through the steps of the process, which upsets H still further. LM6 says: 'If we look at divorce proceedings now, we set you on a course more likely to take you to an end point which may be premature. I'm not getting a sense that's what you want'. H agrees but W is silent. LM6 explains about Consent Orders, but adds: 'It's more important that you think about the marriage'. However, she goes through the way finances are dealt with under section 25 of the Matrimonial Causes Act. They could set out interim proposals in a deed of separation, and LM6 went through the kinds of issues it would need to include, such as setting maintenance against property or house shares and pension. They could have 'full advice of your lawyer' at that point. LM6 observes that 'divorce lawyers are suspicious ... trying to get the best for each' so the more they could agree here the better. H broached the possibility that he might leave a stressful job, but LM6 pointed out that a court would look at his earning capacity and ask why he did it. They conclude by going away with the task of assembling information to be set out in a Form E and to meet again in a fortnight. H states unequivocally that, if they are to part, he wants a loving friendship with W, but also that he would like to 'carve out' a management position from whatever resources they are to share. LM6 warns him that there is a view that the fortunes of children 'should be hitched to a rising star ...' so that his contributions would be expected to rise with his income.

In this case the parties had problems and decisions to make but were not yet in dispute. They were in good communication with each other. They were essentially testing the ground as to what might be involved should they divorce, a prospect which unsettled the husband more than the wife. The bulk of the mediator's input was legal information. The mediator, who later expressed to the researcher an interest in how solicitors might be able to work with both clients as solicitors, drew extensively on her legal knowledge and behaved in exactly the same way as a number of solicitors reported in our study of family lawyers where we wrote:

> In several cases (not always those where the parties were still living together) the client was uncertain at the time of the first visit to the solicitor whether or not he or she wanted a divorce, and desired simply to know how divorce might affect their financial situation or their relationship with their children. The solicitors actively encouraged such clients to go away and reflect on the information they had provided (Eekelaar, Maclean and Beinart 2000: 151).

LM7: A fourth session on finance

LM7 is a former legal aid lawyer, now a consultant in her former practice and mediating two days a week. The mediation observed was the fourth session for this couple and concerned finance and divorce.

The husband (H) owned the matrimonial home, which had been bought with the proceeds of his previous house. He was some years older than his wife, but had not been married previously. The wife (W) owned a house in the European country from which she came, had no capital in England but currently earned a good salary. They had one son aged 15. They appeared to have agreed already to a 60/40 split of assets, so the discussion centred on availability of assets, particularly regarding the house, and the husband referred to his 'financial adviser' talking about equity release, though he did not think that was the way to go. Clearly giving advice, LM7 says: 'About the equity, when you sell, put it into a deposit account and have a deed of trust for x and y percentages to each,' but asks: 'You have advice from a solicitor?', to which the husband (but not the wife) replies: 'Yes.' LM7 gives information about tax relief and child benefit, and later about the government's child maintenance calculator. Regarding arrangements for the child, the couple discuss this between themselves, LM7's contribution being minimal: 'You know the situation ... it's down to the two of you to say what would work. You can try something, see how it works.' She does say that these arrangements need not be part of a separation agreement, but suggests they may be set out in an informal document, and also that they might meet with her every three or six months to discuss how things are going.

It is possible that these parties had been more conflicted at earlier sessions, but there appeared to be sadness but no dispute at this stage: they simply needed help in how to organise their finances, and make arrangements concerning their son. The mediator seemed to do nothing, at least at this stage, which was any different from what a solicitor would do if seeing either one of the parties, except that it concluded with the agreement that she would draft an MOU, which would be sent to the parties' solicitors for approval. The advantage of course was that, by seeing them together, the extent of their agreement could immediately be seen. The costs of the mediation thus far amounted to some £1,800 plus VAT, to which the charges of each participant's solicitors would need to be added. But, as in LM6's mediation above, the participants were not in real dispute. They were effectively asking for, and to a large extent receiving, joint advice, mostly of a legal nature.

LM10: Accreditation portfolio cases

LM10 is a lawyer mediator who was actively mediating when we made arrangements to observe a mediation but gave up her practice before the visit could take place. The work was paid at £18 an hour, which did not cover her travel costs, especially with a high rate of no shows. The service charged £100 for a MIAM (one hour) and from £90 (for people with an income under £24,000) to £200 (for people with an income over £35,000) per person per session plus VAT. The service had three administrative staff and one full-time mediator, and in LM10's view, needed to streamline its costs. She remains confident that mediators are better able than lawyers to recognise the emotional state of families, and to help with ideas about the house, debt and pensions, while supporting their autonomy. She feels it is the job of the mediator to 'bring the children into the room[1] ... take the child's part ...' qualifying this with a concern that 'it infiltrates the autonomy if you go in'. The service had not been in favour of direct child consultation, perhaps through lack of confidence.

LM10, however, remains very committed to mediation and could return to it if take-up improves. Since she was no longer conducting mediations,

---

[1] In the same way a lawyer might be said to bring the other side 'into the room' in a negotiation by maintaining awareness of the other's point of view.

she offered us access to the portfolio she had assembled as part of her training and accreditation requirements. This included three commentaries on cases conducted by LM10 with her trainer as co-mediator, and, among other things, assessment of her own competence which she talked through with us. We comment here on some specific aspects of these assessed cases. For example, in one we noted the statement: 'I took practical measures to communicate with local contact centres to enable the parents to establish their options for supervised contact, which led to an agreement between the parents.' Mediators seem to differ over the extent to which they engage in activity outside the mediation session, for example by consulting experts (apart from drawing up a MOU), but it is a common perception that the practice of mediation is confined to what takes place within the room (other than consultation with children in accordance with section 5.7.3–5.7.4 of the FMC Code).[2]

LM10 also described a financial case where she and her co-mediator had explored the issues in some detail in the first session, and were considering options in the second, when the husband became upset, and the wife needed to withdraw from the room. Because of this incident, the mediators felt the mediation could not continue. But the wife had made an offer before she left, and the mediators decided they would allow the husband to choose to accept that offer and close the mediation at that point. He did this. LM10 remarked that it was 'within the range a District Judge would accept'. It is not stated whether this view was conveyed to the husband, but it would have been entirely reasonable to have done so, and indeed, on the assumption that the wife did or would have agreed, doing it would have been within the principles of the FMC Code. But even if the mediators did not expressly say that they were advising the husband to accept, it is hard to see how providing this information would not have been seen as tantamount to advice. It might be thought that when this occurred, the mediation had finished, as the wife left the room. However, the mediators considered that the offer still formed part of the mediation, which did not close until the offer was accepted.

In a third case, LM10 had sought financial information, saying that she tried to convey to a participant that the questions she was asking would be asked by a solicitor at a later stage and 'it would therefore save money to deal with these matters in mediation'. So here again the task of the mediator coincided with that of a lawyer. Would a non-lawyer mediator be likely to make such a statement with the same confidence? On the children issues in this case, the mediator was able to ameliorate discussion between the participants, and suggested consulting the children. In fact the participants rejected this advice, but were able to work out arrangements concerning the children. On the financial side, a potential sticking point was avoided when

---

[2] See above p 88.

it emerged that the former matrimonial home would be sold. The mediator did intervene quite directively at one point when it seemed that the wife was about to agree a settlement the mediator thought might be disadvantageous: the mediator said she had heard the wife saying she wanted legal advice before agreeing, so she would not allow the agreement. This was a clear example of a mediator attempting to influence an outcome. In the event, the wife accepted a 50/50 asset division when her solicitor had advised 60/40, which is an example that advice, even from a solicitor, is only advice and can be rejected.

II. GROUP 4: LAWYER MEDIATORS PRACTISING MEDIATION AND LAW IN A LEGAL SETTING

LM4: *Child mediation*

LM4 is an accredited family specialist solicitor, describing herself as Resolution- and NFM-trained, working in a law office on a portfolio for accreditation. It is possible to offer mediation within a law firm where neither the person nor their partner is a client of the firm. These parents had never lived together. The father (F) had a new partner, but not the mother (M). The issue concerned the extent of time the child of two should spend with the father: at present she stayed overnight with F at weekends, and F wanted a weekly overnight stay during the week, and ultimately equal care. M believed it was too early to move to this, citing the child's apparent unhappiness at being apart from her. They had attempted an earlier mediation with another solicitor-mediator, which failed. The lengthy, sometimes acrimonious, sometimes sad, discussion at this mediation had the following features. F stated several times that he thought they had come 'to establish the midweek stayover', and expressed his frustration with mediation and anger that this was not happening. Perhaps this expectation was encouraged by the fact that he was paying for both himself and M. LM4 allowed the participants much scope for their angry exchanges, but intervened at crucial points, largely using normalising strategies (for example, saying that the child's behaviour and the parents' perceptions and feelings were to be expected), and occasionally adverting to the undesirable prospect of court adjudication. At one point M suggests fortnightly sleepovers starting next spring, which F angrily rejects, but shortly afterwards LM4 says: 'We could just sit here all day, but it's too expensive. I suggest we move to a fortnightly stay and then a mediation session.' Later, after further exchanges, LM4 says: 'M has proposed overnight Tuesdays fortnightly, starting? F wants weekly but wouldn't decline fortnightly? Right?' F says 'Yes, if it were to work like that, when do we begin?' M suggests: 'Next Tuesday?' That issue resolved (for now), the discussion moves to arrangements over Christmas, when F wants the child to be in his household for crucial periods, but M would like not only the child but F too to be with her and her family. LM4 suggests a complicated compromise arrangement, with which F is very unhappy, but accepts reluctantly. He responds to a proposal for a later mediation meeting saying: 'We haven't achieved anything today, so no point.'

As in the MIAMs reported earlier, one of the participants appeared to expect the process to validate his own position, and was disappointed that it did not. The mediator was adept in keeping the discussion moving, and seeing an opening for possible compromise. However, while the mediator expressed her appreciation of the love and care both parents had for the child there is no overt reference to the need to focus on the child's welfare. But that might have achieved little as both parents clearly thought that they were already doing that. M had a wish that both parents and the child could constitute some kind of family unit, even though there was no couple relationship and never had been. F was busy developing a warm, loving relationship with his new partner and wanting to make his child a part of that unit. But both parents did seem to achieve a better understanding of the other's wishes and feelings during the often bruising conversation. For example, F was moved when M said that the child changed the name of her cuddly toy to include that of the new partner when going to his father's house, and F began to understand how the child was tired by the changeovers despite loving both parents. The mediator had said her aim was to increase the level of trust, and she appeared to have done so.

LM1: A finance and child mediation and two MIAMs

LM1 is a lawyer mediator and a passionate advocate of mediation as 'liberating ... You can do things law can't ... help them move forward'. She had set up a mediation service, with four lawyer mediators, offering mediation once a week in a law office that was not her own and also on other premises including her own legal practice which included legal aid work. Her administrative costs were low, charging for 30 minutes per client per session for administration. There is a constant struggle to timetable, as about 40 per cent of people fail to show up, a similar rate to legal clients. She needed to earn £500 a day to keep the business going at its present levels, but was expecting only £200 the day after our first visit as a result of no-shows. She charges £160 per person for two hours plus half an hour for administration, (compared with her legal practice rate of £185 per person per hour) and with the system on her laptop can scan forms, emails and access a case-filing system. She says: 'I deal holistically ... mediation is gentler.' 'There are litigious solicitors charging £250 an hour; it costs £90 an hour to mediate, collecting and collating information.' Her conversion from assessment to mediation, including legally aided work, is close to 70 per cent.

The first meeting observed did not take place in her own practice. It was the second session with a couple who were still living together, and concerned finance and the arrangements to be made for their 14-year-old daughter after the separation. LM1 thanks the father (F) for bringing financial information, including payslips, following the earlier finance session. On checking what they had agreed so far for their child, the mother (M) says: 'We agreed what was fair.' LM1, however, does not let this stand without further questioning. She asks: 'But is it right for (the child) (C)?' F says they need to see how the routine will settle, as M's work can vary. M wants the arrangements to be 'steady'. LM1 says: 'What I hear is steady routine from M; from F some flexibility because of work and what C needs. Will she have a visit with F mid-week?' M says: 'Yes, I've arranged things to fit C.' It turns out that while she had no objection to F seeing C, M was worried that planning for regular overnights with F would be disruptive during the week because of the father's travel and work commitments, with the implication that during the week it would be better for C to stay overnight with her. F was unhappy about that. LM1 twice disclaims any intention to dictate how this should be resolved: 'I don't have an answer, and you don't,' but adds: 'It might be better to try something and re-write: perhaps ask C in a direct child consultation.'[3] Then: 'It's not my job to tell you how to do it,' adding, 'but her routine is secure while you're in the same house', and gives a veiled warning: 'If you can't arrange it, it might go to court, and that's far-ranging.' LM1's suggestion regarding weekdays is for the parents to think of two or three scenarios, and discuss them with C in a direct child consultation. 'Tell her your ideas to keep her safe and happy. If she's not happy, how will she behave?' F says she is not an unhappy child, and M says they should speak to her. She adds: 'She can see F as much as she wants; I'm not saying she'll never stay over.' After asking for suggestions, LM1 says to M: 'You and C could prepare for a stay.' M: 'Maybe towards the end of the week.' LM1: 'I've heard you say you might try a stay late in the week: you might ask C.' They now turn to weekends. Like M9, LM1 observes that 'there are lots of ways' they could be used (for example, one to M, one shared half and half, one to F), but (unlike M9)[4] does not push any particular format, instead suggesting practical ways in which they might communicate with one another over weekend plans.

Thus far, this mediation adheres closely to the FMC Code. The warning about going to court can be seen as influencing the parties towards agreement, but this is only to be expected. The advice is strictly confined to process: the parents are to construct scenarios (the mediator makes no suggestion about what they may be), and closely observes the guidance in 5.7.2 of the Code that 'mediators must encourage participants to consider the children's wishes and feelings'.

The second part of the mediation was in effect a preparation for the next mediation, which would concern financial matters. The mediator took the

---

[3] This is a consultation with children that follows the provisions of 5.7.3–5.7.4 of the FMC Code.
[4] See pp 105–7 above.

participants through Form E, remarking that if they went to court, this would cost £5,000–£7,000 'just to fill it in', and if they could not agree 'you delegate your responsibility to someone you don't know, the judge'. They start by considering the value of the house, and how soon it might be put on the market. LM1: 'You want to be ready if a buyer turns up.' She then gives a bracing steer towards reaching agreement: 'I know what the law is, and how a court will look at a case. But you are going to do the maths, be your own judge. You will be clear what you are doing, but you will resolve it. You might need legal advice. You'll know what you're doing and why and if you can live with it. It's good for people. I've spent 20 years in courts. I know what it does to people. Lecture over.'

They discuss valuation of the house, and settle on an asking price. LM1 says: 'You both need to go in and sign the forms so it's ready to sell.' F asks for a month to 'tart it up a bit'. Saying she has conveyancing experience, LM1 talks through the mortgage situation, explaining how different kinds of mortgages work. She mentions all the likely sources of capital (including pension), saying: 'I've presented what a lawyer would ask you.' At the end she says: 'You have both given me Form Es. If I work outside this session, it's the same hourly rate, but I wouldn't do it without your agreement. I'll look later. You've done the work so this will come together at the next session.' She says they will have to deal with contents at the next meeting, but suggests they may be able to settle this outside mediation by 'put(ting) different coloured stickies on things you really like and see where you over-lap, and then the less important. Make notes.' As M does not know her state pension entitlement, LM1 says she will forward her the relevant forms, and downloads them on her laptop immediately. M says: 'I don't know how to start a divorce: can I talk to you?' to which LM1 replies: 'OK, over the next two to three sessions.' She says that if there is a dispute, the court can intervene, but 'it's expensive to go to court for maintenance pending suit, a holding position … the last one I did cost £1,200'. The couple are in tears, and LM1 says: 'You are clear the relationship can't go forward. You've cho-sen divorce. If you need advice, see lawyers. If you need information, I've given you sources.'

While there was a certain degree of conflict between the couple regarding the child arrangements, there was no apparent dispute on financial matters. They were still assembling information and learning about the legal land-scape they were entering. They were in the position of people not knowing what path to take, not disagreeing about it. Yet it is hard to see why the first part of the session might qualify for legal aid (contact arrangements being considered a legal dispute),[5] but not the second (and later sessions). The LAA requirement of a 'legal dispute' seems particularly inappropriate in

---

[5] The Legal Aid Agency *Family Mediation Guidance Manual* version 4.0, March 2015: para 2.2.

this context because the object of the exercise is to prevent a dispute arising. Much of the mediator's action at this stage fell within the FMC Code, which states:

> 6.12 Mediators must seek to ensure that participants reach their decision upon sufficient information and knowledge. They must inform participants of the need to give full and frank disclosure of all material relevant to the issues being mediated and assist them where necessary in identifying the relevant information and supporting documentation.

The mediator was clearly 'assisting' the parties in identifying the relevant information. However, she seemed to go beyond that. Although she insisted on the distinction between 'advice' from lawyers and the 'information' she was giving, she clearly considered that her conveyancing experience was relevant for fixing a valuation for the house and explaining to the mother how mortgages worked. She was willing to explain (over the next sessions) how the divorce should be taken forward, and to forward to the mother forms about her state pension. Her reference to the cost of seeking maintenance pending suit was clearly intended to deter any such step. Perhaps most striking was the reference to her court experience, used here to encourage settlement. All this gave added weight and authority to the assistance given by the mediator, in contrast to that given by M7,[6] and is hard to distinguish from advice. It was perhaps natural for this mediator to be willing to do this, as she was also a lawyer. Her actions were no different from what a lawyer might do regarding a client, as we saw in the case of L3.2's discussion with Mrs Y in chapter 3,[7] except that in this case the lawyer mediator would have been taking into account the interests of both clients when 'helping' (to use a neutral word) them in taking forward their divorce. Finally, when discussing the child arrangements, this mediator's reluctance to accept without question a proposal which had not been discussed with the child, and her frequent references to consulting with the child and how this could be done, were very evident. Might this have been the effect of familiarity with the Children Act 1989 or the provision in the Resolution Guide to Practice which puts responsibility for the welfare of the child on the mediator?

The next day started with a visit by a lady in her 50s for a MIAM. LM1 tells her she is charging at the legal aid rate, but the client is not eligible for legal aid. The topic (finance) is suitable for mediation, and the husband is willing to take part. They make an appointment for the following week, subject to confirmation, and LM1 gives her an information sheet setting out the kind of information they should bring in. The next client for an assessment did not appear. LM1 explains to the researcher her plans for a 'pre-MIAM' walk-in family dispute service, giving free diagnosis, options

---

[6] See above pp 101–4.
[7] See above pp 59–60.

and cost estimates. She notes that mediation is low-risk for professional indemnity because it does not involve giving advice.

The next client for a MIAM was a wife (W), but again the husband (H) did not appear. They were divorcing, but still living together. W said they did not have assets in dispute; her problem was H's mental capacity, and that she was at risk of redundancy. LM1 says that, as there was no dispute, legal aid would not be available, and makes an assessment about what mediation would cost her. She adds: 'Mediation is quicker and cheaper. Solicitors are not out of the picture; they are there to help you make the right decisions,' but then adds: 'I can tell you what the law says, also the options, the impact of potential change, loss of job, pensions, tax changes. So you have your solicitor: does your husband?' W says they have the same one. LM1 says they cannot use the same one because of conflict of interest. 'But if you agree, you can use the same solicitor for drafting. I'm mediating, giving information, not advice.'

W says: 'We just wanted someone to talk through it all. We didn't fall out, just (drifted) apart.' She mentions his mental health, which appears to be well controlled. 'He takes his meds and goes to hospital when it's bad.' There is no domestic violence. LM1 says: 'If ever that changes, let me know.' She asks if W knows what mediation is. W replies: 'What we are coming for is information on legal assets, somebody to hear our decisions,' to which LM1 replies: 'I can do that. I can't tell you whether legally you go further.' They discuss a date when they could both come in, and LM1 gives her the form, based on Form E, setting out the information needed if a court were to make an order.

In substance, it seems that if the mediation went ahead, which seemed likely, the mediator would effectively have been acting as a legal adviser to both parties. Indeed, the MIAM itself was not unlike a legal consultation, with the mediator explaining what information a court would need in order to make an order, and offering not only generalised information but also considering 'the impact' of changes in the couple's legal position.

III. WHAT FOLLOWS

The difficulty in categorising the different ways in which mediation is currently delivered according to the models of mediation used can be seen in chapter 5. In this chapter the relationship between mediation and legal training and accreditation adds to the complexity. Legal knowledge and the willingness to use it vary within categories as much as between them. The next chapter expands on the complexity of modes of dispute resolution and assistance becoming available, and raises questions about the desirability of having the expertise of both the mediator and the lawyer in a single provider for the consumer who is likely to be a one-time purchaser under considerable stress.

7

Towards an Integrated Service?

W HEN FAMILY MEDIATION began to grow in England and Wales in the 1980s, it was very distinctive from legal practice in respect not only of its ideology, but also the characteristics of both its practitioners and clients. While practitioners came from a range of backgrounds, most were from caring or helping professions, including early retired volunteers not seeking a second career. Compared with legal clients, mediation services seemed to be used in the early days more by articulate and less conflicted people, often in the more affluent areas of the country. However, from about the mid 1990s, encouraged by the government's promotion of mediation in the context of divorce, lawyers began to become interested in adding family mediation to their professional repertoire. This was seen as a threat by some of the established family mediators. In 2005 Marion Roberts (2005: 520) wrote of 'the Law Society [claiming] control over a new and potentially lucrative area of professional practice, challenging established professional boundaries and therefore core understandings relating to the nature of legal practice and of mediation as a distinctive, discrete, and autonomous form of dispute resolution'.

Since then, as has been seen, non-lawyer mediators and lawyer mediators have been increasingly occupying the same territory of practice. Since LASPO, the population to be served by mediation has moved from being a relatively marginal group to potentially all court litigants, and public funding has sought to re-direct most seekers of legal help away from lawyers towards mediation. In Australia a similar change occurred with the establishment of Family Relationship Centres, which had to deal with a much broader and more demanding population than the early users of mediation, and it is now estimated that up to 80 per cent of cases mediated raise questions about domestic violence.[1] A change in the population served requires some change in the kind of service offered. In addition, in England and Wales, because of the legal aid changes, fewer cases are being referred by lawyers and so lack the 'where do I stand' preparation for mediation. The demand for both free and privately funded mediation remains limited. Nevertheless, mediation is almost always used together with the services of a solicitor at some stage, and often provided in a law office by either lawyer

---

[1] We are grateful to Jon Graham of Relate Australia for this insight.

or non-lawyer mediators. The practice of family mediation appears to be becoming increasingly integrated into legal practice. It is seldom used as a stand-alone service.

But, as described in chapter 3, the lawyers too are changing. There is less total care for a client, a wider range of pricing mechanisms and differentials and more limiting of the services provided to fixed-price and specific tasks. In this new environment, it is not surprising that lawyers are even keener to add mediation to their range of services, relating it more closely to their more supportive approach.

I. TYPES OF MEDIATION

In chapter 4 we described the institutional structure in which mediation services are located in England and Wales, and the objectives that mediation sought to achieve as found primarily in official documentation. We drew attention to what appeared to be problems and inconsistencies in the key distinction between providing information and giving advice, how directive a mediator might be in promoting options in what is essentially private ordering, and noted what we considered to be problems over accommodating legal principles, particularly the paramountcy of the child's welfare, with the distinction between information and advice and other aspects of mediation practice. We now return to some of these issues in the light of our observations and the experience of other jurisdictions.

We start by referring to discussions that have recognised that mediation can take different forms. Parkinson (2014: 37) writes that 'structured' mediation focuses on parties' interests, rather than their preferred outcomes, seeking to reach a settlement that meets as many of those interests as possible. She comments that 'lawyer mediators, in particular, are accustomed to playing an active role in working towards settlement', and adds: 'In structured mediation the mediator can exercise considerable power … There are also risks of mediators steering participants towards a quick settlement rather than spending time building a mutually satisfactory settlement with both or all participants.' Structured mediation, she says, 'was not specifically designed for divorce or family disputes'. In contrast, 'transformative' mediation is designed to enhance participants' appreciation of each other's feelings and perspectives. However, Parkinson observes that this is not necessarily what people seek in mediation, and could take mediators outside mediation's 'ethical boundaries'. It would certainly lie outside the definition for publicly funded mediation,[2] as do 'narrative' and 'ecosystems' approaches, which refer to techniques for reducing tension between

---

[2] See Legal Aid Agency, *Family Mediation Guidance Manual* version 4.0, March 2015: paras 2.2–2.4), above p 81.

[handwritten margin notes: therapeutic]

participants and promoting a higher level of understanding of differing perspectives within their social context.

An alternative typology is offered by Boulle and Nesic (2001: 27–29). They refer to 'settlement' mediation as encouraging 'incremental bargaining' and seeking compromise between the parties' opening demands. 'Facilitative' or 'problem solving' mediation seeks to negotiate in terms of the parties' underlying needs and interests rather than their legal entitlements. 'Therapeutic' mediation seeks to deal with underlying relationship issues. 'Evaluative' mediation seeks to reach a settlement in accordance with the rights of the parties within the anticipated range of court outcomes, which can blur the line between mediation and arbitration. They accept that these models may overlap, even within a single mediation. Others, on the other hand, insist on a purist model which is premised on absolute respect for client autonomy. On this view, the mediator has no interest in the outcome, and any 'steer' by the mediator towards an outcome, even by giving an indication of the possible view of a court, infringes client autonomy and is unethical and not even mediation, but 'settlement broking' (for examples see Stevenson (2015a) and Stylianou (2015)).

Which description best represents what we observed? Not surprisingly, we observed a mixture, and do not think it helpful to try to force a description into any particular categorisation. We see the warnings given about the undesirability of court proceedings should agreement fail (for examples see LM4 and LM1) and the occasions when mediators offered suggestions (or advice) about how agreement might be reached, such as the best way to decide how to distribute the contents of the home (M1 and LM1) or the proposals for shared parenting arrangements made by M9 and LM4's work to move towards a mid-week sleepover in another dispute about overnight stays as efforts to bring about a settlement on which it was hoped the participants could agree despite any reservations they, or the mediator, might feel. But indications that mediators would state whether a solution fell outside legal parameters (M7, LM6, LM10) might reflect a more 'evaluative' approach.

However, these practices were usually accompanied by strategies designed to reduce tension and enhance communication between the participants, as in the 'transformative', 'narrative' and perhaps even 'ecosystems' models. This was particularly evident in the mediations by M7, LM1 and LM6 and the SPIPs (Separated Parents Information Programmes) conducted jointly by M7 and M8, and, perhaps with less success, LM4. So it seems that the mediators combined elements from the different typologies of mediation. There is nothing surprising about that. Indeed, it is entirely consistent with the two aims of mediation set out in the FMC Code:

2.1   Mediation aims to assist participants to reach the decisions they consider appropriate to their own particular circumstances.

124   *Towards an Integrated Service?*

> 2.2   Mediation also aims to assist participants to communicate with one another now and in the future and to reduce the scope or intensity of dispute and conflict within the family.

Similarly, section 2 of the Resolution Guide (2015: 9) states:

> Family mediation is a process in which those whose relationship is ending or has ended, regardless of whether they are a couple or other family members, appoint an impartial third person to assist them to communicate better with one another and to reach their own agreed and informed decisions concerning some or all of the issues relating to their separation, divorce, children, finance or property by negotiation.

However, it is an axiom of mediation that 'Mediation must be conducted as an independent professional activity and must be distinguished from any other professional role in which the mediator may practise (FMC Code, section 5.1.7)'[3] and that 'Participants must be clearly advised [sic: this should perhaps read 'informed'] at the outset of the nature and purpose of mediation and how it differs from other services such as marriage or relationship counselling, therapy or legal representation' (FMC Code section 6.4). In the context which we were observing, the competing role was that of a lawyer, and the distinction between the role of the mediator and a lawyer here is built on the distinction between offering legal information and providing legal advice. As section 5.3 of the Code states: '(Mediators) may inform participants of possible courses of action, their legal or other implications, and assist them to explore these, but must make it clear that they are not giving advice.' Our analysis of section 5.3 suggested that this distinction may not be sustainable.

Our empirical data confirms this view. The distinction has the hallmarks of a formula whose function is to maintain professional boundaries. It seems it may be impossible to maintain in practice. The data provide numerous examples of advice provided by mediators to participants both as regards process and outcome. M1 gave advice to one participant about obtaining a nominal maintenance order, and to both about drawing up their list of assets; M12 said that, unlike lawyers, 'We (mediators) don't encourage wives to claim maintenance,' but went on to say: 'We succeed with getting spousal maintenance and charge back; when the children leave home her income falls off the cliff.' She also said: 'It's harder to get women to look ahead, especially about pensions,' implying that mediators do make some effort to get them to do that. Although she added that 'decisions are down to the people', that is insufficient to distinguish this from what lawyers do, as that is true in that context too. In fact, M12 expressly stated: 'You can give better *advice* if you have information from both,' though still insisting that she gives 'legal principles'. M9 gave advice about taking time to reach

---

[3] The Resolution Guide (2015: 10) has an equivalent provision.

[Handwritten margin notes: "DISTINCTION mediators + lawyers based on info or advice"; "VV imp yes"; "Between info + advice"]

agreement, and eventually about how the living arrangements of the child should be shared. LM7 advised about what should be done with the proceeds of the sale of the home. LM10 (and her co-mediator) gave assurance that an offer was within a range acceptable to a court; and LM1 advised that the parents construct scenarios and how they could decide on distributing household contents, and gave extensive information about mortgages and the divorce process. Much of this is of course advice about process, but process can affect outcome. Some, however, is directly about outcome.

It is not our intention to suggest that the mediators acted in any way improperly or outside their remit in doing these things. We have noted the contrary view of Stevenson (2015), who holds that such approaches should be seen as 'settlement-broking' rather than mediation. To sharpen the distinction, she gives a hypothetical case where a client says: 'Sam is 8 now. He is old enough to decide for himself whether or not he sees his father. I'm not forcing him. It's up to him.' Stevenson suggests that informing the parties that a court would expect that the child should see his father is an example of the former approach. To act ethically, she argues, the mediator should encourage the participants to articulate the circumstances and their perceptions of the child's needs so they can settle on an option and see how it works out with the child. However, we believe that this sets up a false dichotomy. For, while a court would hold an assumption that it is normally in a child's best interests to remain in contact with both parents, this decision would not be taken without regard to all the circumstances, so these would need to be elicited if the information about the possible reaction of a court was to be in any way meaningful. Further, if the purist approach were taken, and it became clear from the additional information that the child was being manipulated and one party overborne by the other, is it really to be supposed that the mediator, who owes some responsibility to the child, would not give some indication about the child's interests, and perhaps seek a consultation with the child in accordance with FMC guidelines? Is a mediator to be totally unconcerned about imbalances of power (see Webley: in press)? The distinction rests on an idealised notion of autonomy as something 'possessed' by each participant untainted by any external influence. Such autonomy does not exist in the real world, and certainly not in mediation when the participants are at least influenced by one another. Nor do you deprive someone of autonomy by offering them advice. The question is only how influence is exercised and to what end. As Raz (1986: 155) wrote: 'Autonomy is possible only within a framework of constraints. The completely autonomous person is an impossibility.'

Therefore, we believe that the criteria according to which the roles of mediators and lawyers are distinguished are unrealistic. The two main grounds upon which the mediators' activities are said to be different from those of lawyers are that mediators provide information (which suggests a neutral act), not advice, and that mediators primarily deal with resolving current conflicts, whereas lawyers are not restricted to this but can offer advice and support in planning for the future, which involves guiding choices between options discussed based on the information or advice available, though at the end of the day the client chooses and gives instructions. The examples given above demonstrate how the provision of information frequently would be, and is intended to be, seen as pointing to actions or decisions which the mediator thinks are in the interests of the participants or a child (or sometimes just one of them). There is little to distinguish this from the way a lawyer delivers advice, apart from the fact that it normally comprehends the interests of two people. The fact that a mediator recommends that the participants consult their own lawyers before approaching a decision does not reduce its character as advice, but can be seen as alerting them to the possibility that they might receive different advice from a lawyer who was less constrained by accommodating the interests of the second person. A less benign reading is that by advising participants to consult their 'own' lawyers the mediator implicitly recognises that any legal information supplied (especially if by a non-lawyer) might be unreliable, and that this step is a safeguard against possible liability for giving negligent advice, for which they may not hold insurance. But mediators, especially if they are lawyers, are likely to be uncomfortable with this reading.

Myers and Wasoff (2011: 5, 7, 100) came to the same conclusion in Scotland. They added a point about transparency, which echoes the views of Greatbatch and Dingwall in a series of papers[4] published from 1989:

> For solicitors, the approach to option appraisal is a transparent process of outlining, on the basis of their knowledge and experience, the pros and cons of different approaches. In the mediation context the process is both transparent and opaque. The transparency of the process lies in the appearance of information sharing, the identification of aims, objectives and issues, and the joint discussion of possible options. The opacity of the process emerges from the way in which practitioners, also drawing on their expertise and experience appear, from their accounts, to subtly lead people in particular directions. This strategy is more indirect than is evident from solicitors' accounts. While a sophisticated approach it may be at odds with the rhetoric of mediation which suggests neutrality, impartiality and couple control (Ibid: 5).

The other respect in which the activity of mediators is closer to that of lawyers than usually understood is when mediators are not primarily seeking to resolve a dispute, but rather to respond to a need for one or both participants for information (or advice) in order to make a decision. As M12 explained in the 'MIAM' she gave to the researcher, mediation was 'an opportunity to sort out face-to-face all the practical and personal things directly but with the help of a mediator'. This clearly does not necessarily envisage a dispute.

---

[4] Greatbatch and Dingwall (1989); Dingwall and Greatbatch (1991); Greatbatch and Dingwall (1999).

In the mediation by M7 the mediator's task was primarily to open channels of communication between the participants rather than to bring them to agreement over contested issues. This was problem solving rather than dispute resolution or even decision making. The clearest example of a mediator acting very much as a lawyer would do was in LM6's mediation, where the couple were essentially exploring the legal and other consequences that would accompany their separation should they choose to separate. But this was also true for LM7's mediation (although there may have been a dispute at an earlier stage), and the second part (on finances) of LM1's first mediation, and seemed to be likely if the second MIAM conducted by LM1 converted to mediation: the wife expressly said: 'We just wanted someone to talk through it all.' And a client in a MIAM may really be seeking legal advice, as in the final MIAM described for M7, which involved quite complex property issues.

II. WHO IS THE CLIENT?

As Myers and Wasoff (2011: 97) observe, there is of course one clear distinction between the position of mediators and that of lawyers in this context, which is that the mediator is able to see both clients together. A lawyer normally could not be instructed by both parties where there is conflict of interest, or a significant risk of conflict,[5] between them but could act as a mediator between them because conducting mediation is not considered to be a 'legal activity' which is defined as including 'the provision of legal advice or assistance in connection with the application of the law or with any form of resolution of legal disputes'.[6] That makes it possible for mediators to engage in an activity (assisting the parties to communicate directly with one another) which is denied to lawyers unless they 'become' mediators and refrain from giving 'legal advice or assistance', which is what they are primarily trained to do. But if it is conceded that legal advice and assistance are not uncommonly provided in mediation, then mediation might sometimes be thought to fall within the definition of 'legal activity', and within the prohibition against lawyers in professional practice receiving instructions from conflicted clients. However, this principle may be permeable. According to the Solicitors Regulation Authority Handbook, 2011, Code of Conduct:

> 3.6 Where there is a client conflict and the clients have a substantially common interest in relation to a matter or a particular aspect of it, you only act if: you have explained the relevant issues and risks to the clients and you have a reasonable belief that they understand those issues and risks; all the clients

[5] Solicitors Regulation Authority Handbook, 2011, Code of Conduct, para 3.5.
[6] Legal Services Act 2007, s 12(3)(i).

have given informed consent in writing to you acting; you are satisfied that it is reasonable for you to act for all the clients and that it is in their best interests; and you are satisfied that the benefits to the clients of you doing so outweigh the risks.

The recognition that clients might have 'a substantially common interest' seems to open the door, if only theoretically, for solicitors to act for both parties in a divorce case. Richard Tur (1995: 151) made a strong argument that 'the law of lawyering and legal ethics should be adjusted to permit one lawyer to act for a divorcing couple, where appropriate, and always with the informed consent of the parties'. This was based on a view that it was too readily assumed that the parties' interests are necessarily opposed in divorce, and that such an adjustment would bring about substantial savings in costs and time. We would put the matter slightly differently. It is possible that the parties' interests at the time of, and after, separation may often be in conflict, but that they will share another interest, namely, that the conflict be resolved and disputes prevented or overcome in a manner that is both fair and minimally damaging to themselves and their children. That could be said to be a 'substantially common interest' under Rule 3.6. It could be further argued that, just as it is thought that a mediator can act 'impartially' with respect to the parties' interests, so it is reasonable that a lawyer might be 'satisfied that it is reasonable … to act for (both) the clients and that it is in their best interests (to do so)'. It follows that for a lawyer to act as a mediator and give legal advice within the mediation would not necessarily breach the rule against lawyers advising conflicted clients.

When a lawyer has only one party as client, whether what is provided is information or advice (and a lawyer may provide either), this is done with a view to furthering the interests of the client (although this may well take into account the interests of others). In such a case Marion Roberts (2014: 111) is correct to say that the role of the lawyer and client 'is inseparable from the relationship of representative', but this does not arise from the fact that the lawyer gives advice rather than information, but because the lawyer normally is concerned to identify and seek the best way to protect the interests of a single client. As Myers and Wasoff (2011: 97) put it: 'The solicitor route is by its nature characterised by particularity'. But if it is possible to identify a common interest, as mediation claims to do in a dispute, the provision of advice, including legal advice, to protect that interest does not make the mediator a 'representative' of either participant. This is so whether the mediator is a lawyer or not, and the fact that this is not a 'reserved legal activity' would also allow a non-lawyer mediator to give such advice.

Lisa Webley (2004) discusses the issue from a different perspective. She raises the question: who is the client in family proceedings? Referring to the statement in the Law Society Protocol on Family Law of 2001 that a solicitor is to 'have regard to the interests of children and long-term family relationships' she observes that this places on the solicitor a duty that goes beyond that owed to the client who gives the instructions. While Webley does not go as far as to state explicitly that other family members can be considered to be 'clients', her comment that this seems to 'widen the net' in respect of the question who the client is (Ibid: 249) indicates that it is not far-fetched to believe it is possible for a lawyer properly to give advice to two (or more) members of the same family. While the passage from the Law Society's 2001 Protocol to which Webley refers no longer appears in the 2010 edition, Resolution's Guide to Good Practice for Family Lawyers in Dealing with Clients (2012: para 5.1) has similar guidance:

> When the client is seeking our help to define what objectives it is sensible to pursue then we can seldom do better than to help them reach out for what is most principled and what, whilst promoting their own interests, also promotes the welfare of the family as a whole, in particular what is in the interests of any children.

If lawyers should seek solutions that not only promote the immediate client's interests, but also the welfare of the 'family as a whole', it is not a great leap to imagine the other family members as being, notionally, 'in the room', and from there to accept that the 'other' party could actually be in the room. So, while it might appear to be a major change to allow a lawyer to accept both parties together as clients, it could be argued that this is to some extent already recognised in such guidance. Our observations support the view of Myers and Wasoff (2011: 11) that 'there is more common ground than one might expect from commonly made claims' between the approaches of mediators and lawyers. The difference is that the mediator, *even if legally qualified*, proclaims not to be acting as a lawyer, disclaims giving legal advice, and advises the participants to consult other lawyers. But these are largely devices to maintain an outward distinction between the professional roles which seem to be converging at this point.

III. A PROPOSAL: 'LEGALLY ASSISTED' FAMILY MEDIATION

The market in divorce services being offered to separating couples has diversified rapidly (see chapters 2 and 3) and the boundaries between the different activities have become more opaque and permeable. People are using DIY online sources to do the preliminary work in a divorce, perhaps then moving to legal service packages at fixed prices, to mediation if in dispute, perhaps from mediation to arbitration and back again, and using expert advice on many matters from tax to parenting, or even purchasing a private financial dispute resolution (FDR) hearing. There are many options (to which we briefly refer below). This could be confusing for people undergoing the stress commonly associated with relationship breakdown. Barlow et al (2014: 6) report of the subjects they interviewed that 'many felt that the full range of options and the implications were not given to them or not well explained'. We therefore think it is important that opportunities should be available for them to be provided with information and advice about these options, and we address this in our proposal below.

We also believe that there is a case for adding to the present options a process that brings together the two key services, those provided by lawyers and mediators, which have so much in common in their working practice, so that clients, particularly those with limited means, can find what they need in one place. While sometimes it may be necessary to involve more than one professional in attending to the various needs of couples who contemplate separation, much of the expense and stress could be reduced if a one-stop service was available. Marc Lopatin has recently developed a scheme attempting to make mediation more attractive by linking it with the provision of legal services both before and during the process under the title 'Lawyer Supported Mediation'.[7] Lopatin's scheme envisages linking legal and mediation services in price-capped 'packages' but still separates the mediating from giving legal advice, and assumes separate legal representation of the participants. But might it not be possible to combine the two key skills, legal expertise and communication skills, in one service? The advertising strategies of many divorce service providers suggest that this could be what many people want. Even Marion Stevenson, who seemed to consider that mediation which sought to influence outcome was not mediation proper, but 'settlement-broking', later conceded that there was a place for 'settlement-broking' 'when clients understand that this is what they are buying' and refers to it as 'a model where they are given support in structuring a fair, reasonable and practical settlement' (Stevenson 2015b, d).

In the Netherlands a group of lawyers have formalised the relationship between mediation and law by forming an association, the vFAS (*Vereniging van Familierecht Advocaten Scheidingmediators*), of lawyers who are also qualified as mediators or mediator advocates who offer mediation with legal advice to couples who wish to and can appropriately work together.[8] Alternatively if parties wish to be separately advised, vFAS offers the services of FAS mediator-advocates separately to each party. These lawyer mediators then are committed to working in a non-adversarial way and negotiating with each other to reach agreement. If a mediation begins but breaks down the parties are free to seek the help of two separate lawyers who may be FAS lawyer mediators. If this form of help also fails to reach agreement the parties will need to go to court for adjudication. All the FAS lawyer mediators are specialist family lawyers of at least five years' standing who have been fully trained as mediators.

---

[7] See Lopatin (2014) for a full account of the scheme, later launched as Dialogue First.
[8] See 'Scheiden Doe Je Samen' from the *Vereniging van Familierecht Advocaten Scheidingsmediators* www.verenigingFASnl. June 2015. postbus 65707 2506 EA DEN HAAG.

When a FAS intervention ceases, the FAS lawyer mediator is not allowed to act for one party against the other, and nor is any member of their firm or any other adviser such as an accountant or counsellor who has been involved so far. The FAS lawyer mediator charges at the same hourly rate whether mediating or giving legal service, but of course the mediation service is cheaper as only one hourly fee is charged. FAS therefore offers choice: mediation with legal advice for both parties together from a lawyer, and legal services for each party separately from lawyers with a commitment to seeking settlement. The service is mainly used by people with property and the charging rates are not low. But legal aid could be available for those on low incomes.

At present in England and Wales, the only way for a divorce practitioner committed to helping both parties together to reach a fair and informed arrangement by using both full legal knowledge and mediating skills is to be a lawyer who has trained as a mediator but has stepped down from the Law Society Roll. This can be seen in the Divorce Negotiator scheme developed by Carol Sullivan over the last three years, where following her own difficult and costly divorce, she decided that there must be a better way through the process.[9] She had practised as a family solicitor, but withdrew from the regulated profession in order to be free to advise the two separating clients together, and she uses mediation techniques to help them move towards settlement. She is able, unlike a formal mediator, to draft consent orders, though not to represent parties in court. In order to do what needs to be done, she left her profession but retained her skills.

Our proposal for a unified, one stop service in this jurisdiction is similar to the Dutch system explained above. We argue that it should be possible for a suitably qualified lawyer to accept two parties contemplating separation, but seeking agreement, as joint clients, and accordingly to advise them jointly in drawing up a separation agreement, should the clients desire this. The prospect of parties drawing up marital agreements with the assistance of a single lawyer is familiar in European countries where the emphasis is upon ensuring that a notary should not see the parties separately, but together. Indeed, in such cases the notaries 'have to explore the intentions of the parties and the facts of the case and have, accordingly, to instruct the parties about their rights and duties' (See Dutta 2012: 172, for Germany; Pintens 2012: 79, for Belgium). By contrast, in England, it has been said that when a pre-nuptial contract is signed 'it is usually without ceremony, but symbolically sees the couple coming together after being with their separate legal teams' (Vardag and Miles 2015: 137–38). The position in Italy regarding separation agreements has been explained as follows:

A consensual separation (*separazione consensuale*) can be reached if the spouses agree, by and large, at least on: getting separated (obviously), assets splitting, and

---

[9] See www.divorcenegotiator.org.uk/about/ (accessed 7 August 2015).

custody and maintenance of children. In this case, they can go to the same lawyer and give him/her power of attorney to represent them in court. Then the lawyer will go into more details and advise the couple on the best legal way to get what they both want. Finally, he/she will draw up a legal agreement on the 'separation conditions' and submit it for judge's approval (so-called *omologa*). After a hearing in court, where the judge will try to reconcile the couple, if he/she holds the conditions of the agreement fair and balanced, separation is granted.

Of course, sometimes spouses cannot reach an agreement on their own, although they would like to or maybe they thought they did and went to the same lawyer for a legal draft, but then realised that they actually did not agree on every single condition. In these cases, the same lawyer can and will, in fact, try to reach a (more) suitable agreement for both parties. There is no doubt that, in doing so, the lawyer will give legal advice. I would argue that this is necessary because the agreement has to hold up in court. If he/she succeeds in getting the spouses to agree on the conditions of their separation, the proceeding will fall into the same category as before.

If the lawyer sees that a consensual separation is not an option, he/she will advise the couple to seek separate legal counsel. The lawyer may or may not retain one of the spouses as a client and represent him/her in the contentious separation proceeding that is about to start'.[10]

But, as our evidence shows that facilitating agreement between two persons who are present together can be a demanding process that requires special skills and training, we suggest that if lawyers were to be permitted to accept two potentially conflicted parties as joint clients, the conditions under which this was undertaken would need to be carefully considered and mediation training provided. So we believe that a lawyer who accepts joint clients in this context would need to have undergone the same mediation accreditation processes as presently apply to family mediators, for, while some cases may appear to be relatively straightforward and amicable, requiring information and advice, the fact that the parties are contemplating separation, or have separated, means that the dispute resolution skills of mediation could become relevant at any time.

We do not think that this service should be provided only by practising lawyers. It should be open to non-lawyer mediators as well, but just as the lawyers should have undertaken mediation training, non-lawyer mediators would need to have undertaken specially focused legal training in order to be able to openly offer good-quality legal advice in the course of the mediation, not covering all aspects of law but only those necessary for this area of work, rather as licensed conveyancers were trained for their specific area of activity following the ending of the solicitors' monopoly of conveyancing.

They could do this since this is not a 'reserved legal activity' which is confined to persons authorised for this purpose under the Legal Services

---

[10] We are grateful to Giovanni Cinà, *avvocato*, for this information.

Act 2007.[11] For convenience, we call this 'legally assisted family mediation'. If legally assisted family mediation fails, the lawyer mediator involved would not be permitted to act as a legal representative for either of the parties, who would need to seek their own separate legal adviser, who may or may not be trained for legally assisted family mediation.

Under this proposal, the conditions for a lawyer to accept joint clients should be essentially the same as those which currently apply if the lawyer acts as a mediator. That is, there should be no domestic abuse, or undue imbalance of power, and information should be openly shared. If these conditions are not met, the couple would not be suitable for legally assisted family mediation. Barlow et al (2014: 32) recommend that MIAMs (which are focused on, and frequently seek to promote, mediation) should be replaced by DRIAMs (dispute resolution information and assessment meetings), to widen the options under consideration. To guard against bias, they suggest they be provided 'independently of dispute resolution services', and should be free. While this would be attractive in an ideal world, our suggestion is more modest. Just as at present a mediation should be preceded by a MIAM, acceptance of joint clients for legally assisted family mediation should be preceded by an meeting in which the lawyer both assesses the parties' suitability for being accepted as joint clients (including screening for violence) and explores other options, some of which are discussed in the next section of this chapter. Many lawyers already hold an 'options' meeting with potential new clients to discuss what kind of service is appropriate. But another step towards joint client work was observed in an innovative legal practice, where a lawyer mediator runs a joint Choosing Options Together (COTS) session, charging £200 an hour for both clients. This process should be encouraged and enhanced, aided perhaps by a better appreciation of the range of options available. If legally assisted family mediation were to be chosen, a further important step would need to be taken involving a judgment whether the parties have sufficiently common interests and willingness to move forward that agreement between them is a realistic possibility. This assessment stage is already an important element in a MIAM. Should the assessment be negative, neither the lawyer mediator making the assessment nor anyone in that person's firm should be able to take on either party as an individual client.

We see this as a new option which could be provided by lawyer mediators who would either be lawyers with mediation training or mediators with appropriate legal training. Our proposal would simply entail removing two current *restrictions*, namely, the assumption that practising lawyers cannot advise two parties jointly, as discussed above, and, secondly, the specific prohibitions in the mediation codes against a mediator offering advice. In place of that the mediator in legally assisted family mediation should be

---

[11] Legal Services Act 2007, ss 12, 13.

permitted or encouraged to offer an opinion on the effects of any matter under discussion on the interests of either participant, and *required* to do so with regards to the interests of any children.

Once again, our evidence suggests that it is difficult to maintain the present distinction between offering information and advice, which we think serves little purpose other than to maintain an artificial distinction between acting as a mediator and acting as a lawyer. This distinction would disappear if the two practices were brought closer together in the way we suggest. Of course neither participant would be obliged to follow the mediator's opinion, and they should be told that is the case, and of their freedom to consult an independent lawyer, tax expert, child welfare adviser or any other source of professional help should they so wish. But this is no different from the current position between lawyer and client. The lawyer currently openly gives advice and takes instructions, while the mediator may only cautiously approach giving advice or an opinion, but in either situation the clients can ignore, accept or reject whatever is offered. It is only in arbitration where the parties choose to agree to accept the view of the decision maker, and in adjudication where they are bound to do so.

Legally assisted family mediation would not replace either negotiation between lawyers or mediation as currently practised. There is therefore no reason why forms of mediation, such as the 'transformative', or those which we have called 'purist', should not continue to be available in those cases where it is appropriate. However, we believe that it would be beneficial if the Resolution and FMC Codes were modified by the insertion of the italicised words as follows, at least if the mediation is given state support, whether by funding or otherwise:

> Family mediation is a process in which those whose relationship is ending or has ended, regardless of whether they are a couple or other family members, appoint an impartial third person to assist them to communicate better with one another and to reach their own agreed and informed decisions concerning some or all of the issues relating to their separation, divorce, children, finance or property by negotiation *within the principles of the law*. (Resolution Guide to Good Practice on Mediation 2015: 9)

> Mediation aims to assist participants to reach the decisions they consider appropriate to their own particular circumstances *within the principles of the law*. (FMC Code: 2.1).

There was much concern when arbitration or mediation by religious bodies was under discussion that the state should not be supporting processes that resolved family issues according to norms that departed from those of the wider community (Malik 2014; Eekelaar 2015). It therefore seems reasonable to expect that if mediation aims to reach a specific outcome (rather than being confined, say, to improving communication between the participants), that the outcome should be consistent with the principles of the civil law.

This addition would require non legally qualified family mediators to demonstrate training in the basic principles of family law.

In legally assisted family mediation, therefore, the mediator would not be 'neutral' as understood in the current model for family mediation, as the outcome sought would fall within the concern of the mediator. But, as we indicated earlier,[12] the mediator can, and should, remain impartial as between the participants. In our view, the modifications suggested in any case make explicit what often presently occurs in mediation, but in a hidden and inconsistent way, which Myers and Wasoff (20011: 5) call 'opaque'. For example, one of the most important principles of the law is that the welfare of the child should be paramount. We referred earlier[13] to the comment by the Family Justice Review that 'all mediation should be centred on the best interests of the child' and noted that suggestions about hearing the child have the potential to oblige a mediator to steer the parties towards an agreement informed by an assessment of the child's interests made in the context of the child's views, especially in the light of the 'responsibility in regard to the welfare of any child of the family' placed on the mediator by Resolution's Guide (2015: 14–15). It would therefore be appropriate to acknowledge that this introduces what is an important principle of law into the conduct of mediation. But that is not the only principle of law that is relevant. The statement in Resolution's Guide (2015: 11) that mediators *have a responsibility* … to inform clients if they consider that the outcome/s they are considering might or would fall outside that which a court might approve or order' suggests that the preferred outcome is an agreement that complies with legal principles.

The final major matters for attention in any move towards integration would revolve around the termination of the mediation. Apart from termination when agreement has been reached, the occasions for termination would be the same as presently set out in Resolution's Guide (2015: 33–34) which include the presence of a power imbalance that cannot be addressed, or if either party lacks capacity to negotiate to reach a 'workable, fair and reasonable outcome', or where there are safeguarding issues concerning children, or deliberate failure to disclose financial information, or where the participants simply cannot make progress. These could be seen as specific instances when there is insufficient commonality of interests to allow joint advice. Apart from such circumstances, which should already terminate mediation under current guidance, the mediator should accept the participants' agreement, as now, even if he or she has earlier expressed an opinion that the agreement, or aspects of it, are not in the interests of either or both of the participants, and draft an MOU on this basis. As regards children, the mediator should accept that the participants may have a different view from the mediator's expressed opinion on the matter, but should be alert to the

[12] Above, p 87.
[13] Chapter 4.

possible need to take steps under safeguarding procedures if they consider that the parents are not acting in the best interests of the children. Also, the mediator could decline to translate the agreement into a Consent Order (which the mediator, if a lawyer, or legally uplifted mediator should be able to draw up) if the mediator considered that any aspect of it was inappropriate for that purpose.

As intimated above, we are proposing legally assisted family mediation as a form of one-stop mediation with legal uplift, whether the mediation is carried out by lawyer or non-lawyer mediators. But there is no reason why mediation should not continue to be provided as it is at present. Mediators who are not lawyers might wish to do this for a number of reasons, from a wish to concentrate in the private sector on therapeutic aspects of mediation to concern that their present insurance indemnity policies would not cover them if they were to accept that they could give legal advice. If this occurred, there would be (at least) two forms of mediation on offer. Clients would choose which was more attractive for them. Legally assisted family mediation might save costs as the participants would have less need to seek additional legal advice from their own lawyers, or for drawing up a Consent Order (whose terms the mediator could discuss directly with both participants).

At present it seems clear that a Consent Order cannot be drawn up by a mediator (even if a lawyer) because this would involve giving 'some form of advice', and thereby breach the FMC Code (Resolution Guide to Good Practice on Mediation 2015: 45).[14] That would change under our proposal for legally assisted family mediation because the lawyer (or legally trained) mediator would be able to give advice to both participants. There might be concern that such a Consent Order, on which the parties had not received independent legal advice, would be less likely to be accepted by a judge, and more vulnerable to challenge even after made by a court.

As regards the readiness of a judge to accept the terms of a draft Consent Order, the reason why judges do not scrutinise them in detail was expressed by Ward LJ in this way in *Harris v Manahan*:[15]

> The statutory duty on the court cannot be ducked, but the court is entitled to assume that parties who are sui juris and who are represented by solicitors know what they want. Officious enquiry may uncover an injustice but it is more likely to disturb a delicate negotiation and produce the very costly litigation and the recrimination which conciliation is designed to avoid.

---

[14] In August 2015 the Solicitors Regulation Authority intimated that a solicitor could draw up a Consent Order for both parties on a joint retainer, but without giving advice, and only if satisfied that various conditions had been met such as absence of undue influence, duress or imbalance of power, or vulnerability, which might be difficult for a lawyer who had not conducted the mediation to assess: www.sra.org.uk/solicitors/code-of-conduct/guidance/questionofethics/August-2015.page.

[15] [1996] EWCA Civ J0524–8; [1997] 1 FLR 205.

It has also been said that 'formal agreements, properly and fairly arrived at with competent legal advice, should not be displaced unless there are good and substantial grounds for concluding that an injustice will be done by holding the parties to the terms of their agreement'.[16] The reference to representation by *solicitors* (in the plural) reflects the current standard practice, and should not be taken to rule out the possibility that a party's voluntary participation in legally assisted family mediation and agreement to an outcome in the light of legal advice given to the parties jointly by one lawyer as proposed here would not equally be grounds for considerable restraint by a court in reviewing the agreed outcome. Similarly, having strongly emphasised the policy objectives of restraining litigation, particularly in family cases, Ward LJ proclaimed that Consent Orders, once made, should be capable of challenge on the basis of bad legal advice only in the rarest cases (causing the 'cruellest' injustice). If that is the view taken about bad legal advice, there seems to be little reason to challenge a Consent Order on the ground only that legal advice had been given to both parties jointly. In any event, since those using this process would need to be inclined to co-operation, they would be less likely to adopt combative methods later (though of course this could happen). Where parties are initially heavily conflicted, they should have separate representation throughout.

IV. AN ADR CONTINUUM

ADR is usually seen as standing for 'alternative dispute resolution', where the resolution processes are seen as being alternative to 'adversarial' ones. But King et al (2009), writing within the Australian context, rejected sharp dichotomies between adversarial (where the parties control the issues to be addressed and the evidence to be considered) and inquisitorial justice (where the judge plays a more active role) (Ibid: 5) or between court-based litigation, where adjudication by a third party is envisaged (seen as 'adversarial') and ADR, where the parties retain control of decision making (seen as 'non-adversarial') (Ibid: 101). They noted (Ibid: 94–95) that ADR tends to be either roundly praised or, conversely, criticised, for example as being 'second-class' justice (Tyler 1988–89) or as promoting a 'harmony ideology' that conceals much coercion (Nader 1993). They therefore sought to develop the idea of 'non-adversarialism', which is not the opposite of

---

[16] *Edgar v Edgar*[1980] 1 WLR 1410 (Ormrod LJ). This approach is likely to be reinforced after the decision of the Supreme Court in *Radmacher v Granatino* [2010] UKSC 42, which applied a similar approach to pre-nuptial and post-nuptial agreements, since separation agreements are a species of post-nuptial agreement. See Miles (2012); Scherpe (2012: 512–13). Scherpe (Ibid: 494) suggests that the requirements regarding independent legal advice in upholding marital agreements may have weakened after *Radmacher*, becoming just one factor in determining what is fair.

rsarialism, but forms part of a continuum, 'a sliding scale upon which ous legal processes sit, with most processes combining aspects of adversarial and non-adversarial practice to varying degrees' (King et al: 5). Since 'alternative' suggested processes that were opposed to or supplementary to 'adversarial' processes, the view that most processes combine elements of adversarial practice suggested that ADR might be better understood as referring to 'appropriate dispute resolution' to emphasise that focus should be upon the best process for the issue in hand (Ibid: 89). King et al saw non-adversarial justice as an approach that focuses on non-court dispute resolution, aimed at prevention rather than post-conflict solutions, and which itself divides into 'hard non-adversarialism' (involving paternalistic judicial management) and 'soft non-adversarialism' with more party control but with emphasis on compromise (Ibid: 6). They pointed out that 94 per cent of applications to the Family Court of Australia in 2001–02 were resolved without judicial determination, and described a movement away from a dispute-resolution court system, towards a problem-solving justice system which is more comprehensive and preventive and much wider than the court process itself, with ADR playing an important part. They explained how, in Australia, as elsewhere, after a period of messianic enthusiasm, then a sceptical reaction, ADR services were slowly moving towards 'professionalisation and standardisation' (Ibid: 96–97, 121). But this is not easy, as our account of the process in respect to mediation in England and Wales testifies.[17] They identified four kinds of ADR—facilitative: with practitioners providing a process for parties to resolve their issue (for example mediation and negotiation); advisory (conciliation and expert appraisal); determinative (arbitration and private judging) and hybrid (where the practitioner combines a variety of roles) (Ibid: 89–90).

Australia was one of the first jurisdictions to adopt a facilitative approach to family dispute resolution, requiring attendance at a non-legal dispute resolution service before going to a court. But already there are hybrid elements. If we look at the relationship between legal and mediation work in Australia, signs of the kind of convergence or at least rapprochement between lawyers and family dispute practitioners we have raised can already be seen. The 65 original Family Relationship Centres, where attendance is mandatory for parental disputes before using the court, with some exceptions, began by excluding legal services from their work, as part of the attempt to move away from a culture of litigation towards more co-operative post-separation shared parenting. But lawyers and courts are now accepted as part of the range of services needed by families. The Coordinated Family Dispute Resolution Service offers early access to publicly funded legal help to parents with issues of violence or abuse (see Moloney et al 2011). Similarly in New Zealand, outside specific circumstances (for example, where the application

---

[17] See chapter 4.

is by consent, or in cases of violence and abuse) mediation is required before filing an application on a parenting issue to the family courts unless a 'family dispute resolution form' is filed (for example, where mediation has been abandoned or the dispute completely resolved). The costs will fall on the parties unless tight legal aid conditions are met. Although not in the legislation, concerns about lack of legal advice led the government to introduce a scheme allowing four hours' legal advice for those who meet the strict criteria of legal aid, which could cover advice during and after mediation, or even the identification of a right to proceed to court without mediation, as in cases of domestic violence. The legislation is silent about the attendance of lawyers at the mediation. If a dispute does proceed to court, judges have the option to order fully subsidised counselling if they believe this will help the parties, but this is expected to be rare (see Atkin 2015; Family Mediation Task Force 2014: 36).

Even where facilitative models are given strong government support, the part which courts play in these processes can vary considerably between jurisdictions, and also how mediation sits within a system, who provides it, who uses it, how users are directed to it. And outcome measures remain elusive.[18] A key element in governmental assessment of the effectiveness of ADR in the UK is reduction in the level of court use in family matters. International comparisons are often made, but these can be misleading if there is no consideration of the way the court is used in different settings.[19] In England and Wales people do not usually attend court for the actual divorce process, but only apply for hearings on matters of finance or parenting which either cannot be resolved, or have been resolved but the parties need assurance of enforceability through a Consent Order. All applicants to court must go to a MIAM to be told about mediation and assessed for suitability. The court welfare service, CAFCASS, will screen applications concerning children for any safeguarding issues. In some other jurisdictions one or both of the parties or their lawyers must attend court for the divorce process even where there is agreement.

But courts may also be used for triage to appropriate support services as well as dispute resolution through both court orders and voluntary mediation. For example in Germany, representation by a lawyer is compulsory, though where divorce is by consent, one lawyer may represent the parties jointly. The actual court proceedings can be preceded by a mediation session at the court (Martiny 2002). Following the reforms of 1998, the court, run by the Land, is not seen as the place which tells parents what to do

---

[18] See Dr Tern Geurts, Ministry of Security and Justice, The Hague, 'The Impact of Mediation', Paper given at The Hague International Meeting on High Conflict Divorce, May 2015, where 1,000 papers on impact were studied but found only 13 published evaluation studies to be of value, and the only randomised controlled trial study in the US reported less parental conflict and less use of court after mediation but no impact on the welfare of the children.

[19] See, eg, Family Mediation Task Force (2014: 35, Annex C).

when they have parenting problems, and it is not focused on quick decision making but instead facilitates access to long-term support by working with the Youth Advisory Service run by the municipality. This offers easy access to a range of support services, and its officers attend court and speak to families with the goal of making gradual progress. There is a constitutional right to advice from welfare officers on visitation, and to protected visitation in high conflict cases. In Germany, reducing court use is not a policy aim, and it is estimated that this way of using the court to gradually lower tension may be more cost-effective than attempting rapid decision making on complex matters. Mediation is available as one of many helping services, and it is used for specific disputes, but not for providing the longer-term help which is often needed by families with problems. The court is the 'hub' for access to help, not just for dispute resolution.[20]

In France, everyone attends court for their divorce with their lawyer, but often for less than 20 minutes (Bastard et al 2015; Biland et al 2005). Mediation is not widely used even though it is a highly qualified profession, with two years' training (in the UK basic training for mediators takes nine days) but demand has remained low. The government prepared legislation to enable judges to send couples to two sessions of mediation without their consent, but the draft law was withdrawn in the face of widespread opposition from many quarters.[21] In Belgium, short-term court-ordered mediation by agreement is used when necessary, but in 2013 the Amicable Settlement in Court procedure was set up by which a magistrate can require parties to meet with him or her to work on reaching agreement which will be given legal certainty. The process is free, legally aided, and if agreement is not reached, the parties come back to court but see a different judge.[22] New court-centred developments are not confined to Europe. In Nova Scotia the judge can hold binding a Binding Settlement Conference attended by parties and their lawyers before a hearing begins, where the judge can lead the parties to an agreement which then becomes binding. A court hearing is avoided, but the judge has acted almost as in the English FDR proceedings.[23] In California, where mediation on children issues is mandatory, the family

---

[20] Dr Thomas Meysen, 'The German approach in family court proceedings and the interplay to support services by the child and youth welfare system', *High Conflict Divorces, Mediation and active interventions from an international perspective* (Ministry of Security and Justice, The Hague, May 2015).

[21] See Proposition de Loi relative à l'autorité parentale et à l'intérêt de l'enfant, Art 17: www.assemblee-nationale.fr/14/propositions/pion1856.asp and discussion by Benoit Bastard: www.huffingtonpost.fr./benoit-bastard/mediations-familiales-divorce_b_5252500.html (accessed 6 October 2015).

[22] Dr Patrick Senaeve, 'The origins of family courts in Belgium and the in court mediation', *High Conflict Divorces, Mediation and active interventions from an international perspective* (Ministry of Security and Justice, The Hague, May 2015).

[23] Lecture by Justice J Williams, Supreme Court of Nova Scotia, Westminster University, 30 April 2015.

courts provide this free and the agreements reached have the status of a court order when signed by a judge.[24] Alternatively, parties with the necessary resources may buy the services of a private judge registered to adjudicate and the order carries the weight of any other court order.[25] In these American and Canadian examples the court remains central, but seeks to avoid contested hearings. In a growing number of jurisdictions in South America and Eastern Europe notaries can grant divorces in uncontested cases as well as act as mediators and arbitrators, although there have been concerns that they may lack the necessary skills to deal with conflicted parties (Kennett 2016, citing Lesseliers 2012).

Mandatory universal mediation for those considering coming to court is increasingly discussed as a policy option, even where mediation can be court ordered and takes place after a hearing. In the Netherlands political pressure for universal mandatory mediation arose after a particularly distressing recent case (Zeist) where a couple had prepared a parenting plan, were not currently in litigation and there was no reason to expect any problems with their shared parenting. The father's arrangements were later changed by the judge and there was a delay in letting him know. He became very distressed, took the children and killed them. Experts in the Netherlands have resisted the mandatory mediation proposal following the failure of mandatory parenting agreements as part of the divorce process to reduce conflict, and also because of the belief that universal provision is rarely necessary or cost-effective. But there is also a development described earlier with lawyers with mediation training joining together in the organisation vFAS. Serious concerns have been expressed over the way evidence of domestic violence is dealt with in mandatory mediation in California (Johnson, Saccuzzo and Koen 2005) and regarding the cost-effectiveness of adding mandatory mediation to the court process (Salem et al 2007; Salem 2009).

In jurisdictions where court use is low, it is not necessarily as a result of the use of mediation but because parenting problems after divorce are seen as child welfare issues, not part of a legal dispute between adults. Child welfare services do the necessary work, and court involvement is minimal. In Scandinavia[26] courts are little used for family matters generally. For example, in Norway 'ordinary' separations do not go near a court, and the mandatory use of pre-court mediation is being reconsidered on the basis that is not value for money. Arrangements for children can be discussed with the welfare authorities who provide a certificate which entitles parents to various forms of support, and the arrangements made can be enforced by a court.

---

[24] See www.courts.ca.gov/1189.htm#acc11728 (accessed 3 August 2015).

[25] Kennett (2016).

[26] Vaula Haavisto, 'The Fasper Project in Finland'; Professor Odd Arne Tjersland, 'Experiences with separating parents in Norway'; Thea Totland, 'The Norwegian legal system including mediation and enforcement', *High Conflict Divorces, Mediation and active interventions from an international perspective* (Ministry of Security and Justice, The Hague, May 2015).

But Tjersland's research found that 40 per cent of those using it did not need conflict resolution, 40 per cent needed advice and received it, and the last 20 per cent stalled and left without agreement. There are also concerns that mediation services concentrate on short-term issues and fail to deal with long-term family problems. In Sweden there are no specialist family courts, but where problems arise a form of mediation known as 'co-operation conversations' is held with a social worker to address parenting problems (Ryrsted 2009). Here there are concerns about the pressure on parents to reach agreement, and a tendency to focus on parental issues rather than children's needs (Ryrstedt 2012). In Scandinavia divorce is less problematised, as financial matters are more open and equal, tax returns are in the public domain, and parents tend to share childcare while living together or apart. So parenting difficulties are the central concern and are seen as an indication that a family has problems, not just a dispute. A similar approach is taken in Finland where parents have autonomy over the arrangements regarding children but can go to the welfare authorities and prepare a written agreement which the courts can enforce. But the children's officers are so overburdened that parents are going straight to court to avoid long delays. If agreement is not reached the judge will co-mediate with a child welfare expert, but there are concerns about the cost of involving welfare authorities in addition to the legal framework.

In England and Wales the slow convergence which we observed and endorse between mediation and legal practice raises many new questions where this kind of international information may be helpful in considering where mediation (in whatever form, voluntary or mandatory, in or outside court, publicly funded or privately paid, with or without a close relationship to child welfare services) might be best placed on the ADR continuum. But mediation not only sits alongside negotiation by lawyers and facilitation by judges, but also alongside other forms of private ordering, including arbitration and 'neutral evaluation', as well as the therapeutic transformative models of mediation and counselling. How will potential users who currently have difficulty in understanding what mediation has to offer cope with these variants?

Lucinda Ferguson (2013) has suggested an alternative image to that of the continuum or 'sliding scale', namely, that of intersecting circles, 'most significant where distinctive, ie where not overlapping'. She points out that many of the methods contain variable mixes of similar elements, for example, state involvement and personal choice, and it could be misleading to suggest that a coherent method of grading can be adopted. In particular, she observes (Ibid: 120) that 'instead of starting with pre-determined categories of dispute resolution and then looking to their content and variation therein, it might be more profitable to start by observing disputing couples and their engagement with dispute resolution. We could then examine those activities to consider what categories of resolution process emerge.' Our observations have indeed suggested that *a priori* categorisation can be disturbed by empirical evidence. Ferguson's model caters better than a continuum for the overlaps between the various processes, and we suggest the following sequence, which reflects *roughly* a diminishing degree of third-party input into (or increasing degree of party control over, and private ordering with respect to) the final outcome, simply for ease of presentation, but accepting that elements can overlap.[27] The Report of the Family Mediation Task Force (2014: 22) uses a diagram which sets out the value of the different services according to cost to individuals, opportunity to solve problems and highest allocation of funding, aiming at the provision of information and parenting plans for all, triage and allocation to dispute resolution services and SPIPs for half, supported dispute resolution and other support for 30 per cent and judicial decision making for 5 per cent.

Our full sliding scale of modes by which problems encountered by parties who are or have separated are dealt with comprises: 1. Adjudication[28] by a court with full representation; 2. Adjudication by court without representation as a LIP; 3. Facilitation by a court in an attempt to avoid adjudication; 4. Neutral evaluation at court but not as part of proceedings intended for adjudication (for example, FDR hearings); 5. Arbitration outside court; 6. Arbitration after mediation (Medarb);[29] 7. Early neutral evaluation or FDR arranged privately; 8. Legally assisted one stop family mediation (see note 29) under our proposal; 9. Lawyer-led negotiation (the 'full legal'); 10. Lawyer-led negotiation (unbundled); 11. 'Managed' divorce via the internet; 12. Mediation (see note 29) under the 'purist' non-legal model; 13. Private negotiation with internet-based legal information; 14. Private negotiation with other professional advice, such as financial advisers; 15. Private negotiation without professional advice ('kitchen table' agreements).

The first two (1) and (2) are the categories to which the rest are usually seen as 'alternatives'. The third (3), facilitation by a court, stands between adjudication and non-adjudication. It occurs in the context of court proceedings that could result in adjudication, but where the judge assists the parties

---

[27] Another characterisation is to see the 'scale' as showing a movement from strong focus on outcomes towards emphasis on the parties' behaviour, such as reaching agreement, improved communication and simply putting up with however things turned out: see Eekelaar and Maclean (2013: 15–23).

[28] Adjudication may be divided into processes that are inquisitorial and those that are adversarial, although many processes contain elements of each style, and that which occurs solely on the basis of evidence presented in court, or that which occurs after the court has received a report by a court-appointed (expert) official, who has conducted an independent investigation, for example (in England and Wales) by CAFCASS. In Sweden in the case of a financial dispute the (non-specialist) court may appoint a 'marital division officer' who is a local lawyer to provide a decision which would be enforceable but appealable: see Maclean, Wasoff, Hunter, Ferguson, Bastard and Ryrstedt (2011: 335).

[29] The 'mediation' categories could be further divided into cases where mediation is compulsory (whether through court order or otherwise) and where it is not and whether the mediation agreement becomes a court order or not, free or paid for.

to settle so that adjudication can be avoided. Hence the authority of the judge is a significant factor in achieving an agreed outcome. We described the process in detail in *Family Justice*, giving examples, and observing that 'by facilitating agreement, the judge guides the parties towards the outcome envisaged by the law, exercising judgment as to how much latitude the parties should have in fashioning their own solutions' (Eekelaar and Maclean 2013: 98). In (4), prior to the hearing of any financial dispute, the parties may be required to attend FDR proceedings before a judge with the express aim of reaching agreement. This outcome is frequently assisted by the judge giving an indication of how he or she would decide the issues in dispute. If agreement is not reached, directions will be needed for preparing for an adjudicated hearing before another judge.[30] The Belgian Amicable Settlements Scheme and the Nova Scotia Bindings Settlement Conferences referred to earlier are variants.

Arbitration (5) has long been widely used in commercial matters, and has developed into a major form of dispute resolution, especially at international level. It has considerable benefits for disputants, including the ability to choose the arbitrator, the location of the proceedings, to some extent the law to be applied, privacy and speed. It does not necessarily come cheap. Lawyers are usually present. It is governed by contractual principles according to which the parties enter into an arbitration agreement under which they select an individual before whom they will present their respective arguments regarding their dispute, define the issues to be addressed, and agree to be bound by the arbitrator's decision, which, if necessary, a court will enforce. The use of this form of dispute resolution in family law was given a boost in England and Wales by the launch of a family law arbitration scheme by the Institute of Family Law Arbitrators (IFLA) in 2012 (see Ferguson 2013), confined to financial and property issues but the arbitrators are expecting to be able to gradually extend their work to children issues.[31] The IFLA arbitrators must have practised for eight years, and have two days' training, or be retired judges. International family arbitration could be attractive for English lawyers if their decisions are enforced abroad under the New York Convention on the Recognition and Enforcement of Foreign Arbitral Awards 1958. It seems to be assumed that domestic arbitral awards in the IFLA scheme are binding, and will therefore be enforced as a court order on application to the court under section 66 of the Arbitration Act 1996.[32] However Ferguson (2013: 128–31) points out that in family law cases the judiciary retains a discretion whether or not to enforce an award in

---

[30] For a useful description, see Family Justice Council (2012).

[31] Although there is no technical bar to doing this the arbitrators are currently working on ways of making the process clear and acceptable before going ahead.

[32] The grounds for challenging the award are restricted to 'serious irregularity affecting the tribunal, the proceedings or the award': Arbitration Act 1996, s 68(1).

the light of its compliance with family law principles and that it is therefore misleading to suggest that arbitration awards in such cases are 'binding'.[33] Surveying the use of arbitration in family matters in a wide range of jurisdictions, Kennett (2016) observes that the 'commercial' model is usually modified for the following reasons: an imbalance of power; the fact that the parties are not repeat players and so are less familiar with the system and dispute resolution methods than commercial parties the involvement of third parties—in particular children; the state's interest in families and the existence of significant mandatory regulation; and the fact that marriage is a special type of contract—notably because of its length and the fact that it can be expected to pass through many vicissitudes.

While the IFLA has clear rules, it is perhaps not surprising in a setting so clearly concerned with private ordering that there should be much variation in practice. The IFLA rule 1.4 states that its rules should not be subject to alteration or amendment without the consent of the parties and the arbitrator, but the default position would then be that they can be changed with that agreement, except for any such change which would be contrary to current law. This opens the way to changing the definition of issues to be included, the processes to be followed and even the binding nature of the award. This follows from the contractual basis of the process, which is subject to little if any supervision or screening for power imbalances. Indeed, in one case described to us, the barristers for both parties negotiated all day as they would have done in court, and reached an agreement which the arbitrator who had taken no part in the negotiations proclaimed as the arbitral award. Perhaps it is considered sufficient protection that in these cases the parties are usually separately legally presented.

The use of arbitration by 'religious' tribunals has raised a separate set of concerns, for, while the jurisdiction of arbitrators rests on the agreement of parties who are separately represented, this could be problematic in a religious context, and the adjudication may involve the application of religious laws that are inconsistent with the principles of the civil law. Ontario has famously legislated that arbitrators must apply Canadian law, which is clearly a restriction on the scope of private agreement, and even without such a constraint it is questionable whether English courts would enforce arbitral awards that were seen to violate fundamental principles of justice.[34] A variant of arbitration, or of adjudication, occurs if parties are allowed, as in California,[35] to select (and pay) their own judge (usually a specially

[33] Ferguson (2013) also draws attention to the implications for understanding the norms that govern the outcomes of family breakdown if their resolution by arbitration, which is a private process, becomes normal.
[34] See the debate concerning the Arbitration and Mediation Services (Equality) Bill 2011, discussed in Eekelaar (2011); Eekelaar (2012); Bano (2015).
[35] See www.crinfo.org/coreknowledge/private-judging (accessed 1 May 2015). These options are fully discussed in Kennett (2016).

authorised retired member of the Bench) who is enabled to deliver a judgment enforceable as any other court judgment. Arbitration (6) with mediation envisages that the participants to a mediation agree that, should they fail to reach agreement, the mediator may make a determination, which they will implement, and which might be enforced by a court. The effect of the mediator transforming into an arbitrator (which is a form of adjudication) on the mediation process needs careful consideration. It is perhaps hard to see why someone would readily enter a form of negotiation process in which they agreed in advance to accept a decision with which they disagreed.

In some US jurisdictions which compel mediation in disputes over children, the mediation is carried out by a 'Child custody recommending counselor', not a lawyer but a professional who combines expertise in psychology and law, who will make a recommendation on matters not resolved by the mediation. Since this does not depend on the parties' prior agreement (because the mediation is mandatory), and as recommendations are frequently adopted by the courts,[36] this almost amounts to an adjudication, thus illustrating the advantages of Ferguson's image of these processes in terms of overlapping circles. Nancy Johnson et al (2005) have warned of the dangers of combining a power to make recommendations with mediation in cases with evidence of domestic violence. Their study showed that in many cases recommendations were made which paid insufficient attention to the evidence of violence.

Early neutral evaluation (ENE) (7) occurs when the disputants pay for a selected individual to hear their respective positions and give an opinion about the merits. The parties are not bound to follow it, and the opinion has no standing in any subsequent court proceedings. It can, however, form the basis for further negotiation between the parties.[37] The process is largely unregulated, but parties tend to approach a senior barrister, seeking his view of what various judges would be likely to decide in their case. Their up-to-date experience is their selling point.

The evidence and analysis of this book has led us to propose developing a stronger, stand-alone form of mediation combining law-based negotiating skills with mediation for dealing with separation disputes in a cost-effective way leading to fair and informed settlement: that is, method 8 on the continuum. But this must be seen together with methods 9–13. We have observed that they share many elements. These, and the other processes that constitute the 'spectrum', or 'intersecting circles', offer people who are experiencing difficulties in a separation a wide range of options from which to choose what is most suitable for their circumstances. However, as Diduck (2014: 619) observes, their freedom to choose is seriously undermined if government policy, whether described as neo-liberalism or marketisation, creates

---

[36] See Johnson, Saccuzzo and Koen (2005).
[37] See www.cedr.com/solve/ene/ (accessed 1 May 2015).

obstacles hindering access to some of them, for example, by permitting (limited) legal aid only for mediation (of a certain type) and not for other forms of assistance.

V. FINALLY—LEGAL AID

Traditionally the purpose of family justice was held to be protecting those made vulnerable by the process of family breakdown. This gradually developed into a policy of promoting 'fair and informed settlement'. But fairness and being informed do not occur naturally: they depend on social conditions and actions. Since LASPO one route for achieving those objectives has been virtually closed for a large section of the population. This book has examined the alternatives that have been emerging. They are not without promise. But their growth has been haphazard, almost chaotic, and the quality often unknown. It is not even clear that some of the measures are cost-effective. As the National Audit Office intimated, the Ministry of Justice may have saved money under one heading, but has no idea of the costs building up elsewhere.[38] We think it is likely that the convoluted method of the public funding of mediation, with its intricate relationship with the provision of legal advice, might well generate more costs than are necessary in order to achieve the same level of service provision, and at the same time fail adequately either to protect the vulnerable or support fair and informed settlement.

This book has focused primarily on the nature and mechanisms of the services for separating families. It has not examined the legal aid system as a whole, although legal aid policy has had a profound effect on those services. Our proposal for legally assisted family mediation, too, has implications for the provision of legal aid in this context. By calling the process 'mediation' it might seem to qualify for legal aid since 'mediation provided in relation to family disputes' and 'civil legal services provided in connection with the mediation of family disputes' are within scope of the scheme.[39] Yet this is possible only if the subject matter is a 'legal dispute'[40] and (as is commonly understood) no legal advice is offered in respect of that dispute. Our proposal challenges this bizarre situation by suggesting that the mediator, if properly qualified, could offer legal advice, and also that a 'dispute' in the strict sense need not necessarily be present. Yet we think legal aid should be available for legally assisted family mediation. Indeed, costs could be saved by concentrating the service in a single provider rather than, as at present, potentially using three (two lawyers and a mediator).

---

[38] See above p 19.
[39] LASPO, Schedule 1, para 14(1).
[40] The LAA's *Family Mediation Guidance Manual* version 4.0, March 2015: para 2.2.

One could imagine that government might be willing to make legal aid available for this process as a means of encouraging this mode of reaching settlement. But if it did so, it would become hard to justify withholding it from an individual who sought legal advice on a family issue as a single client, especially if the other party refuses to attempt to reach a settlement. It is not for us to try to settle the parameters of the legal aid scheme, though it will be clear from our remarks in chapter 1 regarding the justifications given for limiting the scope of the scheme in family cases[41] that we do not think that these represent satisfactory policy, and we have sympathy with the observations we cite by Collins J in *S v the Director of Legal Aid Casework and the Lord Chancellor*.[42] But we conclude that, whatever positions are taken on those wider issues, surely it is time to consider how to make it possible for the anomalies created by professional boundaries to be removed so that a service to both parties, such as that offered by Divorce Negotiator (see above), can be provided without the providers having to leave the accredited and regulated profession of solicitor but by adding the benefit of mediation skills to the process. Instead of lawyer mediators being forbidden to give the legal advice which parties need to frame their settlement-seeking activity, and non-lawyer mediators being ill-equipped to do so, could we either train lawyers to add mediation to their skill set while continuing to act as lawyers, or enable mediators to add legal knowledge to their resources, or preferably both, so that separating parties can benefit from both information about the legal framework and advice and support in making the best possible use of it?

---

[41] See p 8.
[42] (2015) EWHC 1965; see p 10.

Bibliography

Abel, R (2003) *English Lawyers between Market and State: The Politics of Professionalism* (Oxford, Oxford University Press).

—— (2005), 'The Professional as Political' in W Felstiner (ed), *Reorganisation and Resistance: Legal Professions in a Changing World* (Oxford, Hart Publishing), ch 1.

Albeson, J (2014) 'The Sorting out Separation Web App: Fit for Purpose?' 44 *Family Law* 878.

Atkin, B (2015) 'Controversial Changes to the Family Justice System in New Zealand: Is the Private Law/Public Law Division Still Useful' 29 *International Journal of Law, Policy and the Family* 183.

Bano, S (2015) 'Muslim Dispute Resolution in Britain: Towards a New Framework of Family Law Governance?' in Maclean, M and Eekelaar, J (eds), *Managing Family Justice in Diverse Societies* (Oxford, Hart Publishing).

Barlow, A, Hunter, R, Smithson, J and Ewing, J (2014), *Mapping Paths to Justice*, Briefing paper (Exeter, University of Exeter).

Bastard, B, Delvaux, D, Mouhanna, C and Schoenaers, F (2015) 'Controlling Time? Speeding up Divorce Proceedings in France and Belgium' in Maclean, M, Eekelaar, J and Bastard, B (eds), *Delivering Family Justice in the Twenty-First Century* (Oxford, Hart Publishing), ch 16.

Bell, F, Cashmore, J, Parkinson, P and Single, J (2013) 'Outcomes of Child-Inclusive Mediation' 27 *International Journal of Law, Policy and the Family* 116.

Bevan, G (1996), 'Has there Been Supplier-induced Demand for Legal Aid?' *Civil Justice Quarterly* 99.

Biland, E, Mille, M and Steinmetz, H (2015) 'National Paths toward Private Ordering: Professionals' Jurisdictions and Separating Couples' Privacy in the French and Canadian Family Justice Systems' in Maclean, M, Eekelaar, J and Bastard, B (eds), *Delivering Family Justice in the Twenty-First Century* (Oxford, Hart Publishing).

Boon, A (2010) 'Professionalism under the Legal Services Act 2007' 17 *International Journal of the Legal Profession* 195.

Boulle, L and Nesic, M (2001) *Mediation: Principles, Process, Procedure* (London, Butterworths).

Brown, H, 'Standards and Survival: Enhancing the Practice Model' (2015) 45 *Family Law* 202.

Cabinet Office (2010) *Building the Big Society* (London, Cabinet Office).

Clementi, D (2004) *Report of the Review of the Regulatory Framework for Legal Services in England and Wales*, www.legal-services-review.org.uk.

Consultation Paper (1993) *Looking to the Future: Mediation and the Ground for Divorce*, Cm 2424.

Cookson, G (2011) *Unintended Consequences: The Cost of the Government's Legal Aid Reforms* (London, King's College).

—— (2013) 'Analysing the Economic Justification for the Reforms to Social Welfare and Family Law Legal Aid' 35 *Journal of Social Welfare and Family Law* 21.

Coy, M, Scott, E, Tweedale, R and Perks, K (2015) '"Its Like Going Through the Abuse Again": Domestic Violence and Women and Children's "unsafety" in Private Law Contact Proceedings' 37 *Journal of Social Welfare and Family Law* 53.

Cretney, S (2003) *Family Law in the Twentieth Century* (Oxford, Oxford University Press).

Davis, G, Cretney, S and Collins, JG (1994) *Simple Quarrels* (Oxford, Oxford University Press).

Davis, G, Pearce, J, Bird, R, Woodward H and Wallace, C (1999) *Ancillary Relief Outcomes: A Pilot Study for the Lord Chancellor's Department* (Bristol, University of Bristol).

Denning Committee (1947) *Final Report of the Committee on Procedure in Matrimonial Causes*, Cmd 7024.

Denvir, C (2014) *What is the Net Worth?* PhD thesis (London, University College London).

Dewar, J (2010) 'Can the Centre Hold? Reflections on Two Decades of Family Law Reform in Australia' 22 *Child and Family Law Quarterly* 377.

Diduck, A (2014) 'Justice by ADR in Private Family Matters: Is it Fair and Is it Possible? 44 *Family Law* 616.

Dingwall, R (2010) 'Divorce Mediation: Should we Change our Mind?' 32 *Journal of Social Welfare and Family Law* 107.

Dingwall, R and Eekelaar, J (1988) *Divorce Mediation and the Legal Process* (Oxford, Clarendon Press).

Dingwall, R and Greatbatch, D (1991) 'Behind Closed Doors: A Preliminary Report on Mediation/Client Interaction in England' 29 *Family and Conciliation Courts Review* 291.

Dutta, A (2012), 'Marital Agreements and Private Autonomy in Germany' in Scherpe, JM (ed), *Marital Agreements and Private Autonomy in Comparative Perspective* (Oxford, Hart Publishing).

Eekelaar, J (2011), '"Not of the Highest Importance": Family Justice under Threat' 33 *Journal of Social Welfare and Family Law* 311.

—— (2011) 'The Arbitration and Mediation Services (Equality) Bill 2011' 41 *Family Law* 1209.

—— (2012) 'Family Law—What Family Law?' in Probert, R and Barton, C (eds), *Fifty Years in Family Law: Essays for Stephen Cretney* (Cambridge, Intersentia).

 —— (2013) 'Then and Now—Family Law's Direction of Travel' 35 *Journal of Social Welfare and Family Law* 415.

—— (2015) 'Law, Values, Cultures', in Diduck, A, Reece, H and Peleg, N (eds), *Law In Society: Reflections on Children, Family, Culture and Philosophy Essays in Honour of Michael Freeman* (Leiden, Brill Nijhoff).

Eekelaar, J and Maclean, M (1986) *Maintenance after Divorce* (Oxford, Oxford University Press).

Eekelaar, J, Maclean M and Beinart, S (2000) *Family Lawyers: The Divorce Work of Solicitors* (Oxford, Hart Publishing).

Eekelaar, J and Maclean, M (2013) *Family Justice: The Work of Family Judges in Uncertain Times* (Oxford, Hart Publishing).

Evetts, J (2015) 'Professionalism, Enterprise and Markets' in Sommerlad, H, Harris Short, S, Vaughan, S and Young, R (eds), *The Futures of Legal Education and the Legal Professions* (Oxford, Hart Publishing), ch 2.

Family Justice Council (December 2012) *Financial Dispute Resolution Appointments: Best Practice Guidance).*

Family Justice Review (2011) *Final Report* (London, Ministry of Justice).

Family Mediation Council (September 2014) *Manual of Professional Standards and Self-regulatory Framework.*

Family Mediation Task Force (2014) *Report* (London, Ministry of Justice), www.justice.gov.uk/downloads/family-mediation-task-force-report.pdf.

Felstiner, WLF, Abel, RL and Sarat, A (1980–81) 'The Emergence and Transformation of Disputes: Naming, Blaming, Claiming …' 15 *Law & Society Review* 631.

Ferguson, L (2013) 'Arbitration in Financial Dispute Resolution: The Final Step to Reconstructing the Default(s) and Exception(s)?' 35 *Journal of Social Welfare and Family Law* 115.

Finer Committee (1974) *Report of the Committee of One-Parent Families*, Cmnd 5629).

Genn, H (1999) *Paths to Justice* (Oxford, Hart Publishing).

Gibson, C (2000) 'Changing Family Patterns in England and Wales over the Last Fifty Years' in Katz, SN, Eekelaar, J and Maclean, M, *Cross Currents: Family Law and Policy in the US and England* (Oxford, Oxford University Press).

Greatbatch, D and Dingwall, R (1989) 'Selective Facilitation: Some Preliminary Observations on a Strategy used by Divorce Mediators 23 *Law & Society Review* 613.

Greatbatch, D and Dingwall, R (1999) 'The Marginalisation of Domestic Violence in Divorce Mediation' 13 *International Journal of Law, Policy & the Family* 174.

Harding, M and Newnham, A (2014) 'Initial Research Findings: the Typical Levels of Parental Involvement where Post-Separation Parenting is Resolved by Court Order' 44 *Family Law* 672.

Harding, M and Newnham, A (2015) *How do County Courts Share the Care of Children between Parents?* (University of Reading and University of Warwick) http://eprints.port.ac.uk/15618/http://eprints.port.ac.uk/15618/).

Hitchings, E, Miles, J and Woodward, H (2014) 'Assembling the Jigsaw Puzzle: Understanding Financial Settlement on Divorce' 44 *Family Law* 304.

House of Commons Justice Committee (March 2015) *8th Report, Impact of Changes to Civil Legal Aid under Part 1 of the Legal Aid, Sentencing and Punishment of Offenders Act 2012,* (London, House of Commons).

Hunter, R (2011) 'Doing violence to family law' 33 *Journal of Social Welfare and Family Law* 343.

Ingleby, R (1992) *Solicitors and Divorce* (Oxford, Oxford University Press).

Johnson, NE, Saccuzzo, D and Koen, WJ (2005) 'Child Custody Mediation in Cases of Domestic Violence: Empirical Evidence of a Failure to Protect' 11 *Violence against Women* 1022. See also www.ncjrs.gov/pdffiles1/nij/grants/195422.pdf.

Kennett, W (2016) 'Arbitration but not as we know it: Reflections on Family Law Dispute Resolution' 30 *International Journal of Law, Policy and the Family*, Issue 1 (forthcoming).

King, M, Freiberg, A, Batagol, B and Hyams, R (2009) *Non Adversarial Justice* (Annandale, Federation Press).

Legal Services Board (June 2012) *Benchmarking Report 1156.*

Lesseliers, V (2012) 'The Value of Mediation as a Component of the Legal Education' in Schonewille, F and Euwema, M (eds), *Mastering mediation education* (Antwerp, Maklu).

Lester, S (2014a) 'Professional Organisation and Self-regulation in Family Mediation in England and Wales: Part I: Background' 44 *Family Law* 1338.

—— (2014b) 'Professional Organisation and Self-regulation in Family Mediation in England and Wales: Part 2: The 2014–15 Reforms' 44 *Family Law* 1473.

—— (2014c) 'Professional Organisation and Self-regulation in Family Mediation in England and Wales: Part 3: Issues, implications and future challenges' 44 *Family Law* 1610.

Lewis, PSC (February 2000) *Assumptions about Lawyers in Policy Statements: A Survey of Relevant Research*, Lord Chancellor's Department Research Programme.

Lopatin, M (2014) 'Growing Family Law Services in a Post-LASPO World: Mediation as Collateral Beneficiary' 44 *Family Law* 1476.

Maclean, M (2000) 'Access to Justice in Family Matters in Post War Britain' in Katz, SN, Eekelaar, J and Maclean, M (eds), *Cross Currents: Family Law and Policy in the US and England* (Oxford, Clarendon Press), ch 24.

Maclean, M and Eekelaar, J (1997) *The Parental Obligation* (Oxford, Hart Publishing).

Maclean, M, Sidaway, J and Beinart, S (1998) 'Family Solicitors—The Workforce' 28 *Family Law* 673.

Maclean, M, Wasoff, F, Hunter, R, Ferguson, L, Bastard, B and Ryrstedt, E (2011) 'Family Justice in Hard Times: Can we Learn from other Jurisdictions?' 33 *Journal of Social Welfare and Family Law* 319.

Maclean, M and Eekelaar, J (2009) *Family Law Advocacy: How Barristers help the Victims of Family Failure* (Oxford, Hart Publishing).

Maclean, M, Eekelaar, J and Bastard, B (eds) (2015), *Delivering Family Justice in the Twenty-First Century* (Oxford, Hart Publishing).

Mair, J, Wasoff, F and Mackay, K (2015) 'Family Justice without Courts: Property Settlement on Separation using Contracts in Scotland' in Maclean, M, Eekelaar, J and Bastard, B (eds), *Delivering Family Justice in the Twenty-First Century* (Oxford, Hart Publishing), ch 10.

Malik, M (2014) 'Family Law in Diverse Societies' in Eekelaar, J and George, R (eds), *Routledge Handbook of Family Law and Policy* (Abingdon, Routledge), ch 7.4.

Manchester, AH and Whetton, JM (1974) 'Marital Conciliation in England and Wales' 23 *International and Comparative Law Quarterly* 339.

Marshall, TH (1963) *Sociology at the Crossroads and other Essays* (Abingdon, Routledge, reprinted).

Martiny, D (2002) *Grounds for Divorce and Maintenance between Former Spouses: Germany* (Commission for European Family Law).

McEldowney, J (2012) *Family Mediation in a Time of Change: FMC Review Final Report* (Family Mediation Council), www2.warwick.ac.uk/fac/soc/law/research/impact/mceldowney-review-for-family-mediation-council.pdf.

Middleton, P (September 1997) *Review of Civil Justice and Legal Aid. Report to the Lord Chancellor by Sir Peter Middleton GCB* (London, Lord Chancellor's Department).

Miles, J (2012) 'Marital Agreements and Private Autonomy in England and Wales' in Scherpe, JM (ed), *Marital Agreements and Private Autonomy in Comparative Perspective* (Oxford, Hart Publishing).

Ministry of Justice (2010) *Proposals for the Reform of Legal Aid in England and Wales,* Consultation Paper CP 12/10.

Ministry of Justice (September 2014) *Court Statistics Quarterly April–June 2014.*

Ministry of Justice and Family Mediation Council (November 2014) *Marketing Communication Tips for Family Mediators.*

Ministry of Justice and Legal Aid Agency (2014a) *Legal Aid Statistics in England and Wales, April to June 2014,* 25 September.

Ministry of Justice and Legal Aid Agency (2014b) *Implementing Reforms to Civil Legal Aid,* Report by the Comptroller and Auditor General, National Audit Office, November, www.nao.org.uk.

Moloney, L, Kaspiew, R, de Maio, J, Deblaquierre, J, Hand, K, and Horsfall, B (2011) *Evaluation of the Family Relationships Centre Legal Assistance Partnerships Programme* (Australian Government, Australian Institute for Family Studies).

Moorhead, R (1998) 'Legal Aid in the Eye of a Storm: Rationing, Contracting and New Institutionalism' 25(3) *Journal of Law and Society* 365.

Myers, F and Wasoff, F (2011) *Meeting in the Middle: A Study of Solicitors' and Mediators' Divorce Practice* (Scottish Executive, Central Research Unit).

Nader, L (1993) 'Controlling Processes in the Practice of Law: Hierarchy and Pacification in the Movement to Re-Form Dispute Ideology' 9 *Ohio State Journal of Dispute Resolution* 1.

National Family Mediation (2014) *National Statistical Report.*

Norrie, K McK (2012) 'Marital Agreements and Private Autonomy in Scotland' in Scherpe JM (ed), *Marital Agreements and Private Autonomy in Comparative Perspective* (Oxford, Hart Publishing).

Parkinson, L (2014) *Family Mediation* (Bristol, Jordans Publications).

Paterson, A (2012) *Lawyers and the Public Good: Democracy in Action?* The Hamlyn Lectures (Cambridge, Cambridge University Press).

Pintens, W (2012), 'Marital Agreements and Private Autonomy in France and Belgium' in Scherpe, JM (ed), *Marital Agreements and Private Autonomy in Comparative Perspective* (Oxford, Hart Publishing).

Pleasence, P, Balmer, N and Moorhead, R (2012) *A Time of Change: Solicitors' Firms in England and Wales* (The Law Society, Legal Services Board, Ministry of Justice).

Raz, J (1986) *The Morality of Freedom* (Oxford, Clarendon Press).

Resolution (2012) *Guide to Good Practice for Family Lawyers in Dealing with Clients.*

Resolution (2015) *Guide to Good Practice on Mediation.*

Roberts, M (2005) 'Family Mediation: The Development of the Regulatory Framework in the UK' 22(4) *Conflict Resolution Quarterly* 509.

—— (2007) *Developing the Craft of Mediation: Reflections on Theory and Practice* (London, Jessica Kingsley).

—— (2014) *Mediation in Family Disputes: Principles and Practice* 4th edn (Farnham, Ashgate).

Ryder, Mr Justice (2012) *Judicial Proposals for the Modernisation of Family Justice* (London, Judiciary of England and Wales).

Ryrstedt, E (2009) 'Separate Representation and Family Courts—Do We Need Them in the Nordic Countries?' 21 *Child and Family Law Quarterly* 185.

—— (2012), 'Mediation regarding children—is the Result always in the Best Interests of the Child? A View from Sweden' 26 *International Journal of Law, Policy & the Family* 220.

Salem, P (2009) 'The Emergence of Triage in Family Court Services: the beginning of the end for Mandatory Mediation?' 47 *Family Court Review* 371.

Salem, P, Kulak, D and Deutsch, RM (2007) 'Triaging Family Court Services: the Connecticut Judicial Branch's Family Civil Intake Screen' 27 *Pace Law Review* 741.

Saunders, L (2014) 'Dispute Resolution: Mediation and Child Consent Orders' 44 *Family Law* 1187.

Scherpe, JM (2012), 'Marital Agreements and Private Autonomy in Comparative Perspective' in Scherpe, JM (ed), *Marital Agreements and Private Autonomy in Comparative Perspective* (Hart Publishing, 2012).

Sefton, M, Moorhead, R, Sidaway, J and Fox, L (2011) *Unbundled and Pro Bono Advice for Litigants in Person, a Study for the Cabinet Office* (Office for Civil Society Transition Fund). (Quoted with permission from Richard Moorhead given on 18 January 2015)

Smith, R and Paterson, A (November 2013) *Face to Face Legal Services and their Alternatives: Global Lessons from the Digital Revolution*, Report to the Nuffield Foundation.

Stevenson, M (2015a) 'Mediation and Settlement-Broking' 45 *Family Law* 575.

Stevenson, M (2015b) 'A Mediator's Compass' 45 *Family Law* 715.

Stylianou, K (2015) 'Rationale for the Ethics and Integrity of a Family Mediator' 45 *Family Law* 829.

Susskind, R (2013) *Tomorrow's Lawyers* (Oxford, Oxford University Press).

The Law Society (March 2013) *The Legal Services Industry Part 2 Main Sectors 2012*, www.lawsociety.org.uk/policy-campaigns/research-trends/market-assessment-2012-13/.

The Law Society (July 2013) *Legal Services, Part 3: Key Markets*.

The Law Society (2014) Problems Faced by Firms: Law Society's Firm Survey 2013–14, www.lawsociety.org.uk.

Todorova, V (2015) 'Family Justice in Bulgaria: the Old System and New Demands' in Maclean, M, Eekelaar, J and Bastard, B (eds), *Delivering Family Justice in the Twenty-First Century* (Oxford, Hart Publishing), ch 6.

Trinder, L, Hunter, R, Hitchings, E, Miles, J, Moorhead, R, Smith, L, Sefton, M, Hinchly, V, Bader, K and Pearce, J (December 2014), *Litigants in Person in Private Family Law Cases* (London, Ministry of Justice).

Tur, RHS (1995) 'Family Lawyering and Legal Ethics' in Parker, S and Sampford, C (eds), *Legal Ethics and Legal Practice* (Oxford, Clarendon Press) 145.

Tyler, TR (1988–89) 'The Quality of Dispute Resolution Procedures and Outcomes: Measurement Problems and Possibilities' 66 *Denver University Law Review* 410.

Vardag, A and Miles, J (2015) 'The Rite that Redefines the Rights? The Contemporary Role and Practice of Pre-Nuptial Agreement' in Miles, J, Mody, P and Probert, R, *Marriage Rites and Rights* (Oxford, Hart Publishing), ch 6.

Voice of the Child Dispute Resolution Advisory Group (March 2015) *Final Report*, www.gov.uk/governemtn/uploads/system/uploads/attachmentdata/file/421005/voice-of-the-child-advisory-group-report.pdf.

Walker, J, McCarthy, P and Timms, N (1994) *Mediation: the Making and Remaking of Cooperative Relationships* (Newcastle, Relate Centre for Family Studies).

Webley, L (2004) 'Divorce Solicitors and Ethical Approaches—the Best Interests of the Client and/or the Best Interests of the Family 7 *Legal Ethics* 231.

—— (2015a) 'When is a Family Lawyer a Lawyer?' in Maclean, M, Eekelaar, J and Bastard, B (eds), *Delivering Family Justice in the Twenty-First Century* (Oxford, Hart Publishing) ch 17.

—— (2015b) 'Legal Professional De(Re)Regulation, Equality, and Inclusion, and the Contested Space of Professionalism within the Legal Market in England and Wales' 83 *Fordham Law Review* 2349.

——(in press) 'When is Mediation Mediatory and when is it really Adjudicatory? Religion, Norms and Decision-making'.

White Paper (1995) *Looking to the Future: Mediation and the Ground for Divorce* CM 2799.

Wildblood, HHJ Stephen QC, Goldingham, CW QC and Evans, J (2014) '"The way we are": accessing the court after LASPO' 44 *Family Law* 1597.

Woolf, H (1996) *Access to Justice: Final Report* (London, HMSO).

Zander, M (1980) *The State of Knowledge about the English Legal Profession* (Chichester and London, Barry Rose Publishers).

Zuckerman, A (2014) 'No Justice Without Lawyers—The Myth of an Inquisitorial Solution' 23 *Civil Justice Quarterly* 355.

Index